Enterprise Risk Management and COSO

Enterprise Risk Management and COSO

A Guide for Directors, Executives, and Practitioners

HARRY CENDROWSKI
WILLIAM C. MAIR

John Wiley & Sons, Inc.

Library of Congress Cataloging-in-Publication Data:

Cendrowski, Harry.
    Enterprise risk management and COSO : a guide for directors, executives, and practitioners / Harry Cendrowski, William C. Mair.
        p. cm.
    Includes bibliographical references and index.
    ISBN 978-0-470-46065-8 (cloth)
1. Risk management. 2. Corporate governance. I. Mair, William C. II. Title.
    HD61.C443 2010
    658.15'5—dc22

                                                                            2009020135

10 9 8 7 6 5 4 3 2 1

Contents

About the Contributors

Harry Cendrowski, **CPA, ABV, CFF, CFE, CVA, CFD, CFFA**, is a founding member of Cendrowski Corporate Advisors, Cendrowski Selecky PC, and The Prosperitas Group. Harry has served as an expert witness in numerous economic damages analyses, contract disputes, lost profit analyses, business valuations, and partnership disputes. He has served as court-appointed receiver in several multimillion-dollar estates, and as the accountant to the trustee in high-profile bankruptcy cases.

Harry is the co-author of *The Handbook of Fraud Deterrence* and *Private Equity: History, Governance, and Operations,* published by John Wiley & Sons, Inc., and has authored articles in several professional publications. These publications include a chapter in *Computer Fraud Casebook: The Bytes that Bite,* a textbook centered on fraud examination.

Along with Jim Martin of CCA, Harry is a co-author of the Certified Fraud Deterrence Analyst (CFD) training materials for the International Association of Consultants, Valuators and Analysts (IACVA). He serves as IACVA's Director of Fraud and Forensic Services. He is also a co-author of the training materials used by the National Association of Certified Valuation Analysts (NACVA) in certifying Certified Forensic Financial Analysts (CFFA).

William C. (Bill) Mair is a director with Cendrowski Corporate Advisors. Bill is the originator of some of the key concepts applied in the structure of the early risk management and control assessment materials. A mathematician and accountant by education, during various phases of his career Bill's roles have included being a military commander, EDP auditor, educator, author, technology consultant, CPA firm partner, professional standards consultant, expert witness, bank internal audit director, insurance company financial executive, corporate director, public investment company trustee, webmaster, and a number of other functions.

The Information Systems Audit and Control Association voted Bill the fourth most influential person among the pioneers of information systems auditing in a study published by *The EDP Auditor Journal,* while his 1972 book, *Computer Control & Audit,* was voted the second most influential book. Bill is the creator of many systems control concepts and audit techniques now so established as to be viewed as "traditional."

In recent years, Bill has focused on bridging quantitative risk analysis with effective communication to the board level.

Adam A. Wadecki is a manager with Cendrowski Corporate Advisors. Adam specializes in operational analyses, business valuations, and quantitative risk management modeling. He has academic and professional experience in lean manufacturing tenets and the Six Sigma methodology. Adam has helped numerous Fortune 500 companies assess, improve, and monitor the operations of their production facilities. Additionally, in conjunction with the CCA team, he has provided business valuations of publicly traded and private firms that have served as the basis of legal cases, and assisted private equity general partners with their financial due diligence.

Adam is also active in academia. He has authored articles on supply chain management, operational assessments, quantitative risk management, and fraud deterrence, in addition to co-authoring *Private Equity: History, Governance, and Operations.* He has served as a graduate student instructor at the University of Michigan for courses in venture capital finance, private equity, business valuation, and process assessment and improvement.

Adam holds a Master's degree in Operations Research, and graduated *magna cum laude* with Bachelor's of Science degrees in Mechanical and Industrial and Operations Engineering, all from the University of Michigan.

Carolyn H. Rosenberg, Esq. is a partner in Reed Smith LLP's Chicago office. She is a member of the firm's Executive Committee as well as the firm's Audit Committee, and heads the firm's Talent Committee. She frequently advises corporations, directors and officers, risk managers, insurance brokers, lawyers, and other professionals on insurance coverage, corporate indemnification, and litigation matters nationwide and internationally. Carolyn also assists clients in evaluating insurance coverage and other protections when negotiating transactions and represents them in resolving coverage disputes.

Carolyn was selected by *Corporate Board Member* magazine as one of the country's 12 Legal Superstars and the top D&O liability insurance lawyer in August 2001 and she was confirmed as the nation's top D&O liability insurance lawyer by *Corporate Board Member* magazine in a feature on superstar corporate attorneys in July 2004. In addition, Carolyn has been recognized as one of the top lawyers in her field by *Chambers USA 2008–2009: America's Leading Lawyers for Business.*

Efrem M. Grail, Esq. defends entities and individuals in "white-collar" criminal investigations, prosecutions, and administrative enforcement actions involving allegations of securities, health-care, and business fraud; government contracting, false claims, foreign corrupt practices, and domestic political corruption; and tax and environmental violations. Efrem also litigates complex business disputes, handles injunctions and civil trials in federal and state court, and advises on compliance matters.

A former prosecutor, Efrem has represented clients in confidential matters before federal grand juries and in criminal prosecutions nationwide. He has also represented clients before numerous federal government agencies in administrative enforcement actions.

The Allegheny County Bar Association's Public Service Committee and the Allegheny County Bar Foundation's Pro Bono Center selected Efrem to receive their 2007 Pro Bono Award for Outstanding Individual Attorney and their 2005 Law Firm Pro Bono Award as director of Reed Smith's Pittsburgh pro bono effort. In 2008 and 2009, Efrem was selected for inclusion in *The Best Lawyers in America* in the area of White Collar Criminal Defense. In addition, Efrem has been named a "Pennsylvania Super Lawyer" in the area of White Collar Criminal Defense in 2005, 2006, and 2009.

Acknowledgments

We are sincerely grateful to several individuals for their unique contributions to this book. Adam Wadecki was instrumental in helping us develop ideas throughout the manuscript authoring process. He also assisted us in editing and authoring the manuscript. Adam's contributions helped shape the book that now rests in your hands.

We would also like to acknowledge Carolyn Rosenberg, Esq. and Efrem Grail, Esq. of Reed Smith LLP for contributing a chapter to this book. Their insight into how boards and Chief Risk Officers can quickly identify and contain risks is invaluable to directors whose firms participate in our ever-changing, global environment.

Preface

Recent financial crises have proven that risk management practices are essential for organizations large and small. Publicly traded companies, privately-held firms, and nonprofit organizations were all wounded by the events of 2008 and 2009. Scars from these largely unanticipated or "black swan" events continue to manifest themselves in the growing national unemployment rates, low levels of consumer confidence, and the contracting U.S. gross domestic product (GDP). However traumatic these events have been for our economy, they also provide business leaders and risk practitioners with insights into how we can heal these wounds and prevent them from recurring in the future.

We believe the process of risk management fits within the broader context of organizational management. Risk itself is a driving force in strategic, operational, reporting, and governance decisions. It is a critical cog in the organizational machine—one that can operate with little fanfare, or one that can cause a critical failure. In today's highly competitive world, it is imperative that board members, executives, managers, and employees are involved in the risk management process. The knowledge possessed by each of these individuals allows unique perspectives to be married into a single assessment designed for safeguarding the organization against the many forms of risk.

Until recently, risk management was not generally seen as a component central to the operation of many firms. While detailed risk management activities took place in areas of many organizations, holistic risk management has only recently come into vogue. Many professional organizations such as the National Association for Corporate Directors (NACD) are pushing for significant changes in the way board members and executives evaluate risks. These changes are being made largely in response to recent crises that began in the financial services sector. Indeed, the banking sector is also advocating change in risk management policies with the recent finalization of the Basel Committee's second capital accord (Basel II). While the document was not finalized until 2006, the initial capital accord touched off a discussion on the importance of risk management that began nearly 10 years ago. It is our hope that this text continues this discussion of risk management, highlighting its importance to directors and executives while also providing insightful information for practitioners.

This book is organized in two sections. In accordance with the afore-mentioned emphasis on risk management at high levels of the organization, we have grouped material relevant to directors and executives in our first section, "Organizational Risk Management." The second section, entitled "Quantitative Risk Management," is catered to risk management practitioners. We have authored both sections as standalone entities: Readers can elect to focus on either section, or read the book in its entirety.

The first section examines risk management at a macro level. In this section, we emphasize risk management practices most important to board members, C-suite executives (e.g., CEOs and CFOs), and high-level managers. We focus on risk management from a top-down perspective, emphasizing the manner in which executives and directors can cultivate the culture necessary for an organization to possess effective risk management policies. Many pages are spent discussing how these individuals can set an appropriate "tone at the top" that will foster a culture of risk awareness. We have purposefully emphasized understandability over mathematical modeling within this section, given our potential audience members' diverse backgrounds.

The second section details a quantitative framework for analysis that can be used by risk practitioners who perform risk assessments of enterprises, divisions, systems, and processes. This section presents mathematical formulations as well as example assessments of various systems for the practitioner. While the models in this section are mathematical in nature, our goal has been to emphasize practicality over mathematical rigor. The tools illustrated in this section can be employed by practitioners looking for a framework that demonstrates how enterprise risk management policies, similar to those presented in the Committee of Sponsoring Organization's (COSO) Enterprise Risk Management framework, may be implemented.

Our hope is that this book provides a comprehensive resource not only for those in corporate America, but also for individuals in the public sector; risk management practices for governmental organizations are inarguably equal in importance to such practices in private industry.

Many governmental agencies are receiving funds through the American Recovery and Reinvestment Act of 2009 (ARRA). The Obama Administration has made transparency and accountability a primary goal of ARRA in hopes of mitigating risks associated with waste, fraud, and abuse. Decreasing the chance such risks occur will require considerable planning and oversight by administrators, from program inception through conclusion. We believe the quantitative models and framework for analysis contained within this book can help administrators of governmental bodies ensure program goals are achieved, and greater economic impact is realized.

Our risk management framework can also help directors and executives of private companies receiving stimulus funds to mitigate risks. Many private infrastructure companies are receiving major infusions of stimulus dollars for new, capital-intensive projects. Our quantitative models can also assist these firms with mitigating risks associated with cost and time-related overruns that sometimes plague such projects.

Finally, we wish to note that this book is not a comprehensive treatise on risk management techniques or models. Complicated probability models and distributions are not our central focus in this text. Rather, we endeavor to introduce models and risk assessment procedures to the reader that are easily understood and practical in nature. Our goal throughout the authoring process has been to present the reader with a text that is thought provoking, accessible and understandable.

We sincerely hope this book is able to assist the reader in assessing risks irrespective of his or her position or employing organization. We also hope that it will encourage readers to further their knowledge in this essential twenty-first-century discipline.

Harry Cendrowski
William C. Mair
Chicago, IL
September 2009

Organizational Risk Management

R isk management is a necessary part of our lives. Risk is present in any situation in which decisions must be made under uncertainty with imperfect information. Our minds constantly assess risks as we drive our cars and even pay our bills. In each of these instances, the mind enumerates the risks associated with the activity, quantifies the risk, and then compels us to make a decision based on this assessment.

When operating a vehicle, we are never sure that surrounding drivers will operate their cars in a rational manner. However, we enter such a situation with an *a priori* belief that other drivers are indeed rational. After all, they must pass a test to obtain a driver's license. When we're driving down the road, our minds are continually evaluating and updating this *a priori* belief with respect to every car that is within a personal "envelope of concern."

Driving at a steady speed on the highway, we are not very concerned with the actions of those far behind us. While we can see other cars in the rearview mirror, the likelihood that such a driver's actions impact our own decisions is low. If a far-behind driver loses control, it does not impact us, although it could impact a group of drivers behind us. However, we are very concerned with the actions of those in front of us—most particularly, those immediately ahead of our own vehicle—and those to our side. If these individuals make an error in judgment, the consequences to us could be severe. Our envelope of concern is thus concentrated to the front and sides of our vehicle rather than behind it.

With this simple example we have introduced two central notions of risk assessment: probability and magnitude. The probability that a random driver loses control is identical no matter where this driver is located with respect to us. However, the magnitude of the risk differs based on the location of the driver. Our minds evaluate both magnitude and probability when we are assessing risks. This assessment is then used to make decisions based on information we perceive. Whether or not we are conscious of it, our minds quantify these risks, and we make decisions based on this quantification.

Although risk management might come naturally to our minds, it is not an involuntary process within an organization. A business must establish, utilize, and monitor risk management procedures to effectively perceive changes in the firm's environment. Returning to our previous example, it is essential that management and board members develop an envelope of concern for the business's strategic objectives. This strategy should focus on risks caused by competitors within the business's immediate operating environment as well as risks posed by potential future competitors, should the organization's environment change.

Organizational Risk Management

Organizational risk management has evolved considerably in the past few decades, from a nascent stage in the 1960s to very complicated modeling in the current day. Risk management within the United States developed primarily in response to the globalization of the U.S. economy. At the turn of the twentieth century, many U.S. businesses focused on selling goods to geographic areas within the country. Few finished goods were imported from overseas or sold across our border. As transportation methods improved in both speed and efficiency through the 1960s, U.S.-based companies began exporting goods abroad. Foreign companies also began selling their goods within the United States.

Prior to this occurrence of global trade, many U.S. industries operated in an oligopoly: The production power of an industry was concentrated within the hands of relatively few corporations. Within such a framework, corporations were able to obtain healthy profits, primarily due to the lack of competition in the marketplace. However, as international competition increased within U.S. markets, the profit margins of manufacturers began to erode. From 1960 through 2008, the U.S. economy shifted from a small net exporter of goods and services to a major importer. (See Exhibit I.1 for more information.) This shift is reflective of the fact that many U.S. corporations began to face increasingly stiff competition from overseas competitors over this time.

Especially susceptible to foreign competition were those manufacturers producing goods with no discernible quality difference from their overseas counterparts. Many U.S. industries began to experience consolidation and hardships that continue today. Witness the current tumultuous environment faced by the U.S. automotive industry and its suppliers as both recently received tens of billions in loans from the federal government.

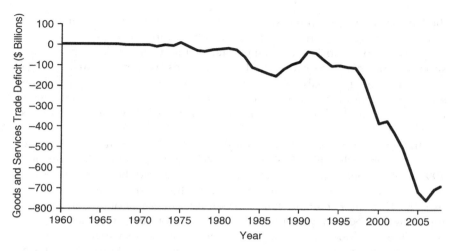

EXHIBIT I.1 Historical U.S. Goods and Services Foreign Trade Deficit, 1960–2008
Source: U.S. Census Bureau.

Modern risk management arose out of this increasingly competitive environment faced by many corporations. In the 1960s, risk management primarily took the form of purchased insurance against *force majeure* events. Today, many corporate executives are worried about not only these types of events but also many others. As shown in the survey results presented in Exhibit I.2, within the United States many corporate chief financial officers (CFOs) are worried about consumer demand and the cost of labor within

EXHIBIT I.2 Top Concerns of U.S. CFOs (Higher Score = Greater Importance)

Rank	Concern	Avg. Importance Score
1	Consumer demand	0.82
2	Cost of labor	0.73
3	Credit markets/interest rate	0.59
4	Cost of fuel	0.58
5	Cost of health care	0.56
6	Housing-market fallout	0.50
7	Skilled-labor shortage	0.48
8	Regulation	0.39
9	Cost of nonfuel commodities	0.30
10	Currency values	0.27

Source: Duke University/*CFO Magazine Global Business Outlook Survey.*

the United States.[1] Natural disasters—a primary subject of risk managers 40 years ago—did not even make the list of CFO's top concerns.

Contemporary risk management takes the form of hedging against shocks in the currency, stock, and commodities markets; evaluating organizational strategy, reliability of financial reporting, and risks in operations; and assessing risks in corporate governance procedures. Accordingly, many professional standards that focus on risk management have been introduced within the past two decades.

In 1995, Standards Australia published one of the first modern risk management standards with AS/NZS 4360: 1995. Canada soon followed suit in 1997 with the publication of CAN/CSA-Q850-97, as did the Institute of Chartered Accountants in England and Wales with their Turnbull Report, released in 1999. This latter standard called for stronger internal controls in financial reporting and better monitoring of risks throughout the organization.

Risk management standards within the United States largely took a back seat until the financial scandals of the 2000s (involving Enron, WorldCom, and Tyco, among others). These events forced the passage of the Sarbanes-Oxley Act of 2002 and in 2004 led to the creation of the enterprise risk management (ERM) framework by the Committee of Sponsoring Organizations (COSO). This latter framework will serve as the foundation of our risk management methodology introduced in the second section of our book.

The Risk Assessment Process

The risk assessment process consists of five steps:

1. Enumeration of risks
2. Qualitative analysis
3. Quantitative analysis
4. Implementation of risk management strategy
5. Assessment of risk management strategy

Risk assessment in organizations is the domain not only of the auditor but of operating managers, board members, and C-level executives. As stated in the Preface, all four of these groups comprise the intended audience for this book.

Auditors assess risks when they perform an examination (commonly called an "audit" when it involves financial statements). In performing an examination, an auditor must select a combination of information from a large body of evidence that limits the risk of a material misstatement. Operating managers must assess risks associated with the internal operations of the business. If performance metrics begin to indicate that the organization is struggling to achieve its mission, managers must prioritize initiatives according to the risks they pose to the organization's health. C-level executives examine risks to the organization's strategic plan from external and internal threats. This also falls within the domain of the board of directors.

Risk Management at the Board Level

The recent economic crisis has put a renewed emphasis on directors' oversight over the day-to-day operations of their organizations. In the words of the National Association of Corporate Directors (NACD), the board:

> is charged with selecting and evaluating senior executives; planning for succession; monitoring performance; overseeing strategy and risk; compensating executives; approving corporate policies and plans; approving material capital expenditures and transactions not in the ordinary course of business; ensuring the transparency and integrity of financial disclosures and controls; providing oversight of compliance with applicable laws and regulations; and setting the "tone at the top." [2]

This is no small order for individuals who often serve as executives at other companies. Though this list of responsibilities is rather long, all its elements essentially fall under a single umbrella: risk management.

Although directors must principally look out for the interests of shareholders, they are also accountable to employees, regulators, suppliers, and customers. Balancing responsibilities to these individuals is no simple task. In the words of the NACD, "Serving as a director is demanding and—in addition to significant substantive knowledge and experience relevant to the business and governance needs of the company—requires integrity, objectivity, judgment, diplomacy, and courage." [3] Moreover, shares of many organizations are held by diverse groups of investors, including individual investors, pension funds, hedge funds, and university endowments. Each of these investors may have different investment horizons, expectations of returns, and opinions on risks the organization should bear in generating returns. Catering to each of these investors can prove difficult without a proper risk management plan.

Sound risk management practices enable board members to fulfill their fiduciary obligations to all stakeholders of the organization. Such practices ensure that information systems properly assimilate data from different parts of the organization, that this data is critically analyzed, and finally, that plans are verified or modified because of the data. Performance measurement, strategic goal setting, and establishment of corporate policies are all outputs of this process, the result of which is increased value for all stakeholders.

The Importance of Proper Risk Management

The importance of true risk management has become heightened in today's competitive economic world. Historically, risk management practices focused on minimizing financial losses to the firm at the micro level, primarily through insurance or hedging contracts associated with specific services or goods. Macro-level, holistic risk assessments performed by senior managers, C-level executives, and boards of directors have only recently come into vogue—although some of these groups still remain reluctant to analyze organizational risks and act on their analysis of them.

The tenets of risk management must be ingrained within a corporate culture in order for such practices to be effective. The tone demonstrated by a company's board of directors and senior managers sets the example for the organization. Unfortunately, recent research has shown that many board members feel radical organizational change is unnecessary, even if systems perceive that the status quo has shifted.[4] Board members are often accustomed to operating within established patterns of behavior, favoring smooth meetings over confrontation incited by fundamental business issues. They generally fail to critically examine and evaluate the organization's *modus operandi*, instead believing that historical operating procedures will properly mitigate a crisis. We believe a heightened awareness of risks is necessary at all levels of the organization within today's economic climate. Without such a dramatic shift in the organization's tenor, proper risk mitigation will not adequately address fundamental issues.

Crises at the beginning and end of the 2000s effectively bookend a period of time in which the importance of risk assessment rose dramatically. The accounting scandals of the early 2000s, the economic crisis of the late 2000s, and the Bernard Madoff Ponzi scheme have shown that the complexity of business sometimes outpaces the knowledge of even the best executives and regulators. Numerous businesses have come to realize that they must understand and manage all risks to the organization, not just as separate threats but also with an understanding of the interaction between risks: Seemingly insignificant risks, when coupled together, can cause great damage.

Many companies hurt by the global financial crisis of 2008 and 2009 employed some form of risk management, but most failed to include a crucial component—sound information—in their risk management practices. Rapid financial innovation, including securitized subprime mortgages, had the effect of increasing noise in market-based data. Few owners of such mortgages or credit-default swaps truly understood the nature of the contracts and the value associated with them; some arguably didn't attempt to understand these risks, which were masked by the overly complicated nature of the contracts.

The practice of gathering sound information, or "Information Integrity™," is paramount to risk management. To manage risk effectively, it is essential that one has sound, reliable data, with a clear sense of how such risks could affect the organization *in the future*. Although we are always forced to drive through the "rearview mirror" in assessing our risks, our envelope of concern, as illustrated in the earlier example, is really the events that come ahead of us rather than those that we have passed.

We must be careful in using historical data to assess risks; blind faith in data extrapolation can subvert any risk management process. Information Integrity™ is paramount—a necessary condition for a proper risk assessment. When "noisy" data is employed in making strategic decisions, the results (as evidenced by the current credit crisis) can be disastrous and systemic in nature. For that reason, risk management practices should include periodic checks of employed risk models. This will help ensure that the risk management process is working and can serve as a correction aid in the event that it is not.

Preview of Section I

Within Section I we present key tenets of organizational risk management. This section introduces a common definition of risk and discusses high-level enterprise risk management strategies. Internal investigations and insurance recoveries are also discussed in Section I.

As stated in the Preface, we have purposefully tailored this section toward directors and executives charged with implementing enterprise-wide risk management procedures. Accordingly, we focus on topics of interest for these individuals.

Notes

1. K. O'Sullivan, "Top 10 Concerns of CFOs," 2008, www.cfo.com/article.cfm/10596933/c_10712531.
2. National Association of Corporate Directors, "Key Agreed Principles," 2009, https://secure.nacdonline.org/StaticContent/StaticPages/DM/NACDKeyAgreed Principles.pdf.
3. Ibid.
4. A. Campbell and S. Sinclair, "The Crisis: Mobilizing Boards for Change," *The McKinsey Quarterly*, 2009.

CHAPTER 1

An Introduction to Risk

R isk and risk management are two terms that comprise a central component of organizations, yet they have no universal definition. In this chapter we discuss these terms, explain at a high level the manner in which a risk assessment is conducted, and discuss factors of which risk management practitioners should be aware in conducting such assessments.

This chapter also serves as an introduction to the body of work presented in subsequent Section I chapters and to our quantitative methodologies that supplement this information in Section II.

Definition of Risk

There is no single definition of risk or, for that matter, a set of heuristics or rules by which one can deem a given level of risk to be acceptable. However, we offer the reader the following definitions of risk, exposure, and events:

Risk = Probability that a problem occurs

Problem = An event or incident that would be harmful to objectives

Incidents or Events = Risk times the opportunities for occurrence, mitigated by the environment and control activities

Consequences = Harm or loss caused by an incident. The reverse of an objective

Exposures = Incidents times the magnitude of the consequences

COSO-ERM uses the word *events* for things that might happen, and could be favorable or adverse. Favorable events are important in some contexts, but we use the word *incident* when referring to adverse events. We also use the word *problem* to discuss the nature of what could potentially go wrong, creating an incident.

Let's begin with an example:

For instance, suppose that a data entry clerk will make an error in 1 out of every 10,000 keystrokes. She is tasked with inputting data containing a total of 1 million keystrokes. The risk of events occurring associated with a bad entry is then $1/10,000 = 0.0001$, whereas the number of opportunities for this event are 1 million. Thus the expected incidents associated with a bad entry are $1/10,000 \times 1$ million $= 100$ events.

The exposure associated with a risk is defined by the expected number of incidents of risk multiplied by the magnitude of the event's consequences. In most instances, this magnitude will be quantified in terms of dollars. Returning to our example, suppose we estimated that correcting each entry cost $0.50 in labor charges. We assume no other exposure due to these risks. Then the expected exposure associated with this risk would be $50.

The risk management literature sometimes uses the word *risk* to denote the nature of a potential problem and other times to denote what we call *exposure*. Generally, when risk management authors refer to *risk* in the singular format, they are referring to the probability of incidents occurring. However, when authors use the word *risks* in the plural, they usually are referring to either the nature of possible incidents or to exposures. These mixed meanings cause poor communication in discussions of risk management. However, within our framework, risk, incidents, and exposure are three different notions, related by the preceding definitions.

Risk management terminology is meaningful only in the context of the future. Incidents that have already occurred are said to have a probability of 1. Historical information will help us understand the probability of occurrence and opportunities associated with the risk, but the exposure of the event may still remain uncertain.

Consider the case of a material misstatement uncovered by auditors in a firm's financial statements. The probability that this event occurs is 1 by definition: The event has already occurred. However, the magnitude of the event is not yet fully understood. Due to the uncertainty in the magnitude, the exposure associated with this risk is uncertain. Even though the auditors may be able to quantify the size of the misstatement, the magnitude of the event remains unknown: Will shareholders punish the company for such an error? Will customers view the company differently? Has the company ruined the goodwill of those within its supply chain?

With this simple example we have also elaborated a potential complexity associated with risk management engagements: The realization of an event can necessitate the estimation of a completely new series of risks and exposures associated with these risks. Knowing what new risks and exposures necessitate estimation requires risk practitioners to have an intimate understanding of the firm's operations. For this reason, risk management engagements may also be called *operational assessments*. The scope and depth of an operational assessment will largely depend on the goals set forth within an organizational risk management strategy.

The Risk Management Strategy

A risk management strategy is composed of three interrelated components: risk identification, risk evaluation, and risk mitigation. The form each of these components takes will differ by assessor and purpose. For instance, risk identification in a manufacturing setting might involve a detailed walk of the plant floor to examine hazards workers may face; risk identification performed by a C-level executive could seek to identify risks associated with the business's strategy. However, irrespective of the form a risk management strategy takes, the identification of risks must precede other actions taken by professionals in executing this strategy.

Risk Identification

Identification of potential risks is the first step in a risk assessment. Without proper identification of risks, a risk analysis will be sorely lacking in its potential implications. When identifying risks, a practitioner should not only elaborate these risks himself, he should also speak with other experts in the field applicable to the scope of the project to hear their opinions on potential risks. By doing so, the practitioner reduces the chance that a risk is not elaborated. *This issue is a risk of the risk assessment itself.*

Risk identification can take many forms, but we proceed with an example for a manufacturing setting. In Exhibit 1.1, we have elaborated a series of potential problems. Note that this list is not comprehensive.

The format of this list will look significantly different depending on the nature of the assessment. If the risk practitioner is focusing only on risks associated with labor strikes, the enumerated list will represent risks associated purely with labor strikes; if the risk practitioner is focusing on more broad, strategic objectives, the list will include higher-level items.

EXHIBIT 1.1 Examples of Potential Problems in a Manufacturing Setting

Problems
Labor strike
Retail market demand changes
Facility damaged by nature
Raw material inventory depleted
Power failure
Change in government regulations

Risk Evaluation

Having constructed lists enumerating potential risks of various problems, the practitioner should next enumerate consequences associated with each of these risks. How will revenue be impacted by these risks? How will customers be impacted? What about suppliers? Employees? All stakeholders in general? This list of consequences can serve as a foundation for an analysis of exposure due to potential risks.

Once exposures have been evaluated, it is important for the practitioner to next elaborate control measures that are currently in place to mitigate these risks. Various frameworks exist to evaluate these controls, but the one we employ in this book is an augmentation of the COSO Enterprise Risk Management Framework. Current control measures can serve to minimize the probability that an event occurs as well as the magnitude of exposure associated with the event. For example, removing causal factors of a fire from an ignition source effectively lowers the probability that such an event will occur. However, having up-to-date fire sprinklers in place to remediate the fire minimizes the magnitude of the exposure: They help prevent the fire from spreading.

Another component of risk evaluation is the act of comparing levels of risk to organizational tolerances. Risk will be present in any organization, no matter how well run that organization is. Risk is not only a function of controllable events, it is also dependent on events for which we have no control—for example, natural disasters. The important issue within the risk evaluation framework is that potential risks, having been enumerated and analyzed, are accepted as tolerable by the organization.

Risk Mitigation

Once risks have been identified and the consequences and controls elaborated, a risk mitigation strategy should be implemented. This strategy should focus on any risks and exposures that the organization deems intolerable. Risk mitigation might involve revising current control measures, implementing new ones, or removing causal factors that could cause risks.

In implementing a risk mitigation strategy, a practitioner should focus on decreasing both the probability that the event occurs and the exposure associated with the event, should it occur. Doing so will best allow the effect of the risk to be minimized.

For a risk mitigation strategy to achieve effective results, it is important that all individuals within the concerned process support proper mitigation procedures. A proper "tone at the top" should be set by a manager prior to strategy implementation, the strategy should be implemented by practitioners, and periodic audits should be conducted to ensure that the mitigation process is in fact occurring according to plan. The nature of the mitigation strategy—and the players involved in it—will largely depend on the scope of the risk management engagement.

The Scope of a Risk Management Engagement

A risk management engagement is a function of the scope and desired precision of the assessment. In compiling a risk management strategy, it is essential for a risk practitioner to first identify the scope of the engagement. Is the practitioner responsible for assessing strategic risks to the organization? Operational risks? Financial reporting risks? Regulation compliance risks? The scope should be mutually agreed on by both the practitioner and the "customer" associated with the assessment. When a risk practitioner is someone outside the organization, it is relatively easy to identify the "customer": It is the person or people calling for the engagement. However, when the risk practitioner is himself a member of the organization desiring the assessment, he must first understand who will be the eventual recipients of his report. He can then contact these individuals to devise a proper scope for the engagement. Once a common scope is achieved among the future recipients of the risk assessment, this scope should be well documented and circulated to keep the engagement focused on its original objectives.

The desired level of precision is another important estimate that risk practitioners must make at the onset of any engagement. An auditor's standard of precision is usually the threshold for materiality. Board members could have very different standards of precision for engagements tasked with assessing strategic risks to the organization. They might want to know with a high degree of precision the risks associated with new product development processes or external threats from competitors.

Of course, many individuals will desire a very high degree of precision; however, they are not willing to expend unbounded costs in achieving this goal. Establishment of a proper budget in conjunction with a risk management engagement can assist all parties in making sure the engagement achieves its desired objectives. In this way, managers and practitioners can optimize the level of risk assessment they want to perform for any given task. Understanding the economics of risk management can help a practitioner with such a cost/benefit analysis. Optimization of risk management costs and benefits can be thought of in a manner akin to standard economic intuition: namely, that the level of the assessment should occur where the marginal benefits associated with conducting the assessment equal the marginal costs. There will likely be decreasing returns associated with the expansion of any risk management engagement. It will generate large marginal benefits for low levels of cost, but as costs begin to increase, these marginal benefits will tend to decrease and level off. Understanding this issue will help managers "right-size" risk assessments with their associated objectives.

Influences in Risk Assessments

Assessing the risk of a given event is a function of many factors. Professional judgment, the quality of information, and bias are but a few that influence a practitioner's estimate of risk.

Professional Judgment

Professional judgment is one of the most important factors a practitioner must use in estimating risk. Here we speak of judgment not as a final assessment of risk but as a factor that should be employed to arrive at a conclusion. Practitioners amass large amounts of experience over their careers; they see the effects of business cycles on the organization, they witness the changes made due to consumer demand shifts, and they understand the organization's culture. Significant knowledge of each of these issues allows a practitioner to critically examine evidence in whatever form it takes.

In the coming chapters, we show that risk assessments must be made using subjective information. If organizations were able to analyze risks using only available objective data, risk practitioners, directors, and executives would have a relatively simple job. Unfortunately, purely objective data does not exist in the context of a risk assessment because of a central issue with the risk assessment process: We are estimating the risk associated with an event in the *future*, not a past event. Analyzing future risks introduces an element of subjectivity into a risk assessment. Past is not always prologue in the context of risk. Therefore, it is the responsibility of the risk practitioner to critically examine past information—and gather new information—about the riskiness of a particular event. He must then exercise professional judgment in estimating the future risk.

The Quality of Information

The quality of information, or Information Integrity^{TM}, is a central component of risk analysis. When a risk manager performs an assessment, he must first compile data from various sources within the organization. This information will primarily take two forms: It can be derived from automated systems or provided by individuals.

Before using the information in a risk analysis, the practitioner should understand and examine the source of the data. Although many organizations are replete with automated systems that provide information to many users, it is important to note that these systems—though seemingly providers of objective information—can be corrupted or influenced by individuals. At the heart of each of these systems is a program that has been devised by an individual for a specific application. An error in this program can cause faulty data. For example, consider the number of computer glitches in a typical operating system. The interface with an organization's automated system is arguably less complex in its design, but it is also subject to fewer quality control checks and testing methods than a standard computer operating system. Moreover, the propensity for programming errors in an automated system is likely a function of its price.

If the price of an automated system is high, the manufacturer can employ more programmers in the debugging function. One could argue that rather than doing so, it is in the manufacturer's best interest to minimize the costs associated with production, and hence, the manufacturer would employ a minimum number of programmers in such a function. However, if a product sells for a higher price than another good in a competitive market, it must be true that consumers perceive a difference between similar goods, since one commands a higher price. If they did not, the higher-priced good would not sell.

Automated systems also face potential corruption from human errors. For instance, though a general ledger system can easily compile all outstanding receivables, it requires that these receivables are first recorded properly by a data entry clerk to ensure information accuracy.

With respect to information obtained from individuals, it is important that the risk practitioner always consider the potential incentives possessed by an individual. For example, if a component of a division manager's salary is a function of the division's sales, he might overstate the sales so that he receives greater benefits. Also consider the example of an engineering manager working to build a prototype of a new product. If a risk practitioner asks this individual if the prototype will be completed on schedule, he might indicate that this is the case, even if he has a privately held belief that it is not true. The risk practitioner is thus always forced to evaluate not only the information he receives but also the source of the information. A practitioner can trust both an individual and an automated system to provide information, but it is important that he adhere to the adage, "Trust, but verify."

Arguably the largest risks within organizations are caused not by physical hazards but by the culture that pervades an organization. In gathering information, it is important to be aware of this culture and how it influences the quality of information received throughout the risk analysis process. This is especially true of executives and board members, who often use information that has been compiled by many individuals. The more individuals who "touch" the process, the greater the likelihood that the data generated by it will be corrupted.

Bias

Bias can be present in information received by the risk practitioner. We talked about *intentional* bias in a previous discussion on the quality of information, but bias can also be unintentional. If information about a population is constructed using sampling, it is important that the sample be representative of the population and free of bias. Careless collection of data can introduce significant bias, however unintentional, into information. Such bias could also be present when an individual provides information received from another source; the bias might be present with the individual creator of the data, independent of any bias from the disseminator. In procuring data for risk assessments, risk practitioners should thus always consider not just the *immediate* source of information but also the *originating source*.

Summary

Risk is a feature that is present in all organizations, no matter how well those organizations are run. The incidents associated with an event can be defined by the probability that the event occurs, multiplied by the number of opportunities for this event to occur. The exposure associated with an adverse event is equal to the probability of the consequences multiplied by the magnitude of the consequences.

In performing risk management engagements, practitioners should strive to minimize these two elements associated with potential risks faced by the organization. They should also be conscious of the quality of information they receive, the bias inherent in any datasets they analyze, and the professional judgment required of those preparing the data.

CHAPTER 2

Key Tenets of Enterprise Risk Management

Discussions of risk within corporate America usually proceed crises. Rarely talked about in times of economic prosperity, risk is generally at the forefront immediately following events many were not able to predict. Witness the recent global economic crisis of 2008 and 2009. Nearly every sector of the American economy was hit by events that began in the financial sector. Financial instruments such as credit default swaps and collateralized loan obligations, created with the intention of allowing firms and investors the ability to further diversify risks, arguably magnified the riskiness of unfavorable events. Massive government bailouts and stimulus packages in the trillions of dollars were required to stem the crisis which, at the time of this writing, has yet to convincingly subside. While the American economy has sustained economic shocks before (e.g., the Great Depression, Black Monday of 1987, and the dot-com bust of 2000), few risk managers predicted a crisis of this magnitude could occur in light of the "financial innovation" which took place over the past 30 years. The sense of astonishment felt by investors, corporations, economists, and politicians at the events of 2008 and 2009 brought risk management out of the shadows and again into the limelight.

Today, risk management practices are frequently discussed within nearly every sector of our economy. However, despite these discussions, many corporations have yet to embrace what is perhaps the most important element of a risk management dogma: a well-entrenched, vigilant corporate culture focused on risk-adjusted decision making. The most important element of such a culture is unquestionably an appropriate tone at the top set by not only the CXOs (the CEO, CFO, and other chief officers) of the organization, but also the board of directors.

Within this chapter we discuss the manner in which executives and directors can set an appropriate tone at the top for the corporations they serve. We also discuss necessary elements of sound risk management philosophies and common pitfalls corporations may encounter in evaluating risks.

Organizational Culture and Risk Management

An organizational culture focused on risk management is *the* essential component of enterprise risk management (ERM). Just as employee tips are the most frequent detector of fraud in an organization (tips unearthed more frauds than internal controls and internal audits combined in 2008), employee vigilance is the most important component of a risk management policy.[1] When employees are constantly watching out for potential risky incidents—both internal and external to the organization—organizations improve the chance that these incidents will be detected early.

Many organizations have robust risk management procedures and policies in place. However, even when these functions are working properly, the information they perceive is, in the words of corporate defense professional Sean Lyons, "at best provisional, imperfect or obsolete, as it is subject to change at any point in time." The corporate world is "faced with ever-changing and more sophisticated threats, representing an unpredictable world filled with uncertainty and danger."

In order to effectively combat this unpredictable environment, Lyons believes that organizations need to value the interests of all stakeholders, including employees at all levels of the organization. When each of these stakeholders is considered to be "an individual, a person, a human being with human needs and expectations," an organization will be able to "foster the necessary foundation of trust vital to the establishment of the essential top-down, bottom-up culture required" for risk management.[2] We believe that such a culture also promotes employee vigilance.

Employee vigilance is a byproduct of an organization's culture. The establishment of such a culture begins at the top of the organizational pyramid with a tone at the top set by management and the board of directors. Although many definitions of organizational culture exist, we suggest that culture can be defined by an amalgamation of three definitions:[3]

1. "[Culture is] the pattern of shared beliefs and values that give members of an institution meaning, and provide them with rules for behavior in their organization."[4]
2. "[Culture is] a set of understandings or meanings shared by a group of people. The meanings are largely tacit among the members, are clearly relevant to a particular group, and are distinctive to the group."[5]

3. "Culture is the set of important understandings that members of a community share in common."[6]

While a single definition of organizational culture does not exist, these three definitions each describe important components of an organizational culture. First and foremost, culture is a pattern of "*shared* beliefs and values" (emphasis added). Ideally, everyone within an organization will share the *same* beliefs and values about the organization's objectives. This is the goal of management and the board of directors: creating a set of beliefs and values that members of the organizational "community share in common." However, while the creation of such common beliefs and values often takes place at many organizations, convincing employees to share in the beliefs of management is often very difficult. If management does not have the respect of employees, it is almost a certainty that employees will not buy into the beliefs and values set forth by management. Furthermore, in large organizations where multiple divisions operate rather autonomously, it may be difficult for these divisions to work toward a common goal.

Cultural values are also "largely tacit" among group members. Culture is not an entirely tangible attribute. Rather, an organization's culture is best exemplified by the unspoken but conscious beliefs of employees. Corporate slogans, mottos, and banners are accurate manifestations of an organization's culture only if the tacit beliefs of employees agree with these representations. In order to create these tacit values among organizational members, managers need to lead not only with their words, but, more importantly, with their actions. Actions demonstrate to employees that managers genuinely espouse the beliefs they articulate, and that employees will be rewarded for making decisions that agree with the corporation's culture.

Creating a culture of risk management requires management to (1) formulate a risk management policy, (2) articulate this policy to employees, and (3) act in accordance with this policy. Many organizations are successful in completing the first two steps, while the third often proves challenging. The results can be disastrous for organizations where employees make unharmonious risk management decisions. If risks are not combated and addressed in a uniform manner by the organization, they cannot be properly mitigated.

In cases where organizations ineffectively managed the recent economic crisis, cultural change is necessary to prevent such consequences from again harming the organization. Nevertheless, changing an established culture can prove difficult. Consider the example of General Motors (GM), a recent casualty of the economic crisis. In 1982, long before the company filed for bankruptcy in June 2009, GM was falling victim to increased competition in the automotive industry. GM stock had plummeted from $78 $\frac{1}{2}$ per share in December 1976 to $38 $\frac{1}{2}$ in December 1981. GM's management recognized that the corporation needed a significant cultural change to adapt to increasing competition. Lloyd Reuss, the general manager of the Buick division in 1982, stated:

"Our biggest challenge is that we're having to change the mindset of literally hundreds of thousands of people, from the guy who's just been hired in one of our assembly plants right on through the top echelon—not only our organization, but our suppliers as well."[7]

Reuss's comment illustrates the magnitude of change that management and the board must incite if cultural change is to be successful. Unfortunately for GM, the corporation was not able to effectively change its culture: If it were not for the government's bailout of the manufacturer, GM would almost certainly be in liquidation at the time of this book's printing.

Emphasizing Accountability

One of the most important components of a risk management culture is a corporate risk management philosophy that emphasizes accountability. Instituting a culture centered on risk management requires establishing accountability at all levels of the organization. Employees, even those at the lowest levels of the organization, should be accountable to their managers and peers. Those at the highest levels of the organization should be accountable to the board. Without accountability, employees are not incentivized to be cognizant of risks, and cannot be properly evaluated with respect to the organization's risk management philosophy.

Accountability is first and foremost established by formal goal-setting procedures within the organization. Goal-setting procedures allow employees to be rewarded for their work when they have excelled at their job, and held accountable when they have made a mistake. They also provide organizations with an organized tool for ensuring that everyone is marching toward the same goal.

Employees should be rewarded when they meet or exceed goals set for them, and they should face consequences in the event they fail to meet their goals. If an organization fails to reward its highest-performing employees, they may begin to vocalize resentment to other employees. This bitterness can quickly spread internally and can cause high-performing employees to leave the organization.

Many firms that are suffering significant hardships in these challenging economic times are cutting employee benefits, merit pay, and, in some cases, salaries. However, firms should be aware that taking such actions against high-performing employees can create incentives for these talented individuals to leave. It also decreases accountability within the organization. Such employees will likely possess other job options even in tough economic environments; if these individuals do not feel valued, they will leave the organization. After some time, the organization may be left with only those employees who do not have outside employment options. This talent drain is in and of itself a major risk to organizations, especially at their highest echelons. A dearth of talent at the executive and director levels can wreak havoc on an organization's goal-setting process.

Directors possess what is perhaps the most difficult of the goal-setting processes. They must ensure that executives are properly incentivized to adhere to the organization's risk management philosophy. When directors set goals for executives, they should first assess the executive's incentives with respect to the goals they wish to set. For example, a CEO whose bonus is based on increases in revenue might be inclined to grow the firm through acquisitions. If merit raises are based on yearly earnings growth, the CEO may make shortsighted decisions that compromise the organization's long-term profitability. Boards should be especially aware of the incentives they create for executives, since these incentives will cascade throughout the organization. If the incentives of executives are not aligned with the organization's risk management philosophy, the firm may not successfully endure a risky incident. Directors must also make sure to properly reprimand executives who haven't achieved their goals. When ineffective executives are not removed from their posts, employees will begin to feel that the organization does not value accountability. This will, in turn, incite a lack of general concern for the firm's well-being in employees, decreasing employee vigilance. In many cases, it is this vigilance that can best help organizations mitigate risks associated with unforeseen or so-called black swan events.

Planning for Black Swans

The presence of accountability within an organization facilitates effective contingency planning in the event a risk-based incident occurs. Accountability ensures that talented individuals will lead the organization through the incident and command the respect of employees during such challenging times. Accountability is especially important in helping organizations deal with black swan events. The term, coined by Professor Nassim Taleb, is defined in the following way:

> *[A black swan] is an outlier, as it lies outside the realm of regular expectations, because nothing in the past can convincingly point to its possibility. Second, it carries an extreme impact. Third, in spite of its outlier status, human nature makes us concoct explanations for its occurrence after the fact, making it explainable and predictable.*[8]

The term *black swan* refers to the belief previously held by "people in the Old World ... that all swans were white." Before black swans were discovered in Australia, many individuals, including ornithologists, believed such birds did not exist. Taleb uses the term *black swan* to illustrate the "severe limitation to our learning from observations or experience and the fragility of our knowledge."[9]

Throughout his book, Taleb asserts that, because the occurrence of black swans is unpredictable, individuals should not focus on predicting them with precision. It is his belief that we should shy away from predicting such events, instead devoting our efforts to early detection and remediation.

Creating a culture of awareness throughout the organization is, we believe, the best way to deal with such black swan issues. This culture of awareness helps prevent managers from becoming complacent with risks. Instead, they will be more likely to seek out risks and bring them to the attention of their peers and executives. Such behavior and mentality are essential in combating black swan events.

Risk management activities help organizations promote a culture of awareness. They also assist organizations in mitigating predictable risks. Dealing with predictable risks is arguably just as important as dealing with black swan events. However, the predictable nature of the risk allows the organization to take advantage of various enterprise risk management techniques. This is the subject of this book's second section on quantitative risk management. Moreover, within the remainder of this chapter, we also emphasize how the creation of a culture of risk management can assist organizations in dealing with predictable risks.

Benefits of a Risk Management–Focused Culture

By creating a culture of risk management at the enterprise level, companies can better (1) identify the risks they face, (2) evaluate the consequences of these risks, and (3) make enterprise decisions with this information in mind. This three-step process is at the heart of enterprise risk management for today's corporations.

Identifying Risks

The first step in an ERM process is the identification of risks. Depending on the type of organization utilizing the ERM process, many types of risk may be analyzed. However, the key component of risk management is to focus the majority of time on risks that are associated with large exposures. Cash flow, earnings, revenue, operational, regulatory, compliance, and strategic risks are often at the top of the list for many large corporations. Generally speaking, roughly five of these elements will constitute the majority of risks the organization faces. If an overwhelming number of risks are analyzed in detail, the risk assessment process may be stale by the time they can each be analyzed.

Every risk a company faces can realize itself in many ways. When analyzing risks, it is important to consider the full range of exposures and outcomes that they may generate. Many times, managers will focus on, and consequently manage, only those risks they feel are most likely, or those they fear the most. Doing so can create a skewed perspective of the company's true risk exposure.

Understanding the underlying distribution of risks is another important element in the risk management process. When assumptions regarding underlying distributions are incorrectly made, the risk analysis process can reach incorrect conclusions. There are many ways such distributions can be estimated. An objective, historical analysis of data may provide some insight into this underlying distribution, but risk assessments will require subjective analysis. Moreover, although extreme outcomes are unlikely to occur, they may cause a major impact to the organization.

Analysis of Risk

Once risks have been identified, the next step in the ERM process is the analysis of risk. Every business has natural risks that it must bear. The difficulty is in assessing which of these risks are indeed natural, and which should be borne by other entities. In deciding what types of risks are natural, managers might ask themselves the following three questions:

1. Does the firm's current strategy allow it to naturally hedge against particular types of risk?
2. Can the firm manage risks more intelligently than an external entity?
3. Are there mechanisms for the firm to hedge risks externally, such as a liquid market?

Analyzing the business's current and future strategy can help executives and boards to answer these questions. For instance, if a firm is currently a vertically integrated manufacturer, its business model contains a natural hedge against supply chain risks.

In evaluating the second question, firms should look not only at their own track record of risk management, but also at the track records of their industry peers and suppliers. Might it be better for another firm to bear risks associated with certain parts of their business?

The last question can be answered by examining available risk hedging markets, and determining if these can be used effectively by the firm to transfer risk. For example, a firm that is worried about oil prices might hedge against oil price risks by purchasing futures contracts.

While managers may have a distinct view of the risks the firm should bear, it is also essential that managers understand the risks investors are willing to bear. For public companies, a typical measure of risk is the firm's beta (β), defined in the Capital Asset Pricing Model as the covariance of the returns to the market with the returns to the stock divided by the variance of the market returns. Beta represents the riskiness a security brings to a well-diversified portfolio. It is an important measure that investors look at in determining the riskiness of a security.

For example, the β of IBM's stock from the beginning of 2004 through the end of 2008 was roughly 1.0. Such a value indicates that the riskiness associated with IBM's stock is roughly equivalent to the market as a whole. In contrast, the β of Amazon.com's stock over the same time frame was 1.9, indicating that this stock was almost twice as risky as the market for a well-diversified investor. Exhibit 2.1 presents comparative plots of IBM stock

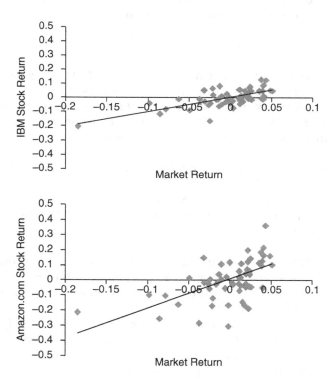

EXHIBIT 2.1 IBM Stock Returns versus Market Returns (*top*) and Amazon.com Stock
Returns versus Market Returns (*right*), 2003–2008 Monthly Data

returns versus market returns (here, we use the S&P 500 for what the Capital Asset Pricing Model calls "market returns") and Amazon.com stock returns versus market returns. Note that the slope of the trend line in the lower plot is nearly twice as steep as that of the chart at the top of the Exhibit.

Given these differences, an investor might welcome Amazon.com taking on a risky project, but frown at the prospect of IBM doing so. If managers at IBM decided to take on a risky project, investors might be inclined to sell their stock if they felt the risks to future earnings were too great.

Understanding Stakeholders' Preferences

Whenever risky decisions are made, decision makers must ensure they fully understand the preferences of stakeholders. For public companies, whose top decision makers include board members and executives, it is essential that these individuals understand the interests of not only individual investors, but also institutional investors.

Institutional investors make finicky business partners. They are the "friend" who pledges endearing support in good times, while disappearing before the bad times get worse. They are quick to buy stock as it climbs, but act with even greater urgency when they sense a stock is heading south. Directors and executives of publicly traded firms who have a large number of shares held by institutional investors should try their best to understand the preferences these individuals hold with respect to risk aversion. If their expectations are not met, they may sell the stock *en masse,* causing prices to plummet rapidly. For decisions makers of large, publicly traded firms, institutional investment can contribute to wild price swings. Recent research has estimated that increasing institutional investment from 1980 through 1996 caused the prices of large company stocks to increase 50 percent more than their smaller stock counterparts.

For closely held corporations, decision makers should be sure they understand the preferences held by key stakeholders. This is especially true in smaller firms where individuals may have invested a significant portion of their wealth in the business.

Making Decisions Using Risk Management Data

Risk management is not an ephemeral exercise that is assessed once or twice a year. Instead, risk management at the most effective level is an ingrained corporate culture established by those at the top of the organization. These individuals, namely, boards of directors and C-suite executives, are responsible for establishing a risk management culture that guides the firm's day-to-day operations.

One way these individuals can help foster risk management ideas within the organization is by changing the format of investment reports they demand. When many high-level individuals evaluate future projects, they ask for net present value (NPV) analyses based on projected cash flows. Instead of deriving a single NPV estimate, these individuals should ask for a range of NPV estimates based on an analysis of probable outcomes. While some managers will evaluate projects by looking at NPV analyses that focus on a downside, base, and upside case, a clear understanding of what these cases represent is not often sought. Does the downside case represent the lowest possible NPV of the project? Does it represent the 25th percentile outcome or the 10th? Does the upside case represent the 75th percentile outcome or the 90th? Does the base case truly represent the median NPV of the project? By asking risk managers to quantify these NPVs, executives and directors can make better decisions about the projects in which they wish to invest. It may also be helpful to ask for a probabilistic estimate of a negative NPV project.

Project investments should also be investigated under a number of financing scenarios. The NPV of a project funded with debt will generally differ from one funded with equity capital: Both investors require different rates of return on their investment. This should be taken into account in the NPV analysis; a single discount rate should not be used. Furthermore, the consequences of funding a project with either type of capital should be investigated. What are the consequences of the firm increasing its debt capacity? Will the company need a cash cushion in the future? Should a bank bear the majority of the risks associated with an investment (through debt instruments), or should equity holders?

Operationally focused decision-making processes can also benefit from sound risk management analyses: Supply chain, manufacturing, and outsourcing decisions should all be evaluated from an enterprise risk management perspective prior to their implementation. For instance, over the past few decades, many companies have outsourced nonadvanced manufacturing to overseas countries under the auspices of cost reduction. However, when fuel prices rose rapidly throughout 2008, some of these firms soon found that they had not anticipated the impact of such price increases on the total cost of procured parts. This trend was especially prevalent within the Tier 1 automotive supply base. If, instead, companies had hedged their bets by procuring goods from multiple suppliers around the globe (as opposed to solely suppliers in low-cost countries), they might have been able to better weather the impact of fuel prices on parts costs.

Moreover, in many large, bureaucratic organizations, operational decisions are generally made by division-level managers, supply chain decisions by a centralized purchasing department, pricing decisions by sales and marketing managers, and financial decisions by the financial staff. As noted above, even when those decision makers base decisions on downside, base, and upside case scenarios, they are ignoring the remainder of the probability distribution. In some cases, managers of these divisions will make decisions independently of other areas of the organization.

Ideally, the heads of each of the aforementioned departments would analyze a proposed project from an enterprise perspective, optimizing their decision from a firm level, not a divisional one. The current fiefdom decision-making process is sometimes reinforced by managerial incentives that reward division-level managers for improvements to their own organization, rather than the organization as a whole. Those companies who have properly ingrained a culture of risk management within their organization will, however, recognize the perils of such incentive schemes, and design incentives that reward individuals most heavily for the performance of the corporation as a whole, not just the performance of their division.

Issues in Managing Risk

Within the previous section we described the manner in which firms can identify, evaluate, and use risk management in the decision-making process. We now present several issues typically encountered by organizations in implementing risk management processes.

The Trap of Historical Data

When attempting to quantify risks in the decision-making process, risk managers will often rely on historical data. The assumption made by such managers is often that history will repeat itself, or that future events will closely mirror history. For example, let's assume that a risk manager's boss had requested a forecast of the S&P 500 index for the upcoming year on January 1, 2008. It's likely that one of the first places he would turn would be to historical data. However, how much historical data should he use in his prediction? The S&P 500 index has been published since 1957; should he include data going back 50 years?

Let's say at a first glance that he decides to use 10 years of data for his prediction. Over this time period (from January 1, 1998, through January 1, 2008), the S&P 500 index increased from 970 to 1468, for an average increase of about 50 points per year, or a compound annual growth rate (CAGR) of 4.2%. The standard deviation of yearly returns to the index was 17.8% per year. Exhibit 2.2 presents information on the S&P 500 index values throughout this time period.

Using the obtained information, he constructs a forecast that estimates the S&P 500 index will likely rise by 4.2%, and provides a range of estimates

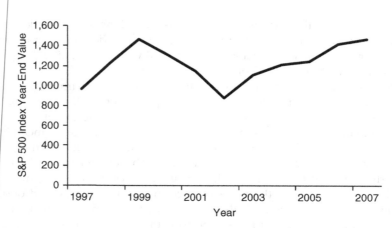

EXHIBIT 2.2 S&P 500 Index Values from 1997 through 2007

to his boss based on the average annual increase and standard deviation of his analysis. The assumptions made in doing so would be that historical data provides a good approximation to future changes, that changes in the S&P 500 are random (i.e., the index is as likely to go up as it is to go down), and changes in the index can be approximated by a normal distribution. How would his prediction have fared? Unfortunately, not too well. As shown in Exhibit 2.3, the S&P 500 index fell by 39% from the end of 2007 to the end of 2008. If he had assumed the index would rise by a mean of 4.2% and had a standard deviation of 17.8% in returns, actual 2008 returns represented an event estimated to occur less than 1% of the time. So, what went wrong with his prediction?

While anyone reading this book is surely familiar with the impact of the economic crisis on the public equities markets, the magnitude of this impact would have been difficult to estimate, even for the best of risk managers. One could argue that a longer time period should have been used for the analysis. If, instead of using only 10 years of data in his prediction, he used 30 years of data, he would have found that the S&P 500 grew at a CAGR of 9.6% per year from the end of 1977 through 2007. Over this time period, the standard deviation of returns was 14.9% per year. This information would have, arguably, caused him to estimate a higher value for the S&P 500 index than if he had used only 10 years of data.

On the whole, the prediction model that was built contained numerous errors. If the true volatility of the S&P 500 index at the end of 2007 were greater than in previous years, he would have substantially underestimated the probability of a decrease in the index's value. Moreover, if the true mean return of the S&P 500 index were considerably different at the end of 2007

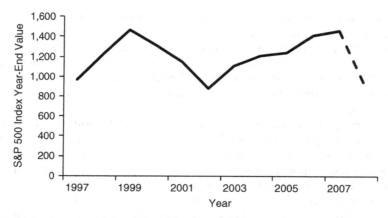

EXHIBIT 2.3 S&P 500 Index Values from 1997 through 2008

than in previous years, his estimates would be highly inaccurate. Lastly, irrespective of these issues with the data, the implicit assumption made in the above forecast was that changes in the S&P 500 index were normally distributed random variables. Normal distribution or Gaussian curves follow the familiar bell curve shape. However, was it fair to assume that the future distribution of S&P 500 returns follows such a shape? What if the distribution were not symmetric about its mean? What if it were skewed in some manner, like those distributions pictured in Exhibit 2.4? If such distributions had been used to construct the aforementioned predictions, the analysis would have yielded very different results.

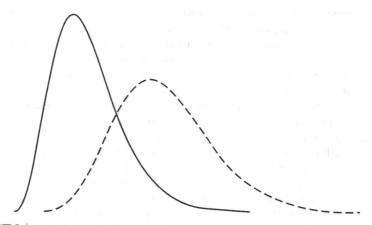

EXHIBIT 2.4 Sample Skewed Distributions

For many companies, rapid financial innovation over the past 30 years has caused changes in the underlying distribution of many types of risk. For example, if one were to estimate the riskiness of real estate prices just a few years ago by using historical data, the effect of collateralized debt obligations and collateralized loan obligations on real estate prices would not have been captured in this analyses—these tools have only been in existence for a very short period of time.

Returning to a metaphor first used in the introduction to Section I, it is often necessary for board members and executives to "drive through the rearview mirror" when analyzing forecasts. Oftentimes, these forecasts will be constructed by lower-level employees, bubbling up through the organization until they hit the top of the organizational pyramid. By the time they find their way into the C-suite, the assumptions underlying the forecasts may have been lost in translation. These assumptions are a crucial component of the analysis; they should not be overlooked. Accordingly, we recommend that any forecasts provided to the board or executives include a discussion of explicit assumptions underlying the analysis. By doing so, decision makers can better understand the manner in which estimates were derived and analyses calculated.

Incorrect Estimation of Inflection Points

When making decisions regarding strategy, boards and executives must often anticipate demand for future products. Before making a decision, these individuals will be presented with numerous forecasts prepared by analysts that contain top-line (i.e., revenues) and bottom-line (i.e., net profit) estimates associated with future product sales. Forecasting such estimates in relatively steady lines of businesses may not present a large challenge for analysts; however, forecasts which estimate these figures for new lines of business may prove especially challenging.

In many circumstances, the estimation of revenues associated with a new product is more difficult than the estimation of the costs of production. If the good is a non-transformational technology, a forecaster could contact outside vendors to see how much the product would cost to build. This estimate could then serve as an upper bound on the costs of the program. Internal cost estimates could be used to validate these costs.

The costs of direct labor for future products are generally well understood by analysts, as are other variable costs including materials (though quite variable in recent times, material costs are generally well forecasted by analysts). Depending on the indirect cost data collected by a firm's accounting system, the estimation of overhead costs may prove challenging; however, the difficulty one encounters estimating these costs often pales in comparison to the estimation of future revenues associated with new products.

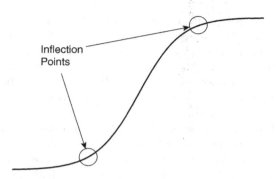

EXHIBIT 2.5 Sample S Curve with Inflection P

If the product is a transformational technology without competitors in the marketplace, the estimation of revenues will prove especially difficult. Sales of new products rarely increase in a linear manner. Oftentimes, sales will increase incrementally and linearly, suddenly exploding once an inflection point is reached. They will stay at this level for a period of time before tapering off at another inflection point. The curve that describes this phenomenon has an S shape as depicted in Exhibit 2.5.

Current forecast methods employed by analysts often disregard these inflection points in favor of linear trend lines. For instance, in a discounted cash flow analysis, it is typically assumed that revenues for a particular product will grow linearly over the explicit forecast period. The results of such analyses could prove disastrous for companies unprepared to deal with the consequences.

When analyzing forecasts that have been prepared for them, directors and executives should be especially wary of these linear trend lines used to predict revenues. Instead, they should focus on identifying where the market is with respect to the two inflection points shown in Exhibit 2.5. Oftentimes, the left-handed part of this S curve is much longer than most imagine. Believe it or not, the internet was over 25 years old when the first dot-com IPO, that of Netscape Communications Corporation, took place on August 9, 1995. However, once this inflection point has been reached (as was experienced in the dot-com boom), sales may take off more rapidly than expected. If the organization's supply chain and manufacturing operations are not prepared for such rapid change, potential customers may switch to substitute products if they are readily available.

Managing Risk in Silos

Many organizations analyze risks separately according to the type of risk in question. Market, compliance, regulatory, operational, and credit risks are often measured by risk managers in separate parts of the organization by different individuals. Discussions between these individuals may not occur, although executives and board members will most certainly review an aggregated version of their work. Management of risks in such a manner can lead to gross underestimation of the correlation between risks. The only way to accurately assess these correlations is for the organization to implement a practice of enterprise risk management.

The global financial crisis has helped ERM transition from an interesting management concept to an important management practice. However, despite continuing convergence surrounding this sentiment, many corporations lack the organizational structure necessary to truly espouse an ERM philosophy.

The position of the chief risk officer (CRO) or the chief risk management officer (CRMO) is one that many financial institutions have created in recent past. Unfortunately, the majority of corporations who possess such officers fall within the financial sector; few corporations in other areas of the economy possess such a position. Perhaps most obvious to outside observers is the lack of such a position at major automotive companies or their suppliers. Despite the fact that both GM and Chrysler failed miserably to predict the current market crisis, neither firm has created such a position to assist the companies in detecting and mitigating future risks. Many automotive suppliers, who received $5 billion from the federal government in 2009, also lack such a position.

By creating a CRO position, a firm signals to its employees the importance it places on risks. This action demonstrates to employees that the corporation values high-level risk management so greatly that it has appointed a specific individual to oversee and manage the risks faced by the organization.

For those firms that possess CROs, these individuals often report to one of three individuals: the CEO (this occurs about 49% of the time), the CFO (as do 28% of CROs), the COO, or the board of directors.[10] It is our opinion that it is in the best interests of an organization for the CRO to report to the board of directors, similar to the internal audit department. By having the CRO report to the board rather than the executive team, the impartiality of this individual is greatly encouraged. For instance, if the CEO has presented the board with a potential acquisition opportunity, together with a set of financial projections for the acquisition, it would be in the best interest of the board to have the CRO deliver an unbiased analysis of the deal. This can only be facilitated if this individual reports to the board.

Curiously, for all the recent attention risk has received in corporate America, the structure of boards of directors has changed little in reacting to this change of focus. Board committees and structure largely remain the same. Given the yet unchanged status quo, under what committee does risk management fall? The audit committee? The finance committee? Other ad hoc committees? In general, the participants on these committees already have a full plate. Meeting the SEC requirements for Sarbanes-Oxley Act compliance requires a considerable amount of time. For directors who serve on boards of multiple companies, they may not have the time necessary to oversee the organization's enterprise risk management.

For those companies looking to demonstrate the importance of risk management to employees and investors, it may be best to form a board level risk committee. This committee would review data regarding enterprise-level risks caused by issues in the firm's internal and external environments. On the internal risk side, the risk committee might review and assess the probability of labor issues occurring in the future, changes in turnover signifying employee discontent, issues with production costs or quality levels, or product recalls, among other issues. With respect to a firm's external environment, the risk committee might review the impact of decisions made by competitors, anticipated changes in market demand levels, or shocks to the supply chain. The existence of the risk committee itself provides a powerful signal to executives, employees, and investors that the company is focused on mitigating risks.

Although the boards of several Canadian, European, and Australian companies have already adopted separate risk management committees, these committees are not yet seen on a diverse array of boards in the United States. Financial institutions lead the way in the adoption of standalone risk committees in the United States; other industries have yet to adopt similar governance structures. Many boards of directors still designate responsibility for risks to existing committee members. Regulatory, compliance, financial, operating, and strategy risks, among others, are delegated to various board committees, primarily based on the skill set of those on the committees. This allows for the evaluation of specific risks by individual board members, but it does not facilitate a holistic, enterprise-level risk assessment process.

For example, suppose the finance committee of a particular company is charged with evaluating the organization's operational risks while the compliance committee is charged with evaluating regulatory risks. Each committee is then apprised of these specific risks and evaluates the potential consequences associated with these risks. However, will these estimates accurately take into account the magnitude of risks the organization may face? Will they evaluate the impact of interaction between risks? In the case of an airline, operational risks (repeated mechanical difficulties with aircraft) may trigger regulatory risks (FAA compliance). Together with the creation of a CRO position, standalone risk management committees can help the organization streamline the process through which risks are identified, evaluated, and acted upon. They can help ensure that the organization fully understands the extent and nature of the risks it faces every day.

Overlooking Risks

Boards and executives rely on data compiled by chief risk officers, risk managers, and risk practitioners when evaluating organizational risk. However, even when these individuals do everything within their power to identify, evaluate, and report risks, they may still come up short on meeting these objectives if other employees fail to report risks. Fraud-related risks present a particular challenge for these individuals given the nature of the risk.

No one wants to suspect a fellow employee of committing a fraudulent act. While the human nature that exists within each of us would like to give a peer the benefit of the doubt, the truth of the matter is that cautious skepticism plays a key role in risk detection. If an employee notices that a co-worker has been acting suspiciously, they may not report the issue out of fear of retaliation, or because they feel their own personal judgment is in error. However, if the suspicion turns out to be correct, the magnitude of the unchecked fraud could soon reach a material level, unbeknownst to risk managers within the organization. One could argue that objective internal control systems should largely be responsible for identifying such risk. However, it is important to remember that these internal control systems were designed and oftentimes are monitored by people.

Risks in other parts of the organization may also go unreported because employees are not incentivized to report them. For instance, is it in the best interests of manufacturing executive to report quality control defects if he himself is in charge of the quality control process? In instances like this, employees may attempt to deliberately hide or disguise risks because it is in their own best interests to do so. Were AIG investment managers who underwrote many credit default swap contracts honest in assessing the riskiness of the securities they created?

Creating a culture of risk management throughout the organization can greatly assist executives and board members in controlling risks in a cost-effective manner. Risk management practices could conceivably—not practically—be structured to keep track of every risk the organization may face. However, such practices would undoubtedly be cost prohibitive. They may also stifle innovation in fast-moving organizations focused on bringing disruptive technologies to market. Within these fast-paced environments, employees need to be able to make decisions rapidly, but with vigilance. If an organization has been effective at creating a culture centered on risk awareness, pockets of risk are likely to be detected wherever they reside. Even the best risk management practices and processes can be subverted by an insular corporate culture that is unfocused on risk management.

The Human Element

The human element introduces an important factor in risk management processes and procedures, and in an organization's culture. No matter how strong an organization's risk management function is, there always exists room for error. Risk management estimates are derived by fallible individuals. They *will* make mistakes, they may have trouble articulating their findings, and their personalities may clash with others whose views are contrary to their own. Even Nobel laureates make grave mistakes and misestimates, as demonstrated by the spectacular failure of Long-Term Capital Management (a fund whose partners included laureates Robert C. Merton and Myron Scholes) in the late 1990s. Risk management is never perfect.

Nonetheless, awareness of the human element within risk management can mitigate this risk of the risk assessment process itself. For instance, key organizational decision makers must often rely on information that has been prepared for them in making operational decisions. It is of utmost importance that this information is of high integrity in order to ensure that sound decisions are made. Directors must frequently rely on information from high-level executives in making decisions, while executives must rely on information from senior managers within the organization throughout the decision-making process. This information is generally based on numerous financial estimates made by preparers in compiling data. In order to assess the accuracy of such estimates, decision makers should ask themselves the following four questions:

1. Do the preparers and/or distributors of information have hidden agendas supported by their incentive structures? Are their remuneration packages based on the optimization of short-term goals or long-term goals?
2. How have previous estimates compared with realized financials? Does there appear to be bias in previous estimates?
3. How do pro forma financial estimates compare with those of competitors and analyst reports of public companies?
4. What accounting estimates have been used in the preparation of such estimates? How do these compare with those of competitors? What is their net effect on the financial estimates? For instance, last in, first out (LIFO) inventory valuation will tend to understate net income in periods of rising material costs, but overstate net income in periods of decreasing material costs. If pro forma estimates are being compared with those of competitors who use first in, first out (FIFO) accounting, appropriate adjustments should be made to ensure an apples-to-apples comparison.

The human element may also come into play at the board level in the strategic decision-making process. An organization may have a well-established policy regarding its risk tolerance and a robust risk management function. However, if a CEO believes strongly in a certain project, he may elect to take it on irrespective of the organizational risks or policies. For this reason alone, board members should actively participate in high-level strategic decision-making processes. Directors can check the power of the executive team should they feel these individuals are not operating in accordance with the organization's stated goals.

A Failure to Communicate

Movie buffs and Paul Newman fans who have seen *Cool Hand Luke* will remember the movie's tagline, "What we have here is a failure to communicate." Unfortunately, the failure to communicate and understand risks also plagues many businesses in America. Even the most astute risk manager who can construct very accurate models will be rendered ineffective by his inability to communicate risks.

The recent economic crisis perhaps best demonstrated this issue of communication and the manner in which it can cause organizations to misunderstand the risks they face. While derivatives trading arms of financial institutions employed highly analytical risk models to make investment decisions, many boards and CEOs of these organizations did not understand the securities their trading arms were buying and selling. Hence, they could not properly assess the risks associated with these instruments.

Indeed one of the largest barriers risk management has had to overcome is its complexity. Many books that include "risk management" in their title contain pages and pages of detailed mathematical models. Some risk management papers and textbooks are difficult for even the smartest mathematicians to understand. For directors and CEOs, individuals whose time is constrained by the many demands they must meet each day, such complicated models may require too much time to dissect when a critical decision is on the line.

A report by UBS to its shareholders in 2008 explained that, "A number of attempts were made to present subprime or housing-related exposures. The reports did not, however, communicate an effective message for a number of reasons, in particular because the reports were overly complex, presented outdated data or were not made available to the right audience."[11] In short, the reports reviewed by key decision makers at UBS failed to accurately convey the risks of UBS's business *in an understandable manner*. We note that UBS's stock decreased by roughly 60% from April 2007 through June 2008.

However, even when a risk practitioner is able to properly articulate his findings, directors and executives need to remember that these findings are not facts—they are estimates. Numerical estimates derived from risk analyses represent only one dimension of an enterprise risk management strategy: They should not be treated as *the* definitive component of an analysis, but rather *a* component. Use of numerical estimates in conjunction with other risk management tools, however, greatly improves the reliability of the risk management process.

Summary

Within this chapter we have discussed the key tenets of an enterprise risk management framework and also common pitfalls experienced by corporations in implementing such procedures. The most important component of an enterprise risk management philosophy is a corporate culture focused on mitigating risks. Only when such a culture is present can organizations best prevent, detect, and mitigate risks that arise in their line of business.

Notes

1. Association of Certified Fraud Examiners, *2008 Report to the Nation*, www.acfe.com/documents/2008-rttn.pdf.
2. S. Lyons, "Risk Management's Role in Corporate Defense" (Society of Actuaries, 2008).
3. Adapted from J. Martin, *Organizational Culture* (Thousand Oaks, CA: Sage, 2001).
4. S. Davis, *Managing Corporate Culture* (Cambridge, MA: Ballinger, 1984).
5. V. Sathe, *Culture and Related Corporate Realities* (Homewood, IL: Irwin, 1985).
6. M. Louis, "Perspectives on Organizational Culture," in *Organizational Culture*, ed. P. J. Frost, L. F. Moore, M. R. Louis, C. C. Lundberg, and J. Martin (Beverly Hills, CA: Sage, 1985).
7. Quote from Lloyd Reuss appears in J. Harbour, *Factory Man* (Society of Manufacturing Engineers, 2009).
8. N. Taleb, *The Black Swan: The Impact of the Highly Improbable* (New York: Random House, 2007).
9. Ibid.
10. C. Lee and P. Shimpi, "The Chief Risk Officer: What Does It Look Like and How Do You Get There?" *Risk Management*, www.rmmag.com/Magazine/Print Template.cfm?AID=2855.
11. R. Stultz, "Risk Management Failures: What Are They and When Do They Happen?" October 2008, http://papers.ssrn.com/sol3/papers.cfm?abstract_id= 1278073.

CHAPTER 3

Mitigating Operational Risks Through Strategic Thinking

M itigating operational risks is often predicated on outdoing business adversaries. In the global economy, many businesses face significant risks from competitors out to steal their market share and their ideas. Without sound strategic practices in place, executives and boards can quickly find themselves in the unenviable position of watching a rival prosper at the expense of their own firm. Good strategic thinking—and the resulting implementation of such thinking—can greatly assist businesses in maintaining their competitive edge and keeping rivals at bay.

Within this chapter we introduce a novel framework for strategic analysis using contemporary economic techniques. Our analysis herein is based on the ideas of Dixit and Nalebuff (1991)[1] and Porter (1980).[2] The economic science of game theory will form the basis of our analysis. Our goal is not a rigorous mathematical treatment of the discipline; rather, we endeavor to present the reader with practical knowledge that can easily be employed in practice. Indeed, one of the likely reasons why game theory is an underexploited tool in many competitive strategy books is the cloak of bombastic jargon that masks the intuitive, underlying theory. We hope our illustrative examples serve to remove this mask and allow the reader to develop a comprehensive understanding of strategic decision making predicated on its insights.

Strategic Behavior

Throughout our careers and in our personal lives, we are faced with choices. The moment we develop cognitive reasoning is the instant we begin to make choices for ourselves. The choices and decisions we make on a daily basis are myriad: "What should I eat for dinner?" "When should I propose to my girlfriend?" "What career path should I choose?" Though the answers to these questions may, at some point, seem evident, the decision-making process invoked by our minds evaluates these decisions in light of our surroundings.

We are continuously surrounded by other decision makers who influence our own choices. For example, the answer to what career path we should choose will likely be influenced by the thoughts of our close friends and family. The answer to when one should propose marriage will likely be influenced by the pressures exerted by one's own family members and by one's significant other's family. In our working lives, we are required to make decisions in uncertain environments. Irrespective of our employer or position, these decisions are influenced by our surroundings.

Fundamental strategic decisions made by executives, managers, and directors should also be made with thought given to the decisions of competitors. All too often, these individuals evaluate significant business projects based on canonical finance methods: Net present values or internal rates of return are calculated; earnings before interest, taxes, depreciation, and amortization (EBITDA) are scrutinized; discount rates are projected; and free cash flow forecasts are perused. However, none of these typical methods of financial analysis—on its own—takes into account the impact of strategic decision making in its analysis. They say nothing about the effects of competitors' decisions on the forecasts, nor the likelihood of competitors' decisions. Using the tenets of game theory, however, we can analyze the effects of strategic behavior on financial decisions. We define strategic behavior as the act of making decisions in light of decisions made by others participating in the decision maker's environment. For businesses, an analysis of competitors' actions would be a necessary condition of strategic behavior.

An Analogy to Sports

Watching sports can provide a viewer with a profound understanding—and appreciation—for strategic behavior. Every Saturday afternoon, loyal college football fans can witness strategic behavior taking place on the field, down after down. Within a down, one team must select an offensive play they will execute (a run or a pass), and the opposing team must select a defensive play they feel will best hamper the offense's success.

Decisions made by coaches and coordinators are based on mounds of data. These individuals, along with the players, have watched hours of film of the opposing team, dissecting their strengths and weaknesses. Coaches hope to exploit weaknesses of the opposing team while devaluing their strengths. They do this by calling plays they feel are most appropriate to the opponent. For instance, if a coach knows that the opposing team has a mediocre quarterback and a star running back, he may elect to run more defensive plays that will guard against the run rather than the pass. Conversely, if the coach knows the opposing team has a star receiver, but lacks a solid running back, he will likely guard against the pass. The strategies coaches employ, and the plays they call, will vary from game to game based on the opponent the team faces. Coaches make these decisions because they are in tune with thinking strategically about the behavior of their opponent.

The game of basketball arguably best demonstrates the art of strategic behavior in sports. On each play in the game, five players are on offense, and another five are on defense. Within the limits of certain rules, defenders can guard whatever offensive player they choose to defend against, and offensive players can determine whether they should pass or shoot the ball. Star basketball players like LeBron James, Kobe Bryant, Michael Jordan, and Shaquille O'Neal are almost always guarded by multiple defenders. Defenders, knowing that these individuals can make shots with high degrees of success, converge on the star player whenever he has the ball in hopes of forcing more difficult shots. This action necessarily leaves another offensive player wide open while two defenders are double-teaming the strong player. Strategic behavior is also evidenced in basketball when defensive players (and their coaches) elect to put only one defender on a star player if this individual is having an off night, or not making shots with a high degree of success.

It could be argued that strategic behavior causes star players to appear less valuable than their less talented counterparts. The statistics star players produce (e.g., points per game, rebounds, or assists) are generated (many times) while they are being defended against by multiple players; statistics of less talented players may be generated when they're not being defended against at all!

Risk Mitigation Through Strategic Behavioral Analysis

Having examined strategic behavior in the world of sports, we now turn to exploring the notion of risk mitigation through the analysis of strategic behavior. The essential component of strategic behavior we investigate is the interdependence of decision making among participants. We refer to strategic interaction among participants as a game. In these games, we will be interested in making decisions that are in our best interests, taking into account the actions of our competitors.

Consider the case of a firm (Firm A) looking to introduce a product to the marketplace. There currently are no similar products on the market, except for those produced by a competitive firm, Firm B. Firm A must make a decision with respect to the project: Should it expend the necessary research

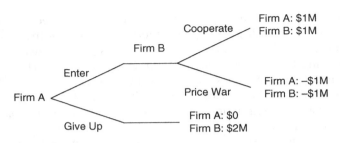

EXHIBIT 3.1 Strategic Decisions of Firms A and B

and development costs needed to bring its version of the product to market, or should it divert its resources elsewhere? To answer this question, Firm A should perform an analysis that takes into account the decisions of its rival.

Let us assume that financial analysts believe the product will yield a net present value (NPV) of $2 million to Firm B in the event it is a monopolist—that is, in the event that Firm A does not produce a competitive product. In the event Firm A does produce a competitive product, Firm B can elect to join forces with Firm A and cooperatively serve the market demand, in which case both firms will earn $1 million. Or Firm B could elect to start a price war with Firm A. If a price war ensues, both firms will lose $1 million on their investment. We assume in this example that Firm A's decision precedes that of Firm B.

In order to make this scenario a bit more concrete, we illustrate these decisions in Exhibit 3.1.

In this exhibit, Firm A's decisions are represented by the first node: It can elect to either enter the market or give up on its hopes of developing the product. Firm B's decisions are illustrated by the "Cooperate" and "Price War" actions of the second node. In order to best understand what Firm A should do, we should first look to understand the actions of Firm B at node 2. More specifically, we can see that if Firm A elects to produce the product, it is in Firm B's best interest to cooperate (and earn $1 million) than to start a price war (and lose $1 million). We can thus anticipate the action taken by Firm B given that Firm A elects to produce a product. With this information in hand, Firm A can now make a more informed decision about the product: namely, that it is better to enter the market, in which case Firm B will likely cooperate with Firm A, than not to enter the market. Doing so yields Firm A a payoff of $1 million versus no earnings at all.

While this example may seem a bit academic in nature, its implications for business decisions are rather profound. Many of the risks faced by companies are predicated on actions based on such strategic decisions. In order to make the best decisions from a profitability standpoint, managers and directors need to first understand what responses are in the best interests of competitors. They can then make decisions that reflect this analysis.

Competitive Analysis

According to Porter (1980), competitive strategy "involves positioning a business to maximize the value of the capabilities that distinguish it from its competitors." Porter believes that a "central aspect of strategy formulation is perceptive competitor analysis." Before making major decisions, managers should first ask astute questions along these lines: "In what product areas should we avoid competition because we know the competitor will respond aggressively?" "How should we interpret the strategic decisions of our competitor?" "Are the threats made by our competitor to our market position credible?"

In many cases, the demand for answers to such questions is overlooked by the financial analysis tools used by decision makers. In fact, the general structure of the board of directors reflects this fact. While there are ad hoc committees that are tasked with accomplishing specific goals (e.g., nominating and audit committees), often ad hoc committees are not used to evaluate changes in competitive strategy. Such decisions are then relegated to standing committees that have much on their plates. Committee members who participate and evaluate decisions regarding business strategy might not receive the amount of information that they would if a specific ad hoc committee were started to examine core business decisions and risks. This committee would gather information about competitors in a detailed manner that would allow for better-informed decisions to be made.

Moreover, when evaluating potential competitive strategy decisions, executives and board members sometimes fall into the trap of believing they understand their competitors because they compete with them every day. They feel that the strategy played by an opponent might mimic previous moves without little formal basis or analysis.

In reality, competitive analyses of markets should critically analyze the decisions of not only current market players, but also *anticipated* market players. These latter would-be competitors are too often overlooked when financial projections are made regarding a particular line of business. Although this type of analysis will likely prove difficult, it can be addressed by asking the following questions:

- What firms have a corporate strategy that would encourage them to compete in this market?
- What firms have supply chains that could accommodate participation in this market?

- What firms could overcome barriers to entry relatively cheaply?
- What firms might attempt to merge or acquire their way into this market?

Analysis of these questions that attempt to forecast *future* market players will allow executives and board members to better solidify their financial projections and provide a sound basis for market decisions. We now discuss issues in greater detail that executives and board members can use to predict the behavior of possible future competitors. We present them in a scorecard format for purposes of practicality.

Scorecard for Competitive Analysis of Future Market Players

Exhibit 3.2 presents the aforementioned scorecard for competitive analysis of future market players. Within this scorecard are 10 items that we recommend board members and executives use for evaluating the future actions of potential competitors. The potential competitor should be evaluated along each of these 10 dimensions and scored on a qualitative scale. We now present a series of questions that can assist an individual in scoring a potential competitor along each dimension.

1. *Historical financial performance.* How has the competitive business been performing recently? Have sales demonstrated recent trends? Are the managers having issues with controlling costs? What earnings have they been able to deliver to stakeholders? What is their current cash flow position? Such questions can serve to identify whether a competitor's leadership is anxious for change or is content with the status quo.
2. *Stated organizational goals.* Within every 10-K statement there is a discussion titled "Management's Discussion and Analysis." This section provides important insights into the organizational goals of the

EXHIBIT 3.2 Competitive Analysis Scorecard

Issue	Item	Score
1	Historical financial performance	
2	Stated organizational goals	
3	Attitude toward risks	
4	Organizational culture	
5	Strategic importance of new market	
6	Diversification plans	
7	Incentive systems	
8	Beliefs of leadership	
9	Regulatory concerns	
10	Contractual commitments	

company. Do the statements made in this section indicate the company may become a future competitor? What do its organizational vision and mission statements indicate about management's beliefs about growth? Does the line of business in question agree with organizational goals? Is the company seeking to grow revenues, increase market leadership, or focus on core operations? What benefits can the organization derive from this business?

3. *Attitude toward risks.* Does the company have a history of risk taking indicative of market entry? Have investors rewarded risky or safe behavior? Do earnings display a smooth or lumpy pattern over the past five years?

4. *Organizational culture.* How is the company organized? Is it a bureaucracy or one with a relatively flat organizational structure? If it's a bureaucracy, would the comments of high-level leaders indicate they're interested in expanding into new markets? If it's a flat organization, what is the general view of all employees?

5. *Strategic importance of new market.* How would serving this new market benefit the company? What synergies could it reap across its divisions? Would its cost structure prohibit such expansion or encourage it? Does the new market agree with stated strategy goals? For instance, Hyundai and Kia Motors have established a reputation of providing low-cost, high-value products to consumers. Would one expect them to introduce an $80,000 sports car given their historical strategy? What strategic importance would such an introduction serve?

6. *Diversification plans.* Has management and the board articulated a strategy of diversification in order to smooth earnings? Is the company investing significant amounts of capital into research and development in noncore areas? Has the company experienced institutional investor stock sales as a result of poorly performing core lines of business? Can the company easily diversify its operations? Does it have the excess capacity to do so, or can it cheaply acquire it?

7. *Incentive systems.* How is management incentivized through compensation? Are they paid primarily in cash, restricted stock, options, equity, or—in some cases—debt? Do their remuneration packages emphasize growth in earnings, revenues, or share price? How are employees compensated? Are they rewarded for taking risks?

8. *Beliefs of leadership.* What types of executives have historically been promoted by the company? What reputation do they have? Are they risk-loving or risk-averse managers? Do their views differ from those historically viewed as important to the company? Do they have convincing personalities? Could they persuade investors and the board that a new line of business is in the best interests of the company?

9. *Regulatory concerns.* Would the introduction of a new line of business create regulatory issues among federal or state governmental bodies?

Would it create antitrust issues for the competitor? What is the competitor's relationship with politicians? Does it have political reach in many states, or is it concentrated in a few?

10. *Contractual commitments.* Does the company have contracts with organizations to supply goods that would constrain its production facilities? What commitments does it hold with its retail customers and upstream suppliers?

Once each of these 10 areas has been critically evaluated by the board and executives, participants in the decision-making process can fill out the scorecard in Exhibit 3.2. We suggest scoring each of the 10 items on a scale of 1 to 5 points (a score of 5 would indicate that an item would highly suggest a future competitor would enter the market). Points should then be totaled and averaged across all individuals who participated in the process. Average scores in the range of 35 to 50 should indicate that an organization should be especially wary of a potential competitor entering a market. Conversely, scores between 0 and 15 should indicate that a potential competitor is unlikely to enter the market. Between these two ranges (average scores of 15 to 35), the company should use further competitive intelligence techniques to discern the motives of its potential competitor.

We wish to note that while the scores derived from this analysis may appear to be quantitative in nature, they are, in fact, qualitative. Although the end result of this analysis was a number between 0 and 50, numbers from 1 to 5 could easily have been interchanged with values such as "very low," "low," "medium," "high," and "very high." Quantitative estimates regarding the impact of each scorecard element have not yet been made. These estimates will be discussed in a later section in this chapter.

Scorecard for Analysis of Current Market Players

Having discussed a scorecard for forecasting future market players, we now offer a scorecard for assessing the strength of current, known market players. This scorecard is shown in Exhibit 3.3.

When businesses formulate changes in strategy associated with new lines of business, it is often best to enter markets where the firm can achieve its objective without sparking a reaction from competitors. This strategy, however, is easier said than done. Aside from venture capital–backed firms and those firms interested in pursuing transformational technologies, many areas of the consumer market are served by organizations. In determining which of these nontransformational markets to enter, new firms should assess potential reactions from current market players before making relatively irreversible decisions about market entry.

EXHIBIT 3.3 Scorecard for Evaluating Current Market Players

Issue	Item	Score
1	Stability of the business	
2	Current market strategy	
3	Organizational values	
4	Beliefs about demand	
5	Historical reactions to market entrants	
6	Beliefs of leadership	
7	Financial position	
8	Business alliances	
9	Operational position	
10	Employee talent	

The scorecard presented in Exhibit 3.3 is designed to assist executives and board members in assessing the potential consequences of entering a known rival's market. We now present a series of 10 questions that can assist these individuals in scoring potential competitors.

1. *Stability of the business.* Does this line of business represent a source of stable cash flows and earnings for the company? Does the business offset fluctuations in the company's portfolio? Are gross and net profit margins healthy? Have the revenues been growing? Are investors pleased with the earnings generated by the business?

2. *Current market strategy.* How does the company maintain its position? Does it compete on cost or product differentiation? How would it react to a new entrant? Has it successfully defended against entrants in the past? Does the company invest in large amounts of research and development to ensure that its product lines are up to date?

3. *Organizational values.* Does the competitor have an emotional identification associated with a particular marketplace? What is the root of this emotional identification? Does it focus on specific geographical markets associated with this emotional identification? Are the founding policies of the company still active today? What do these policies indicate with respect to the firm's actions in light of a new market entrant?

4. *Beliefs about demand.* Does the competitor believe the current market is increasing or decreasing in size? Does it believe the market is saturated? What are analyst predictions about the market? How has the company reacted to changes in demand? Has it built new facilities to accommodate increased demand, or has it allowed prices to increase rather than supply the market with additional goods?

5. *Historical reactions to market entrants.* How has the company histori- cally reacted to new market entrants? Has it responded by differentiating its products or cutting prices for consumers? Has the company suc- ceeded in running out newer entrants? Has it acquired or merged with some entrants in hopes of achieving better horizontal integration?

6. *Beliefs of leadership.* What types of strategies have worked for a busi- ness's leaders in the past? Have its executives been successful at cutting costs? Might it adopt similar strategies to run out new entrants? In what businesses have its leaders previously worked? Will they apply tactics from previous jobs to fend off new entrants?

7. *Financial position.* Is the company in the financial position to fend off a new market entrant? Does it have significant cash on hand? Can it afford to raise barriers to entry through research and development? Can it afford a price war?

8. *Business alliances.* Does the company have alliances with its competi- tors that would intensify its market position (e.g., joint ventures)? Does it have supply chain participants that are satisfied with their current lev- els of production and sales? Would these supply chain partners defend their partner in the event of a new market entrant, or would they defect?

9. *Operational position.* How robust are the company's operations? What levels of capacity utilization are currently being experienced? Does the company's geographic location assist it in maintaining market share? Will major capital expenditures be required in the near future, draining the firm's free cash flow?

10. *Employee talent.* Does the firm have talented employees that help it maintain its market position? Would talented employees be willing to defect to a new competitor? Are they satisfied with their employer? What do the employees desire that the current firm does not offer?

Once these areas have been critically evaluated by management and the board, the scorecard shown in Exhibit 3.3 can be filled out in a similar manner to the previous scorecard that focused on potential competitors. The results of these scorecards can then be employed in the strategic decision- making process. Doing so will help directors and executives mitigate risks posed by competitors—those competitors that are known, and those that may potentially enter the market.

Benefits of Unpredictability

We have detailed the importance of strategic behavior in decision making and provided the reader with qualitative ways in which strategic behavior of competitors can be analyzed. However, before we proceed to discuss the manner in which our previous qualitative assessments can be used by directors and executives, we would like to point out a central issue in the analysis of corporate strategy that can have profound effects on the decision-making process: predictability. Each of our previous scorecards designed to assess competitors employed past information as a window to future decision making. An implicit assumption we made in the preceding analysis was that past events provide insights into the future.

On the football field, if an offense continually runs the ball, isn't it more likely that the defense will eventually defend against only the run? However, if the offense continually mixes its plays between runs and passes, the defense will be left to guess which strategy the offense will employ in a given situation. In this instance, and many others in business, unpredictability is an asset that can be exploited by organizations looking to catch competitors off guard; predictability can cause even the most efficient and talented organizations to falter. In the previous football example, an offense will likely have a difficult time scoring if they continually run the ball despite having a star running back and offensive linemen.

Dixit and Nalebuff (1991) offer a better example that showcases such predictability issues and perhaps best resonates with every American. They use the example of an IRS audit. Let us for a moment suppose that the IRS used an analytic formula to determine whether it should audit a taxpayer. If this formula remained static over time, it might be possible that individuals and corporations would eventually discover the formula—or major components of it—and, hence, simply engineer their tax returns to avoid an audit. The IRS would then be left auditing the most honest taxpayers: Those who did not engineer their returns would be more likely to receive an audit notice than those who falsified their returns.

Within the realm of business, unpredictability has many benefits. However, these are not without their shortcomings. A company that can keep a new product under wraps may be able to surprise competitors with a transformational technology. Because its action was unpredictable, competitors may not have anticipated their rival's action. As a result, their response may be delayed, and the entering company may have a monopoly on the market instead of encountering competition.

Unpredictability, however, is something that may be difficult for publicly traded firms to achieve. Because of the laws surrounding business disclosure, firms must disclose some of what their private counterparts would deem to be proprietary strategic objectives. Investors are always interested in the future actions of the company, as well as its future directions. They relish predictability in earnings while condemning unpredictability. They also heavily scrutinize decisions of management regarding expenditures they may feel are ancillary to the business. Among these are frequently research and development expenses. Thus, for firms that are not looking to raise capital in the near future, it may be beneficial to go private. In addition to saving on compliance costs, the firm may be able to keep future product plans and strategies closer to the vest. This could assist the firm in mitigating operational risks associated with competitive strategy.

Quantification of Strategic Risks

Our previous discussions have offered insights into qualitative analysis that may be performed by directors and executives regarding strategic risks. We now discuss how these qualitative assessments may supplement traditional financial analysis through quantitative means.

When financial analysts are tasked with forecasting the profitability of a particular project (be it the introduction of a new product or the improvement of an existing one), a frequent evaluation tool is a net present value (NPV) analysis. This analysis generally demands explicit revenue and cost forecasts of a specific time frame. The present value of the revenues is then calculated net of all costs at a given cost of capital.

Incorporating the insights from this chapter into these financial analysis tools requires that multiple NPV analyses be calculated based on probable scenarios. The outcomes calculated in Exhibit 3.1 could have been derived from a NPV analysis of each explicit scenario. However, a key insight from this analysis is that, in order to make a decision incorporating strategic behavior, forecasts must be made for one's own company, but also for rival firms. Doing so will allow one to better evaluate the strategic decisions of rivals, and hence mitigate risks associated with the decision-making process.

Returning to our example from Exhibit 3.1, let us now imagine the game structure depicted in Exhibit 3.4.

What can we now anticipate as the NPV of our project? Notice that the only difference between Exhibit 3.1 and Exhibit 3.4 is the payout Firm B receives in the event of a price war. Exhibit 3.4 potentially reflects the analysis performed by a team of product experts that potentially states that Firm B will likely win in the event of a price war; a price war will not prove

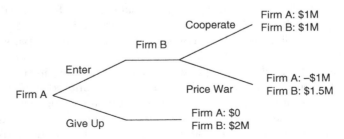

EXHIBIT 3.4 Revised Game Structure from Exhibit 3.1

too costly for Firm B, whereas Firm A will suffer greatly in this price war. As an analyst for Firm A, what can we now anticipate will be the NPV of our project?

Looking at the second node indicating decisions made by Firm B, we see that it is beneficial for Firm B to instigate a price war. By doing so, it increases its NPV from $1 million if it cooperates to $1.5 million. With this knowledge in mind, we at Firm A can make a more informed decision regarding the project. Knowing that Firm B will start a price war, we should give up the project (which has an NPV of $0) rather than fight the war (which has an NPV of –$1 million). Had we not thought about this issue in a strategic manner, we could have elected to take on the project with the hope of high profitability, and later found ourselves in the middle of a costly, bitter price war. Our resources could have been better placed elsewhere.

Estimation Procedures

While the type of analysis we have just discussed is well suited to many strategic decision-making processes, it does require a considerable degree of forecast estimation. This may prove especially tricky when a potential rival may select from a continuum of actions (in which case, the rival has what game theorists would call a large "strategy space"). In such a case, it will generally be best to focus estimation procedures on inflection points within the strategy space. We define an inflection point as the point at which a firm is indifferent between two actions.

The best method for understanding such inflection points is for an analyst to understand the key decisions a competitor would make that would switch its best response strategy. For instance, returning to Exhibit 3.4, Firm B will always find it advantageous to start a price war if the NPV of this activity is greater than $1 million. If this is the case, Firm B will be better off to select the price war (and achieve an NPV greater than $1 million), rather than cooperate with Firm A (and achieve an NPV of $1 million exactly). If we can be reasonably sure that Firm B will reap benefits greater than $1 million if it starts a price war, there's no need to estimate the exact magnitude of Firm B's benefits; we can be reasonably sure that it will take this path. Instead, we can focus our efforts on estimating the impact to our NPV of Firm B's actions. This will improve the expediency of the analysis and also encourage analysts to focus on these key inflection points.

Summary

Within this chapter we have examined the ways in which executives and boards can mitigate operational risks through strategic behavior. By acting strategically, firms can bolster the analytical methods they use to make strategic decisions and better anticipate the reactions of their competitors. In order to make their own actions less predictable, firms may elect to utilize unpredictability to their benefit, although this may prove difficult for publicly traded companies.

Notes

1. A. Dixit and B. Nalebuff, *Thinking Strategically* (New York: W.W. Norton, 1991).
2. M. Porter, *Competitive Strategy: Techniques for Analyzing Industries and Companies* (New York: Free Press, 1980).

CHAPTER 4

Mitigating Risks in Internal Investigations and Insurance Coverage

Carolyn H. Rosenberg, Esq.
Efrem M. Grail, Esq.
Reed Smith LLP

Chief risk officers (CROs) and heads of risk management face numerous decisions in times of crisis. When confronting a crisis, CROs should consult their firm's chief legal counsel prior to launching an internal investigation. In conjunction with the chief legal counsel, the CRO should (1) assess the types of risk faced by the organization, (2) develop a plan to discover the facts, (3) carry out the investigation and analyze any uncovered facts, and (4) develop short- and long-range plans for remediation. The chief legal counsel can also assist the CRO in maximizing potential recovery rates through insurance claims.

We begin this chapter with a hypothetical scenario that a head of risk management may face. This scenario provides a realistic background from which we examine each of our four suggested steps.

Scenario

You are the head of risk management at "the Company," a publicly traded U.S. corporation. You open your first email of the morning. You are about to have a very bad day.

From: Remote Plant Manager
To: Risk Manager

We really need some help down here in the Company's remote production facility. I just read in the local paper that our lead raw materials purchaser, Buyam Stuffalot, was arrested over the weekend for embezzling $9,000 from his local church!

Buyam makes a good salary here at Remote Plant. I can't believe he needed the money!

He has always been a good employee, never late. It's strange—this week was the first time anyone can remember he hasn't been here to open his own mail, and that's only because he was in jail!

It gets weirder. Yesterday, a couple of our employees got some strange-looking checks from our vendors—made out to Buyam! We've also gotten some inquiries from Central Purchasing at headquarters, a thousand miles away from here, about some vendors no one there can recognize. Those vendors are the same ones that the lead buyer has been purchasing raw materials from for years! How could the purchasing department claim they didn't recognize those vendors?

So, I asked the two accounting clerks who work with Buyam processing the paperwork for materials purchases. They claimed not to recognize any of the invoices. We had IT run the backup tapes for purchasing in the past three months, and each of those vendors shows paid by check authorized by those same two employees!

This is bigger and more confusing than what I am used to. On top of all of this, some reporter called from New York asking about Buyam's arrest. It seems she was monitoring local papers, and said she thinks that "there's more to this than just a petty theft." I can't imagine what, but you know how Wall Street reacts to the media. Please advise.

Courses of Action

Panic, although reasonable at this juncture, is not an option. Very soon, the Company will have to respond to this brewing crisis: quickly, confidently, and completely. And although the email correspondence from the field is short on facts, it carries enough information to form the beginning of an action plan. However, before you even put fingers to keyboard, you as a seasoned risk management professional should realize this is a situation that merits input from the Company's chief legal counsel: Don't try whatever is to be done next alone. Even the little you know now should lead to the inevitable conclusion that nothing good can come of this, that it will almost certainly require confidentiality under the attorney-client privilege and its work product doctrine protections, and that it is likely to have significant consequences for all involved.

In consultation with counsel, then, you must immediately initiate the following four steps:

1. Assess the types of risks and delineate the scope of the potential harm at issue: What is the worst-case scenario?.
2. Develop a plan to discover the facts, in order to move from the hypothetical and the potential of what could happen to actual knowledge and understanding of what indeed did happen, and the consequences that very well might come to pass as a result. This requires investigation: Of what? By whom? How? In what depth? How soon?
3. Carry out the investigation and analyze the facts that are discovered. Determine what, if any, reporting is required or prudent in the exercise of good business judgment. Take necessary action now, in the immediate time frame; decide what must be done tomorrow, in the short term; and then decide what to do and who to tell next week and next month, in the medium term and long term.
4. Develop a short- and long-range plan to remediate any harm, both actual and potential, to all of the Company's assets, including its tangible and intangible ones. Put all potentially relevant insurers on notice and take steps to maximize potential insurance recovery. In the longer term, consider a root cause analysis to determine the ultimate cause, identify any system weaknesses, and correct any deficiencies in procedures and compliance processes that may have led to or contributed to the situation in the first place.

Together with legal counsel, you as the representative of the Company's risk management function can very quickly access the information available and anticipate the following.

Assess the Risks

From what you know already, you can deduce that a number of serious problems may exist.

Fact

Buyam, a senior-level Company employee/officer, is charged with a theft-related offense involving moral turpitude (intentional falsehood).

Consequences

- Although everyone is presumed innocent until proven guilty in a court of law, you work for a regulated company listed on a national securities exchange. You don't have the luxury of waiting months or years for

Buyam's trial. One who is suspect in one area is suspect in all others. What has Buyam been up to? What commitments has Buyam bound the Company to that must be reexamined in light of the accusation of dishonesty? What opportunities have there been for Buyam to embezzle funds from the Company?

■ What should various constituencies, such as clients and customers, be told about Buyam? What adverse publicity will result from the newspaper stories and gossip?

■ Why did Buyam need $9,000, given his seemingly adequate salary from the Company? Did he have a drug problem? If so, were drugs used on Company premises? Did he have a gambling addiction? Did he have a secret sexual relationship? If so, could it be with an employee? Did he have a mental breakdown?

Facts

Buyam was never late for work; the Company discovers checks from vendors made out to Buyam.

Consequences

■ Is Buyam taking kickbacks? Has Buyam extorted payments from vendors? Or could there be some otherwise innocent explanation for the very suspicious financial instruments?

■ If in fact there is a financial fraud perpetrated on the Company, how widespread is it? How long has it been taking place, and how many different parties are involved? Who has benefited from the scheme? Who else knows about it, and if they don't, why not?

■ If a financial fraud exists, is it the result of some failure in the Company's internal controls and financial accounting/auditing procedures, or in spite of them? Does this incident mask a larger problem of a failure of process? Is there a culture of noncompliance at Remote Plant, or are Buyam's circumstances isolated?

Fact

Longtime vendors' invoices are not recognized by Central Purchasing department at headquarters.

Consequences

■ Is this practice widespread or an anomaly? How and why has this happened?

■ Is this only a breach of Company policy on centralized purchasing? Or does it indicate a more sinister objective, such as diversion of Company assets?

Fact

Accounting employees claim not to recognize invoices from the vendors who sent Buyam checks.

Consequences

- Are these two employees the correct people who should recognize the invoices? If so, have they been asleep at the switch?
- Has there been a corruption of the Company's electronic controls and a breach of the Company's information technology (IT) security?
- Did Buyam learn employees' computer passwords and subvert the information and security controls of the Company's IT systems in order to breach data security? Is the accounting department involved in this scheme?

Fact

Previous statements contained in the Company's periodic securities filings claim that accounting and auditing procedures, and internal financial controls and data security protections, are adequate.

Consequences

- Will this incident have a material impact on the Company's finances or its representations to the investigating public and the Securities and Exchange Commission (SEC)?
- What adverse publicity will result from this incident? Will it be contained, or could it lead to a drop in the share price?
- If the latter, are the members of the board of directors subject to liability in a shareholder suit for the diminution of the value of Company shares?
- Is there insurance coverage for the types of harms contemplated? If so, should carriers be put on notice of this incident in order to trigger potential coverage obligations? Is the coverage adequate under the circumstances? Are there other sources of contribution or recoupment?

Develop a Plan

At this point, the Company's general counsel or an assistant counsel should prepare a memorandum directing in-house or outside counsel to conduct a confidential investigation, subject to the attorney-client privilege, stating the basis for the investigation, and also stating that the purpose of the investigation is to provide legal advice to the company.

Counsel should then distribute written instructions to any persons assigned to work on the investigation, advising that (1) they are to help the attorneys conduct an investigation, (2) they must treat all information as privileged and confidential, (3) they should not discuss the work and confidential matters with others, (4) they should not copy their paperwork and should deliver everything to the lawyers upon completion, and (5) they should mark all investigative materials and communications as "privileged and confidential."

The development of a forensic work plan is critical to the success of the internal investigation. It should identify the scope of the investigation, its objectives and its initial investigative techniques and steps. The work plan can be modified to fit the circumstances as the investigation proceeds.

It is preferable to obtain written data before any interviews take place, and to do so discreetly to preserve and maintain evidence. Generally, one should interview and confront suspects only as a last step. Whenever possible, the investigation should attempt to obtain evidence from outside third parties for accuracy and verification.

Carry Out the Investigation and Analyze the Results

Review the Company's Charter, Bylaws, and State Employment Regulations

Before any interviews take place, the investigation must take into account how to deal with employees who seek legal counsel either before or after the interview. State statutes, corporate bylaws, executive employment contracts, and individual indemnification agreements may impose on a company an obligation to indemnify its directors, officers, employees, and agents for personal losses resulting from claims of wrongdoing in their official capacities. That obligation may go hand in hand with an obligation to advance payment of legal expenses. A corporation's ability to recruit and retain the best directors, officers, and employees is greatly affected by its willingness to indemnify such agents in connection with their actions on behalf of the corporation and advance payment of related legal defense expenses.

Deal Openly and Honestly with Employees and Other Witnesses

At the outset of every interview, counsel should advise each witness that (1) the attorney represents the corporation or, for example, its directors' independent committee; (2) counsel is not the employee's lawyer and does not represent the employee's interests; (3) statements made to counsel must be truthful; (4) statements made during the interview are confidential and protected by the attorney-client privilege and oftentimes by the work product doctrine, but the privilege of confidentiality belongs to the Company; and

(5) the Company can unilaterally choose to waive its privilege and disclose all or part of what the employee has said during the interview to external auditors, the government, regulators, or others of its choosing.

Investigation counsel should consider telling witnesses at the outset of the interview that the Department of Justice has taken the position that employees can be indicted for obstruction of justice under federal law if they lie to private counsel conducting an internal investigation, where they know that their statements may be shared with government prosecutors and administrative enforcement agency lawyers.

Investigation counsel cannot give personal legal advice to employees, even to say whether they should seek the advice of individual counsel. Counsel should remind witnesses that the counsel does not represent them in their individual capacities.

Counsel should always memorialize the substance of each witness interview as soon after the interview as possible and in a manner consistent with the attorney work product doctrine and the ultimate purpose of the investigation. Best practices for internal investigations dictate that the lawyer never interview or even speak with a witness alone, in order to avoid becoming a witness in one's own case as to what a witness said during an interview.

Be Independent

A poorly executed investigation perceived to be biased or self-interested will raise far more questions than it answers. Such an investigation will accomplish few, if any, of its goals and be quickly viewed by the public, shareholders, Wall Street, and the government as a whitewash or a sham. Companies can face increased liability in court actions for their improper attempts to influence or falsify results of an internal investigation.

Analyze the Findings

At the conclusion of the investigation, counsel and its investigation team should complete any summary or reports, including expert reports, setting forth the conclusions resulting from the investigation and the basis for the conclusions. Such a report would typically be prepared only at the request of the company and with the approval of legal counsel. The investigative report may include, where possible, identification of internal control and/or operational deficiencies that can be remedied after the close of the investigation. These often should be included in a separate document addressed to the appropriate constituency.

Consider Disclosure Obligations to the Government and the Company's Auditors

The Securities Exchange Act of 1934 requires that companies that issue publicly traded securities file with the SEC on Form 8-K announcements of major events that shareholders should know about. (See, for example, www.sec.gov/answers/form8k.htm.) This would include the requirement to release and file with the SEC news of extraordinary events of a material nature. Some events may require immediate disclosure. In addition, industry-specific regulatory agencies have their own mandatory reporting obligations, such as environmental requirements to disclose toxic discharge.

Moreover, Section 10A of the Securities Exchange Act of 1934 requires that every public company audit include "procedures designed to provide reasonable assurance of detecting illegal acts that would have a direct and material effect on the determination of financial statement accounts."

If an auditor "detects or otherwise becomes aware of information indicating that an illegal act (whether or not perceived to have a material effect on the financial statements of the issuer) has or may have occurred," then the auditor must determine whether it is likely that an illegal act has occurred, and if so (1) "determine and consider the possible effect of the illegal act" on the company's financial statements, including possible fines and penalties; (2) bring such issue to the attention of management and the audit committee, unless "clearly inconsequential"; and (3) conclude whether management and the audit committee have taken "appropriate remedial actions."

If the auditors determine that (1) the illegal act is material, (2) management has not taken appropriate remedial steps, *and* (3) the failure to take such remedial action is reasonably expected to lead to something other than a clean opinion, then the auditors must report to the board of directors and the board must within one business day furnish the auditors' report to the SEC.

Failure to report exposes auditors to consequences such as administrative sanctions and civil exposure.

Maintain the Attorney-Client Privilege and the Work Product Doctrine Protection of the Report

At the same time that counsel must consider disclosure of the report, counsel must also always be vigilant to protect against a privilege waiver.

DISCLOSURE TO THE GOVERNMENT　Almost every court that has considered the doctrine of *limited waiver* has rejected it. This means that voluntary production of privileged and/or work-product-protected material to the government will likely mean loss of the privilege and/or work product protection in any and all subsequent proceedings. Production of privileged investigation materials to the government resulting in a waiver, then, must be made only under well-considered circumstances, with the full knowledge and informed consent of the Company.

DISCLOSURE TO PUBLIC RELATIONS STAFF OR GOVERNMENT AFFAIRS CONSULTANTS A court may extend the attorney-client privilege to protect documents shared with public relations (PR) staff or government affairs consultants. Courts have reasoned that PR consultants are "integrated members of the team assigned to deal with a company's litigation and legal strategies." Under such circumstances, courts have held that there is "no reason to distinguish between a person on the corporation's payroll and a consultant hired by the corporation if each acts for the corporation and possesses the information needed by attorneys in rendering legal advice."

DISCLOSURE TO AUDITORS Disclosure to auditors does not necessarily waive the work product privilege, although it likely will destroy attorney-client privilege protection. One court has noted that "any tension between an auditor and a corporation that arises from an auditor's need to scrutinize and investigate a corporation's records and bookkeeping practices simply is not the equivalent of an adversarial relationship contemplated by the work product doctrine." The court also noted that to find that the disclosure to the auditors waived the work product privilege would discourage companies from making the disclosures necessary for the auditor to conduct a proper audit.

INADVERTENT DISCLOSURE There are three views on waiver of the attorney-client privilege by inadvertent production or disclosure to adverse parties:

1. *Strict:* Once a document or communication is disclosed, the privileged is waived.
2. *Liberal:* Inadvertence or carelessness can never constitute an affirmative waiver, since by definition an inadvertent waiver can never be a knowing relinquishment of a right.
3. *Balancing test:* Courts examine the circumstances of the waiver, taking into account the reasonableness of the precautions, the extent of the disclosures, and the measures taken to rectify the problem.

THE ILLUSORY PRIVILEGE OF SELF-CRITICAL ANALYSIS Some courts previously recognized a public interest in encouraging internal inquiries in the interest of self-governance, in the form of a so-called self-criticism privilege. However, litigants who have relied on the self-criticism privilege have been almost uniformly unsuccessful in the courts.

Develop a Plan to Correct Deficiencies and Remediate Harm

Maximize the Potential for Insurance Recovery

Insurance may provide valuable protection for current loss and potential claims. To maximize recovery, you will want to do the following.

GATHER ALL POTENTIALLY RELEVANT INSURANCE POLICIES OR INDEMNITY AGREEMENTS Key policies may include commercial crime or fidelity bond policies for internal theft, data privacy and security or cyber coverage for claims due to potential breaches of security and access to private data, commercial general liability (CGL) and property policies for potential business interruption and product recall claims, and directors' and officers' (D&O) liability insurance for potential breaches of fiduciary duty against directors and officers or securities claims based on financial fraud or SEC-related proceedings.

Any indemnification agreements with vendors or other third parties who may owe contractual obligations to the company should also be reviewed as well as any insurance policies where the Company may be an additional insured.

PROVIDE TIMELY NOTICE OF CLAIMS OR POTENTIAL CLAIMS TO PRIMARY AND EXCESS INSURERS Insurance policies include provisions for reporting claims, occurrences, or losses, and should be adhered to carefully. Failure to comply may result in a coverage dispute or denial of coverage, depending on the policy requirements and applicable case law.

Provisions differ by policy. For example, a fidelity bond policy will specify when the initial notice is to be provided, and a proof of loss must be filed within a designated time period of reporting the initial loss. D&O policies allow reporting of potential as well as actual claims. If the claim develops, it is parked in the policy in which the initial notice was provided. Claims and potential claims should be reported to both primary and excess carriers across all programs to avoid later challenges of late notice.

OBTAIN CONSENT TO DEFENSE ARRANGEMENTS Some insurance policies have a "duty to defend," meaning that the insurer must provide a legal defense for insureds under the policy. Other types of policies provide for reimbursement, where the insured assumes its own defense obligations, subject to the insurer's advancement or reimbursement of defense expenses. The insured typically is required to obtain the insurer's consent to defense arrangements, which may not be unreasonably withheld. Communication with insurers at the earliest stage of a claim is important to address defense arrangements. For example, if policies with both duty to defend and reimbursement obligations apply, the insured can assess how best to manage the defense arrangements. Similarly, if the insurer proposes specific counsel but the insured objects, depending on the coverage defenses raised by the insurer and applicable law, the insurer may be obligated to pay the cost of independent counsel for the insured or the insured may have to retain and pay for separate counsel to monitor the defense.

ADHERE TO COOPERATION OBLIGATIONS AND RESPOND TO REQUESTS FOR INFORMATION AND COVERAGE DEFENSES Although the language of insurance policies differs, an insured generally has an obligation to cooperate with all reasonable requests of insurers. Insurers also typically have a right to associate—that is, to consult with defense counsel or, in some cases, participate—in the defense and settlement of claims involving or potentially involving their coverage.

These responsibilities of the insured may differ depending on the type of policy and whether the insurer is defending the claim. Insureds should recognize, however, that the policy language, relevant case law, and individual, specific circumstances will dictate what is required or reasonable in a given context. For example, insureds typically do not have an attorney-client privileged relationship with an insurer, especially in a non–duty to defend situation. Consequently, an insured would need to be very careful in sharing information with insurers. Confidentiality or joint defense agreements may provide some protection of sensitive disclosures, but knowledgeable counsel should be consulted to provide guidance. Insurers may also seek to interview witnesses, employ investigators, and seek out defense counsel's analysis or fee statements. Again, these requests must be carefully examined with an eye toward insurance coverage and privilege considerations.

Insureds should also promptly respond to letters or other communications raising coverage defenses or denying coverage. Potential exclusions or other terms and conditions may not apply or may limit coverage only for part of a claim. Even if it is too early in the process to discern the full extent of coverage, an insured should make a record disagreeing with the carrier's restrictive coverage positions, and reserve its right to supplement its response. Moreover, a strong letter replying to coverage challenges may result in a reversal of a coverage denial. Obtaining the insurer's position, especially early in the process, may also help expedite a coverage determination through litigation, mediation, or arbitration if informal negotiation is unsuccessful.

OBTAIN CONSENT TO SETTLEMENT OR PAYMENT OF JUDGMENT Know your rights and obligations. Insureds should check for any so-called hammer provisions, which may limit the insured's recovery if the insured refuses to settle where the insurer is able to resolve the underlying claim. Conversely, where the insured desires to settle but the insurer does not readily agree to pay the claim, the insured should review the consent provisions of the policy. Typically consent to a settlement cannot be unreasonably withheld, but policies may also specify that the insurer has a right to participate in the negotiation of a settlement or that an offer to settle requires insurer consent. Managing the insurer-insured relationship throughout the claim process in a thoughtful and diligent way will typically put the insurer and insured in a better position to reach agreement than if the insurer is not promptly brought into the loop.

RESOLVE COVERAGE DISPUTES   If informal negotiation does not resolve a dispute, the policy may dictate the next steps to follow. Policies may contain provisions requiring that an insurance dispute be mediated, arbitrated, or litigated in a particular jurisdiction, or that a certain state's or country's law be applied to the coverage dispute. These provisions should be identified early in a dispute so that strategy can be considered. Moreover, excess policies may include a different provision for resolving disputes than does the primary coverage policy, making resolution of a major claim potentially challenging. Knowing the applicable rules early on will make navigating the settlement course easier.

CONSIDER LESSONS LEARNED FOR RENEWAL   Terms, conditions, exclusions, or other difficulties in resolving claims may be considered in negotiating coverage with the same or other insurers for the next year. In addition, insurance applications may request information about current pending or potential claims. Such applications or requests for information should be reviewed with counsel, as applications and attachments may be disclosed in litigation discovery. Worse, they may become the basis for potential actions by insurers to rescind or void the policy.

Develop a Plan to Ameliorate Deficiencies Contributing to the Problem

Once a crisis has passed, it's essential to determine why a problem occurred and how to avoid it, and ones like it, in the future. Risk managers, knowledgeable counsel, and, as appropriate, consultants, can assist in the following.

ASSESSING ROOT CAUSES   There may be a systems concern, a reporting issue, or a compliance problem. Probing to assess the fundamental cause or causes can be a useful exercise for preventing future problems.

FIXING THE SYSTEMS OR CONTRIBUTING CAUSES   Hindsight typically provides perspective. Problems are also often not unique. Taking advantage of what has worked for other companies can be of value. Sharing information through formal and informal networks or professional associations may be helpful. Auditors, lawyers, consultants, and internal committees can be helpful in correcting deficiencies.

COMMUNICATING THE MESSAGE AND PRIORITIES Implementing a program or new way of handling a situation may require training, goal setting, and repeat communication. Setting the tone and key values at all levels of the company, including with remote plants and outposts, vendors, consultants, and service providers, can provide compliance and deter wrongdoing.

MEASURE THE EFFECTIVENESS OF REFORM Change is worthwhile if it works. Measuring the effectiveness of revised processes and programs is important so that tweaks and further refinements can be made as needed. Moreover, instilling confidence in and support for shared goals is enhanced when progress is shown.

Whether the alleged wrongdoers are brought to justice, claims are made and paid, and the Company thrives is not yet known. But as head of risk management, you are part of a team responsible for taking steps to appropriately put best practices into play.

Conclusion

The information in this chapter provides risk managers with an assessment of risk; a plan of investigation with the assistance of legal counsel and any necessary investigators, accountants, and/or consultants; with adequate advice on required disclosures to directors, government, auditors, shareholders, customers, the media, and company insiders and employees; with timely notice and claims to insurers; and with well-reasoned follow-up with carriers.

In our hypothetical example, Buyam Stuffalot may have perpetrated some scheme on the Company; his actions may have caused a loss. He isn't the first to do so, and he won't be the last. Your ability to respond in a meaningful, competent, and comprehensive manner will preserve and add value to the Company—maybe even save part of its existence, and the jobs of employees along with it. And isn't that what risk management is all about?

Quantitative Risk Management

I n this section we examine quantitative, scalable risk assessment modeling procedures. The first chapters in this section discuss key components of our quantitative risk management methodology, while the remaining chapters discuss potential applications of our methodology.

Within this section we concern ourselves with developing an assessment framework that seeks to quantify risks to the organization and provides a methodology for checking the predictive power of our models. These risks might pertain to financial reporting, operations, compliance with laws and regulations, operations, or the safeguarding of assets. Although state-of-the-art risk assessment tools used by professionals currently include quantitative risk assessment methods, these types of risk assessments often focus on micro-level risks. Technological advances have made it easier for organizations to quantify risks from *force majeure* events such as hurricanes and severe weather patterns, using models that break existing weather conditions into "cells" and simulate their interactions. They have also helped the construction industry better forecast decay in steel-reinforced concrete bridges using nonlinear regression models; the airline industry to better comprehend the fracture toughness of aircraft materials using models of strain developed from stress testing; and the health-care industry to model outbreaks of new flu strains using relational models of disease transmission. However, these types of risk modeling are *not* the subject of the second portion of this text. Rather, we focus on a quantitative approach to assessing risks at all levels of the organization according to their causes.

The methods in this section are intended to augment the COSO Internal Control (COSO-IC) and COSO Enterprise Risk Management (COSO-ERM) Frameworks by adding quantitative assessment and interdependent systems features. The additions are an expansion of the Control Activities component of COSO-IC, but the other COSO-IC components remain unchanged. Furthermore, the methods in this book do *not* conflict with most of the various frameworks espoused for security, financial information, or information technology. The correlations are explained in the forthcoming chapters.

COSO-IC is intended to be a high-level view of internal control and deliberately does not, for example, concern itself with the technology used to support information processing or control implementation. Most commonly, a methodology known as CobiT serves to fill this gap. We also addresses CobiT's framework within this section.

Because the Sarbanes-Oxley Act (SOX) applies only to public companies in the United States, so too do COSO's frameworks. The American Institute of Certified Public Accountants (AICPA) has issued auditing standards applicable to internal controls of private companies. Still other pronouncements exist that are more narrowly directed to security and information technology. These other pronouncements do not directly reference COSO's frameworks, but they are compatible with it.

Most readers who have experience in performing control and risk assessments should already be familiar with most of the concepts described in the first chapters in this section regarding control frameworks. However, we provide a brief refresher for readers who have not had the opportunity to study or apply the qualitative assessments specified by these frameworks and to give all readers a common starting point.

As previously stated, our quantitative assessments are designed to assist managers in understanding the specific and ultimate risks in the areas of financial reporting, operations, and governance. We extend existing qualitative frameworks (e.g., COSO-IC, COSO-ERM, and CobiT) to a quantitative methodology, allowing the reader to better understand the impact of risks to the organization.

Why Is a Quantitative Approach Important?

The use of a quantitative approach offers several advantages over a purely qualitative one:

- Risks and controls can be modeled to predict specific levels of residual risk.
- The model provides a communication structure by which several people can collaborate and pool their knowledge of systems, risks, and controls.
- The model can be validated by comparing it to observed incidences.
- The model can be used to identify and focus on only those controls necessary to achieve the objectives of external financial reporting or other selected objectives.
- The model can be used to plan audits more effectively by quantitatively understanding the risks of material misstatements.

- The model can be used for "what-if" scenarios to test sensitivity, optimize costs and benefits, and consider alternatives for improved design.
- The logic behind the assessment is documented for review and discussion.
- Quantitative measures can reduce the extent of debate arising from differing assessments.
- Multiple instances of a system can be assessed and compared.
- The exposures from multiple systems can be aggregated for the entire enterprise.

Some skeptics question the possibility that a quantitative model of such a complex problem can ever be reliable. However, at the same time, they accept the conclusions of professional judgment in qualitative assessments.

Research has suggested that to be considered experts, individuals should have 10 years of concentrated experience in the specific discipline of their expertise. Without this experience, an individual who makes a "professional judgment" might do so without the necessary background on which to base this judgment. It is essential that board members, managers, and risk management professionals keep this in mind when they are selecting risk management experts to perform assessments. Moreover, directors and managers should select a committee of risk practitioners to perform risk assessments, as individuals on their own may not be able to elaborate all relevant risks; a committee of risk practitioners will be more likely to capture all risks faced by the organization.

The authors have great admiration for the capabilities of the human brain. It can estimate, in an instant, the exact force, direction, and elevation to send a basketball swooshing through a net. It is not as accurate at performing similar estimates for a cannon to hit a distant target. For that, the human brain invented the first computer.

Professional judgment also has its limitations. The financial statements of a public company are usually the product of many systems, which often are quite complex by themselves as well as in their interrelationships. We do not believe that intuition, judgment, or any other solely qualitative assessment could be better than one that enlists the aid of quantitative relationships. This does not mean that we endorse blind acceptance of quantitative results, for they, too, can omit or distort essential issues. It does mean that quantitative measures will usually produce sounder answers than "guesstimating."

Predicting Residual Risk

Our business and personal lives are filled with desires to predict what is going to happen. We seek weather predictions to know what to wear and to plan activities. We predict the next month's and quarter's profits to inform top management and investors. Predicting risks is no different.

A quantitative approach affords us the possibility of predicting what we deem residual risks, or those risks that remain after internal control systems have had a chance to prevent, detect, and correct potential issues. Other qualitative approaches do not allow for such estimation techniques.

Collaborating with Subject-Matter Experts

The explicit listing of risks and controls in our quantitative model provides a structure for people from different disciplines and viewpoints to contribute and blend their knowledge. This is especially evident when accountants and information technology experts work together. A single person is rarely so broadly knowledgeable as to prepare a model alone. Usually someone skilled in modeling works together with several subject-matter experts to construct a model that is complete and realistic. Subject-matter experts contribute their experience and knowledge regarding potential problems, their risks, effectiveness of control design, reliability of control implementation, and likelihood of various consequences.

Validity of Modeling

With the tools built into Excel® and other computer software, one need not be a meteorologist or a mathematician to build a predictive model. Building a model that works with reasonable reliability, however, is still a tricky task. Every model should be validated or "proven" before it is relied on. This can be accomplished via two methods.

Some mathematical models are regression equations containing relatively few variables. Such models can be validated by making a series of observations and then comparing them to the model's predictions. The accuracy of the model can be measured by calculating coefficient of correlation or by graphing the differences. In preparing such a plot, one can verify how predicted values deviate from actual values. Most control assessment models contain too many variables to permit the use of regression techniques. Instead, we apply the techniques of *cross-validation* in our quantitative model.

Cross-validation requires that a practitioner partition a dataset into subsets for future use. Analysis is performed on a subset of the total available data and then validated using data from a separate subset. For example, a practitioner may first acquire historical data regarding the actual occurrence of incidents. Then, using cross-validation techniques, he can exclude the most recent period and use the prior periods to predict values for the most recent period. If the actual data for the most recent period and the prediction are approximately equal, that presents evidence that the model is valid.

An alternative approach is to use recent data to predict the forthcoming period and then wait to see whether what happens is approximately equal to the prediction. This approach requires waiting, but it might be necessary if insufficient historical data is available to apply the first approach. This approach is also appropriate for ongoing monitoring of recurring predictions.

If the results from either of these validation methods are significantly different from reality, the model must be reconsidered and revised to improve it.

Focusing on Objectives

Many financial information application systems serve operating and compliance objectives as well as financial reporting ones. The accuracy and integrity needed for the operating and compliance objectives often exceed the level needed for financial reporting within the boundaries of materiality. How can someone pick out just those controls necessary to financial reporting? Most of the time they will err in the direction of selecting more controls than necessary. Using quantitative methods, the selection of so-called *key controls* and the scope of testing can be substantially reduced from the numbers commonly selected.

Performing Sensitivity and "What-If" Analyses

With a quantitative predictive model, one may alter key parameters and see what would probably happen if those parameters changed in the real future. This also allows tests of relative sensitivity to the variables. Alternative controls can also be considered and measured. This approach can assist in improving the economy and efficiency of the plan of control.

Documenting for Review

In typical practice, a risk and control assessment is based on a study of lists or a matrix of risks and related controls. The actual conclusions reached in the assessment usually are intuitively based on the assessor's experience and professional judgment. Aside from trust in that judgment, a reviewer has nothing explaining the reasoning behind the judgment.

With a quantitative model, however, a reviewer can see the specific estimates and calculations that lead to a prediction. These values can be reconsidered by the reviewer, and the reviewer can use the model for sensitivity calculations.

Reducing Debates

When assessments are based on intuitive judgment and are not particularly susceptible to meaningful review, differences in opinion are bound to occur. Typically, these differences are settled by the party with greatest influence—usually the outside auditors. However, they do not necessarily represent the most knowledgeable conclusion. Auditors will admit that they never met a control they didn't like. They tend to select a large proportion of the controls as "key." A quantitative approach can predict the exposure value and often reveals that only a few controls are really necessary to reduce exposure to an immaterial amount.

Multiple Instances

Some systems operate in multiple instances within the same organization. Good examples are the branches of a bank, agencies of an insurance company, and warehouses of a distributor. Each uses the same suite of applications and operating procedures. Often, each connects electronically to central computer application systems. The primary differences between instances are the quantity and mix of transactions, the manner in which the local staff implements the prescribed controls, and the tone of local management.

Once a quantitative model has been developed and validated for these applications, it can be applied to each instance by changing only the opportunities, inherent risks, and associated dollar values to fit the current instance. Generally, the effectiveness of the control designs will not change, but their implementation will very likely differ by case.

Aggregate Exposure

One of the more difficult tasks of a large-scale risk assessment is to determine the aggregate risk to the enterprise from the combination of all the systems and residual problems expected by each. Although a qualitative approach might recognize sources of major risks, assessing the cumulative risks from a large number of sources that are individually immaterial is more challenging.

The estimated exposures from each assessment of a portion of the whole are easily added together in a quantitative assessment.

Cost of Benefits

With these many potential benefits, why would anyone *not* employ quantitative assessment? Some of the organizations that hesitate are concerned about added costs. In reality, the added cost is usually negligible. Most of the cost of control and risk assessment is in the documentation and testing. Quantitative modeling does not require any additional system documentation over that for the qualitative approach. Testing might even be cheaper because very often the quantitative assessment better shows how to limit the number of key controls.

The only additional time required is for the actual input of values for which "high, medium, and low" or "red, yellow, and green" (from a stoplight perspective) were assigned in rating qualitative controls and risks. Even this step should involve only a few hours per system. Quantitative modeling should save costs in the end while affording the organization utilizing such a model many benefits.

Summary

In Summary, the authors believe that a truly quantitative approach to risk management is not only practical, but is essential to the determination of what amounts to reasonable assurance of adequate control.

Because our quantitative approach is highly compatible with the COSO Framework, retrofitting our approach to existing qualitative assessments is very feasible and can be accomplished with modest effort and cost.

CHAPTER 5

Recognized Control Frameworks
COSO-IC and COSO-ERM

In the words of COSO's first chairman, "Although a lot of people are talking about risk, there is no commonly accepted definition of risk management and no comprehensive framework outlining how the process should work, making risk communication among board members and management difficult and frustrating."[1] We have already offered a definition of risk in Section I; we now introduce two comprehensive frameworks for risk assessment, COSO's *Internal Control—Integrated Framework* (COSO-IC) and *Enterprise Risk Management—Integrated Framework* (COSO-ERM). Both serve as the foundation for later chapters on qualitative and quantitative control evaluations. Other control frameworks are introduced in the next chapter.

All the frameworks introduced in the next two chapters assist professionals in assessing expected risks as well as the exposures associated with these risks. They also provide the foundation for our quantitative framework presented in subsequent chapters.

Although the descriptions in the following chapters represent the status of these control frameworks at the time these chapters were drafted, we encourage readers to check for any updates to these frameworks subsequent to the publication of this book.

Control Frameworks and Professional Standards

The Foreign Corrupt Practices Act (FCPA) of 1977 provided a definition of internal control, later modified by COSO-IC and COSO-ERM. We therefore discuss the implications of the FCPA prior to introducing both COSO models.

The Foreign Corrupt Practices Act of 1977

Federal investigations by the SEC in the 1970s uncovered large bribes paid by U.S. companies to foreign officials. Lockheed Corporation, already reeling from slow sales of its L-1011 commercial jetliner, nearly collapsed after a U.S. Senate subcommittee found that it had bribed officials of foreign governments in hopes of winning military aircraft contracts. Other investigations found "over 400 U.S. companies admitted making questionable or illegal payments in excess of $300 million to foreign government officials, politicians, and political parties."[2]

The result of these investigations was the passage of the Foreign Corrupt Practices Act of 1977. The act's antibribery provisions "make it unlawful for a U.S. person, and certain foreign issuers of securities, to make a corrupt payment to a foreign official for the purpose of obtaining or retaining business for or with, or directing business to, any person." Since 1998, the act also applies to "foreign firms and persons who take any act in furtherance of such a corrupt payment while in the United States."[3]

The FCPA was the first instance in which the term *internal accounting controls* was used in a federal regulation for public companies. It also made management responsible for ensuring that such controls existed and were functioning correctly. Although the act did not further discuss what constituted a system of internal accounting controls, it heightened the importance of proper documentation for SEC-regulated companies. The FCPA states that all public corporations shall:[4]

- Make and keep books, records, and accounts, which, in reasonable detail, accurately and fairly reflect the transactions and dispositions of the assets of the issuer
- Devise and maintain a system of internal accounting controls sufficient to provide reasonable assurances that:
  - Transactions are executed in accordance with management's general or specific authorization
  - Transactions are recorded as necessary (1) to permit preparation of financial statements in conformity with generally accepted accounting principles or any other criteria applicable to such statements, and (2) to maintain accountability for assets
  - Access to assets is permitted only in accordance with management's general or specific authorization
  - The recorded accountability for assets is compared with the existing assets at reasonable intervals and appropriate action is taken with respect to any differences

The FCPA omitted any enforcement provision regarding internal control, and that aspect was widely ignored by corporate managements. The internal controls addressed in the FCPA were specific to corporate accounting functions. It was not until more than a decade later—with the introduction of the COSO-IC Framework—that the definition of internal control was expanded.

COSO-IC

The origin of the COSO-IC Framework was a 1987 report by the National Commission on Fraudulent Financial Reporting, commonly known as the *Treadway Commission* after its chairman, James C. Treadway. The Commission, sponsored by the American Institute of Certified Public Accountants (AICPA), the Institute of Internal Auditors (IIA), the Financial Executives Institute (FEI), the American Accounting Association (AAA), and the Institute of Management Accountants (IMA), had been formed to assess the conditions that permitted such notorious financial reporting failures as the Equity Funding scandal of the 1970s and the widespread problems of the savings and loan industry.[5] The report emphasized the key elements of an effective internal control system: a strong control environment, a code of conduct, a competent audit committee, and a strong management function. One of their major findings was that no consensus existed as to the meaning of *internal control.*

Among other things, the *1987 Treadway Report* called for a more complete pronouncement defining internal control. The five organizations that formed the COSO committee hired Coopers & Lybrand (C&L) in 1992 to integrate existing internal control frameworks into a common reference for practitioners. The committee was tasked with developing a conceptual framework for internal control, along with a standard by which companies could assess the effectiveness of their internal control systems. After three years of work, the eventual result was COSO's *Internal Control—Integrated Framework*, which set forth a new definition of internal control:[6]

> *Internal control is a process, affected by an entity's board of directors, management, and other personnel, designed to provide reasonable assurance regarding the achievement of objectives in the following categories: effectiveness and efficiency of operations, reliability of financial reporting, and compliance with applicable laws and regulations.*

COSO-IC defined the term *internal control* in a broader manner than the FCPA's definition of internal accounting controls. COSO-IC's definition specifies that internal controls should govern the "effectiveness and efficiency of operations," arguably what was previously labeled in accounting literature an internal *administrative* control. (At this point, we strongly recommend that readers of this book also read the COSO-IC Framework. It contains many important insights and is fewer than 100 pages long.)

Although most of the Treadway Commission's recommendations were implemented in some fashion or another, hindsight shows us that they were not entirely effective. Again, in 2002, Congress looked at the fraudulent reporting by Enron, WorldCom, and many other corporations. This prompted passage of the Sarbanes-Oxley Act of 2002 (SOX). The SEC chose to endorse the COSO-IC Framework for use under SOX in its *Final Rule: Management's Reports on Internal Control Over Financial Reporting and Certification of Disclosure in Exchange Act Periodic Reports.*

The COSO-IC Framework describes a valid and useful perspective.[7] However, it has always been intended as a conceptual framework addressing all the major objectives of an organization. It does not provide organizations with a substantial program for internal control assessments. It is a framework, not a complete structure. Moreover, the COSO-IC Framework describes static relationships—not an active process—for sustained implementation of internal controls. Compliance with SOX involves a distinct process of assessment, but the COSO-IC Framework only addresses the relationships.

COSO-IC OBJECTIVES   The original COSO-IC Framework as published in 1992 recognized three primary categories of objectives for internal control:

1. Effective and efficient operations
2. Reliable published financial statements
3. Compliance with laws and regulations

COSO-IC's financial reporting and compliance objectives are primarily subject to internally originating problems and thereby are amenable to internal control, whereas the operations objectives are subject to many external influences that might be beyond the influence of internal controls. However, internal controls should be able to perceive these changes in an organization's external environment and provide guidelines as to how they should be addressed.

In 1994, a fourth objective was added in an addendum, *Reporting to External Parties:*

4. Safeguarding of assets

This objective was added after the Government Accounting Office (GAO) expressed concern that management reports contemplated by the originally published COSO-IC report did not address controls related to the safeguarding of assets. COSO-IC's authors had followed a trend started with the introduction of Statements on Auditing Standards (SAS) No. 55 in 1988, which eliminated the safeguarding of assets as a primary control objective. Previously, SAS No. 1 had included the safeguarding of assets as one such objective.

SAS No. 55 also revised the definition of internal control and expanded the responsibility of the auditor for considering internal control in a financial statement audit. SAS No. 1's classification of internal control into *internal accounting control* and *administrative control* was superseded by a single term: *internal control structure*. This structure consisted of three components: (1) a control environment, (2) an accounting system, and (3) control procedures. SAS No. 55 significantly influenced COSO's members, and the COSO-IC Framework reflects many ideas set forth in this standard.

It is also important to note that COSO-IC's financial reporting objective applies only to *published* reports. In the context of SOX, these are the reports filed with the SEC and distributed to investors. For non-SEC reporting entities, the objective applies to reports provided to private investors, lenders, banks, regulators, and other constituents. It does not apply to purely internal reports used solely in the management of operations. Such reports serve the operations objectives.

We believe that this nuance is the cause of some of the excessive costs many companies experienced in complying with SOX. Many internal accounting systems serve both internal management and external financial reporting. However, the tolerances needed for high-quality management information are often more stringent than the standard of materiality applied to external reporting. Therefore, one can find that accounting application systems have many more and much stronger controls than would be required only for SOX assurances.

For example, most companies holding inventories track the items in stock with a perpetual inventory system. In many of these cases, the values used for individual items are *standard costs*, which are important aids to management but are not acceptable for public reporting. The company may adjust standard costs to conform to GAAP or might compile its "public" inventory value by entirely separate, redundant means. In either event, many of the controls over the perpetual inventory system would not be "key" to an assessment of controls for SOX.

The COSO-IC Framework further delineates whether various management activities fall within their definition if internal control. The exclusions they list include:

- Entity-level objective setting: mission, value statements
- Strategic planning
- Activity-level objective setting
- Risk management
- Corrective actions

We agree that setting objectives and strategic planning are essential management functions and not internal controls. The exclusion of risk management was reversed in 2002 with the publication of COSO's Enterprise Risk

Management Framework. We disagree, for reasons explained later, with the exclusion of corrective actions in the 1992 framework.

COSO-IC'S CONTROL COMPONENTS   The COSO-IC Framework describes five interrelated components, shown in Exhibit 5.1. All should be present and effective to provide adequate internal control.

COSO-IC'S CONTROL ENVIRONMENT   The first component of COSO-IC is the control environment.

Another name for the control environment is the "tone at the top." This, essentially, is *leadership*: an organization's board of directors, CEO, CFO, and other managerial positions. The COSO-IC Framework then describes seven factors that give insight to this environment:

1. Integrity and ethical values
2. Commitment to competence
3. Management's philosophy and operating style

Control Environment
Board of Directors—Integrity and Ethical Values—Commitment to Competence—
Management's Philosophy and Operating Style—Organizational Structure—Assignment
of Authority and Responsibility—Human Resources Policies and Practices

Risk Assessment
Inherent and Residual Risk—Likelihood and Impact—Methodologies and Techniques—
Correlation

Control Activities
Integration with Risk Response—Types of Control Activities—General Controls—
Application Controls—Entity Specific

Information and Communication
Information—Strategic and Integrated Systems—Communication

Monitoring
Separate Evaluations—Ongoing Evaluations

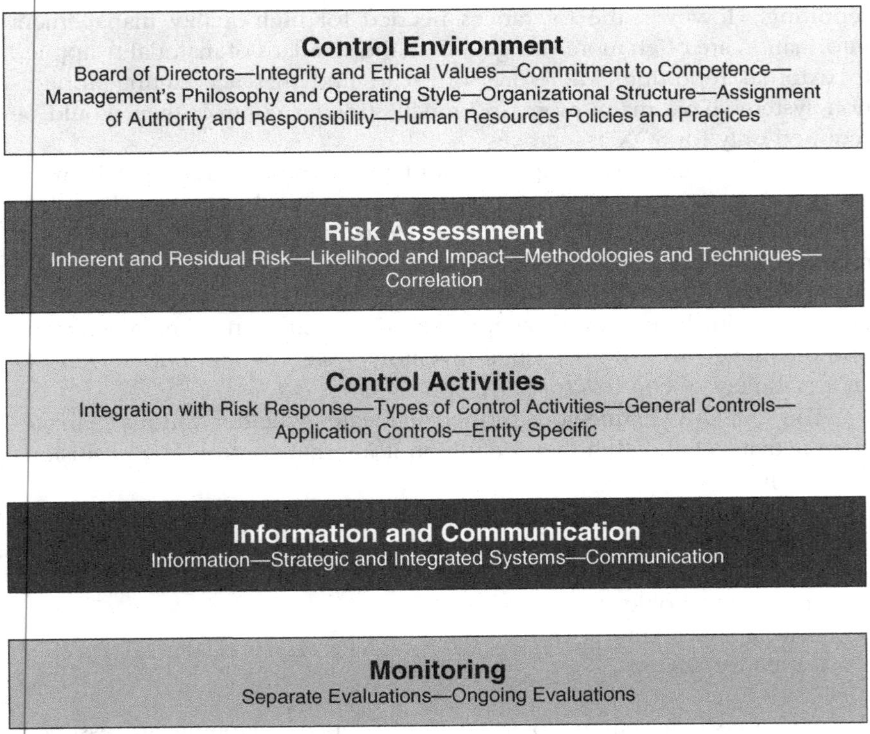

EXHIBIT 5.1 COSO-IC's Five Components

4. Risk appetite
5. Organizational structure
6. Assignment of authority and responsibility
7. Human resources policies and practices

Many of these factors can be declared and distributed in printed words. Unfortunately, they include factors that are more important in actions than in words. For example, Enron's management was very outspoken about their high integrity and impeccable ethics. The company was cited as a model for corporate governance. However, management's actions differed from their words.

Some factors are subject to strong, contradictory forces. In particular, executive compensation that is highly dependent on short-term enterprise performance creates a strong temptation to manipulate financial reporting. When the batter is also the umpire, scorekeeper, and paymaster, who can be surprised when strikes are called only when the batter's swing clearly misses? Anything he does not swing at obviously must be called a ball. In spite of this conflict of interest, legislators and public commentators keep demanding that high executive compensation be tied directly to corporate performance. A solution to this dilemma is to have the performance metrics cover a long-term period, such as three to five years. Many stock option plans already do this. Compensation through restricted stock is another option.

The COSO-IC Framework notes that "... some of the items are highly subjective and require considerable judgment ..." Although an assessor might observe some revealing situations, the assessor must also be conservative in terms of reliance. One of the essential requirements of SOX is that controls that management considers "key" to their assessment must be tested. Many of the factors in the control environment are not susceptible to testing, so they cannot be relied on.

The process described in this book incorporates the control environment concepts of the COSO-IC Framework but changes the sequence of the way it is viewed. This book looks first at COSO-IC's risk assessment, then evaluates the effects of the control environment on those risks.

COSO-IC'S RISK ASSESSMENT A SOX compliance assessment concerns itself with risks that affect financial reporting reliability. Other assessments may focus on other limited sets of risks.

The specific objectives of financial reporting are usually summarized as a list of accounting *assertions*. These can vary by public accounting firm, but COSO-IC lists them as:

- Existence or occurrence
- Completeness

- Rights and obligations
- Valuation or allocation
- Presentation and disclosure

We can see how some persons might be confused by situations encountered while considering risks to these assertions. The essential concern of SOX is the quality of financial reporting rather than related operating issues such as loss of assets through waste, inefficiency, or bad business decisions. For example, shrinkage of inventory due to damage or breakage is an operating risk, whereas recording or estimating these values is a financial reporting objective. This means that when financial reports rely on a perpetual inventory system, physical security of inventory is also a financial reporting control objective.

The quantitative assessment process in this book accepts the relationships in COSO-IC's amended 1994 publication (COSO-94) regarding risk assessment. The only difference is that, as noted, we quantify the risks in the step *before* we quantify the effects of the control environment.

The framework for risk assessment in COSO-94 was changed in 2002 with the publication of *COSO Enterprise Risk Management* (ERM), but COSO-94 was not changed or withdrawn.

COSO-IC'S CONTROL ACTIVITIES   The discussion of control activities in COSO-IC is quite brief—barely over eight pages. Though what is there is very good, it falls short of what is needed to implement an assessment for SOX or most other assessment mandates. We try to supplement some of this shortfall in this book, and many other sources can be found to address other aspects of control.

COSO-IC's materials regarding control activities explicitly exclude correction activities from control activities. The COSO-IC Framework says that internal controls should prevent and detect, but it states that correction activities are not part of internal control. This is like saying, "Bring me problems, but don't bring me solutions." We believe that the activities that serve to correct problems not otherwise prevented by internal controls are a critically essential part of the total function of internal control. For example, errors in retail securities transactions are always settled in favor of the customer. When a security pricing error occurs (and they do), a mutual fund processor must roll back all transactions affected by the error, correct the price, and then roll forward all the affected transactions using the corrected values. This could cover a few days or many months. Error correction in this environment requires careful planning and a system that is designed to process such corrections.

Readers should note that AICPA Auditing Standards differ from COSO-IC by, among other things, including correction as one of the primary control activities.

Another widespread issue with COSO-IC's control activities is their treatment of computer information technology (IT). The COSO-IC Framework recognizes a distinction between general controls and application controls. COSO-IC names data center operations, systems software, acquisition and maintenance, access security, and application development and maintenance as areas of general controls. It also addresses programmed control activities within computerized applications as the other major category of IT controls. Note, however, that the COSO-IC Framework dates from 1992, before the Internet had a significant effect on most business operations and when even internal networks mostly relied on now-obsolete technology.

The COSO-IC Framework addresses the dependence of programmed application controls on general controls. Beyond this recognition, the COSO-IC Framework provides few specifics regarding the controls over either general IT functions or applications. As a result, many practitioners have adopted CobiT[8] as their guide for IT controls. CobiT is the acronym for *Control Objectives for Information and related Technology.*

Most of this book focuses on aspects of control activities and addresses ways to relate the complex dependencies of information applications on general controls.

COSO-IC'S INFORMATION AND COMMUNICATION The COSO-IC Framework's discussion of this control component gives numerous examples of the necessity and variety of information systems, but it does not provide much in the way of a conceptual framework for those functions. We agree that controls must generate information regarding their performance and that timely communication of control activities is essential.

COSO-IC'S MONITORING The emphasis on monitoring might be the most important contribution to the state of the art by the COSO-IC Framework. We agree that monitoring risks and control activities is the key to maintaining sound internal control, especially in an environment of changing conditions and risks.

The COSO-IC Framework also cites recurring control assessments as a part of control monitoring. SOX requires quarterly management assurances regarding changes in internal control. Such interim control assessments should be a key feature of these assurances.

The control assessment process described in this book involves monitoring in three of its aspects. First, we recommend that managers monitor the incidents routinely detected by detection control activities so that they recognize changes in the level of problems that might be caused by changes in transaction frequency and inherent risks. Second, monitoring of detected incidents should be used to continuously validate the model. If forecast and actual incidents differ by significant levels, all the factors in the model should be reviewed. Third, an internal auditing function serves to monitor controls with in-depth assessment and testing of effective control design and implementation.

Other omissions have been acknowledged by COSO subsequent to 1992. We previously mentioned that in 1994, COSO added an appendix with another primary control objective: safeguarding assets. This is the COSO version to which the SEC refers in its rules.

The control category of monitoring is so important to effective risk management and efficient testing of assessments that COSO published materials focused on monitoring in 2009.

Managing Risk and Internal Control

Internal control is not the sole approach to managing risk. Several alternative responses exist:

- *Abstention/avoidance.* This is your mother's advice. If it might hurt, don't do it.
- *Informed acceptance.* Where risks are so trivial or monstrous that no other actions are worthwhile.
- *Insurance.* Particularly suitable for rare incidents.
- *Risk transfer.* Many financial instrument, currency, and commodity risks can be managed using hedges.
- *Asset/liability management.* Balance offsetting risks from financial instrument holdings and obligations. This is rather like an internal hedge but is not subject to the hedge accounting treatment of GAAP.
- *Internal control.* Activities designed to reduce potential adverse consequences. This is the focus of risk management in this book.

Management might have the option to avoid business risks by abstaining from whatever activity brings the risk, but management cannot apply that strategy to avoid the risks of misstatement in financial reporting. They might avoid currency exchange risk by selling or closing a foreign operation, but they still have to report to their investors. If a public company turns private, it can avoid the direct authority of SOX, but starting in 2007 private companies receiving external audits also must document and assess their controls, giving assurance that they can produce reliable financial statements for their bankers, lenders, owners, contributors, and supporters. Additionally, private companies issuing public debt are also subject to SOX, since they must register with the SEC to offer publicly traded debt instruments.

The SEC invites improved and different frameworks in its rules, quoted below:

> *The COSO Framework satisfies our criteria and may be used as an evaluation framework for purposes of management's annual internal control evaluation and disclosure requirements. However, the final rules do not mandate use of a particular framework, such as the COSO Framework, in recognition of the fact that other evaluation standards exist outside of the United States, and that frameworks other than COSO may be developed within the United States in the future, that satisfy the intent of the statute without diminishing the benefits to investors. The use of standard measures that are publicly available will enhance the quality of the internal control report and will promote comparability of the internal control reports of different companies. The final rules require management's report to identify the evaluation framework used by management to assess the effectiveness of the company's internal control over financial reporting.*
>
> *Specifically, a suitable framework must: be free from bias; permit reasonably consistent qualitative and quantitative measurements of a company's internal control; be sufficiently complete so that those relevant factors that would alter a conclusion about the effectiveness of a company's internal controls are not omitted; and be relevant to an evaluation of internal control over financial reporting.*

The implementation rules issued by the SEC cite *Internal Control – Integrated Framework*, published in 1994 by the Committee of Sponsoring Organizations of the Treadway Committee as an acceptable framework. However, the SEC's discussion of the COSO-IC Framework has a decidedly grudging tone, and the COSO-IC Framework seems to be "recommended" mostly because little else is widely available.

The AICPA cites the COSO-IC Framework in its auditing standards regarding internal control but makes a few subtle but important changes. The National Association of Insurance Commissioners (NAIC) also cites the COSO-IC Framework in its Model Audit Law, but NAIC openly invites insurers to apply other frameworks, including a framework developed internally by the insurance company.

The SEC discussion of the COSO-IC Framework states that other control frameworks also can be acceptable and specifies the following criteria for consideration of acceptability. These other control frameworks must:

- Be free of bias
- Contain reasonably consistent qualitative and *quantitative* measurements (emphasis added)
- Ensure that relevant factors are not omitted
- Be relevant to financial reporting

Interestingly, the COSO-IC Framework contains no discernable quantitative measurement criteria. COSO-ERM contains more information than the original COSO-IC report, but readers will note that the methodology in this book again adds some elements.

COSO-ERM

OVERVIEW   In 2004, COSO released additional materials addressing *enterprise risk management* (COSO-ERM). This is a broader application of COSO's original framework, applied to a comprehensive view of an enterprise, to include strategic issues. It also slices more deeply into the original COSO-IC methodology of risk assessment. It breaks that single element into four new ones:

1. Objective setting (comparable to selecting relevant avoidable consequences)
2. Event identification (comparable to identifying potential problems)
3. Risk assessment (comparable to calculating inherent risk)
4. Risk response (comparable to accepting or improving the control design)

These new elements are valid and legitimate clarifications of effective risk assessment and management and were only briefly addressed in the 1992 version of the COSO-IC Framework. (See Exhibit 5.2 for further information on the elements of COSO-ERM.)

COSO-ERM does not, however, provide guidance on how control activities should ensure that risk assessment controls are effectively managing organizational risks. Risk Assessment provides an appraisal of the inherent risks in a system. The control activities should be accompanied by an appraisal of the residual risks in that system.

IMPROVED FRAMEWORK   In this book, we further revise the COSO "cube," expanding on the elements within control activities. These expanded elements are:

- Control function
- Control design
- Control implementation

A revised chart in the style of the previous COSO components charts would appear as shown in Exhibit 5.3.

Holistic Risk Assessments and ERM

Assessing risks in a holistic manner is paramount to proper risk management. Risk managers have historically taken a narrowly tailored focus when

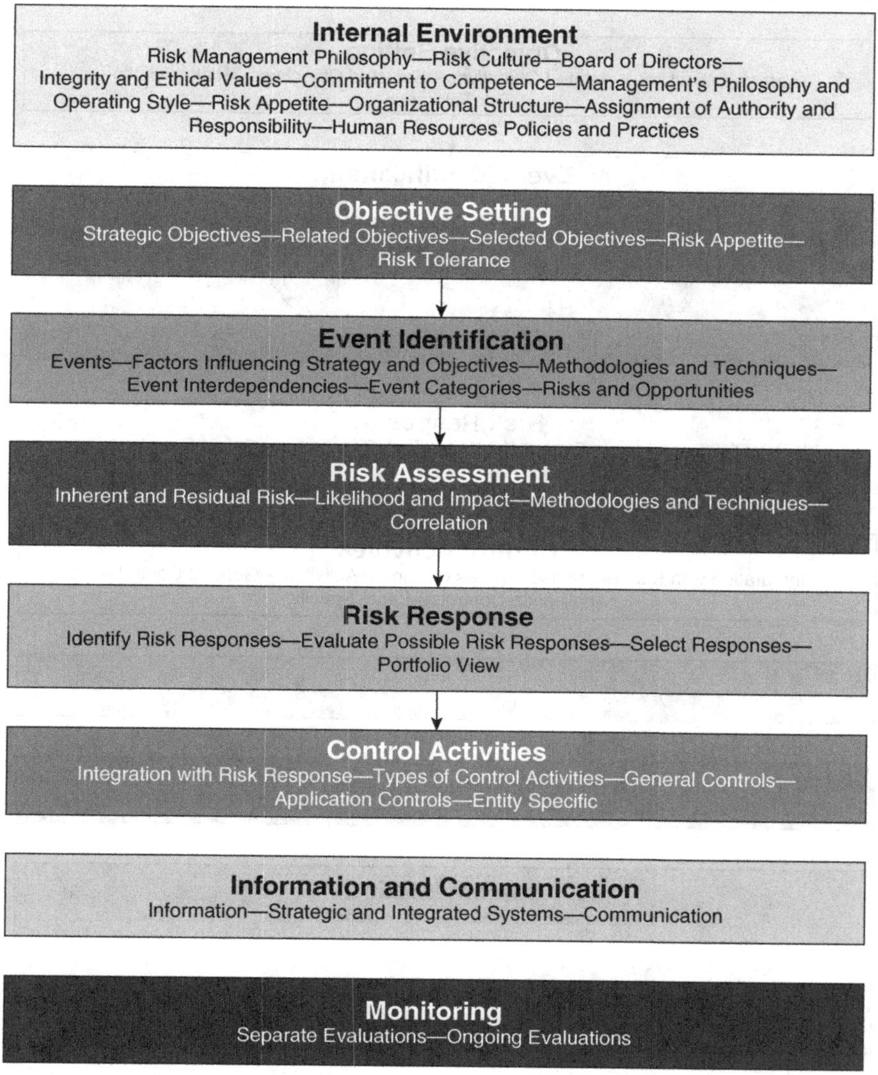

Internal Environment
Risk Management Philosophy—Risk Culture—Board of Directors—
Integrity and Ethical Values—Commitment to Competence—Management's Philosophy and
Operating Style—Risk Appetite—Organizational Structure—Assignment of Authority and
Responsibility—Human Resources Policies and Practices

Objective Setting
Strategic Objectives—Related Objectives—Selected Objectives—Risk Appetite—
Risk Tolerance

Event Identification
Events—Factors Influencing Strategy and Objectives—Methodologies and Techniques—
Event Interdependencies—Event Categories—Risks and Opportunities

Risk Assessment
Inherent and Residual Risk—Likelihood and Impact—Methodologies and Techniques—
Correlation

Risk Response
Identify Risk Responses—Evaluate Possible Risk Responses—Select Responses—
Portfolio View

Control Activities
Integration with Risk Response—Types of Control Activities—General Controls—
Application Controls—Entity Specific

Information and Communication
Information—Strategic and Integrated Systems—Communication

Monitoring
Separate Evaluations—Ongoing Evaluations

EXHIBIT 5.2 The COSO-ERM Model

Source: © Committee of Sponsoring Organization of the Treadway Commission. Reprinted with permission.

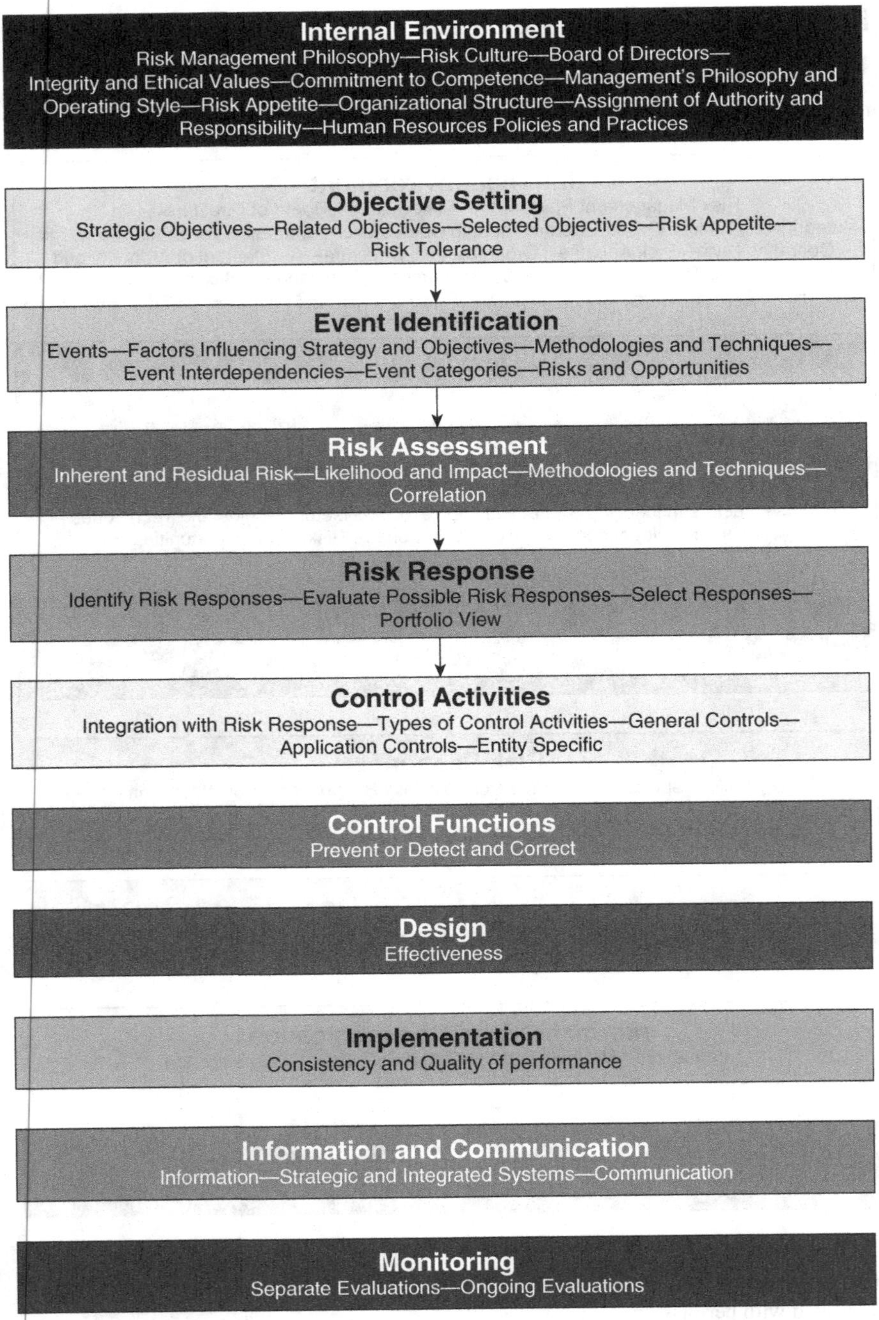

Internal Environment
Risk Management Philosophy—Risk Culture—Board of Directors—
Integrity and Ethical Values—Commitment to Competence—Management's Philosophy and
Operating Style—Risk Appetite—Organizational Structure—Assignment of Authority and
Responsibility—Human Resources Policies and Practices

Objective Setting
Strategic Objectives—Related Objectives—Selected Objectives—Risk Appetite—
Risk Tolerance

Event Identification
Events—Factors Influencing Strategy and Objectives—Methodologies and Techniques—
Event Interdependencies—Event Categories—Risks and Opportunities

Risk Assessment
Inherent and Residual Risk—Likelihood and Impact—Methodologies and Techniques—
Correlation

Risk Response
Identify Risk Responses—Evaluate Possible Risk Responses—Select Responses—
Portfolio View

Control Activities
Integration with Risk Response—Types of Control Activities—General Controls—
Application Controls—Entity Specific

Control Functions
Prevent or Detect and Correct

Design
Effectiveness

Implementation
Consistency and Quality of performance

Information and Communication
Information—Strategic and Integrated Systems—Communication

Monitoring
Separate Evaluations—Ongoing Evaluations

EXHIBIT 5.3 The Revised ERM Framework

performing risk assessments. Often risk assessments are performed by each division of the organization by separate staffs. Only when the assessment travels up the "chain of command" is the information aggregated in a manner conducive to assessing these risks holistically. Dire consequences can result from organizations failing to recognize the importance of the interaction between various risk factors. Good risk management processes could exist within all levels of the organization; however, if these tasks are undertaken via a "silo approach," without any interaction between risk management staffs, proper estimation of risks is impossible.

The COSO-ERM Framework was designed from the onset with the intention of assisting organizations in performing holistic risk assessments. COSO-ERM defines enterprise risk management as "a process, affected by an entity's board of directors, management and other personnel, applied in a strategy setting and across the enterprise, designed to identify potential events that may affect the entity, and manage risk to be within its risk appetite, to provide reasonable assurance regarding the achievement of entity objectives." At the heart of this definition is the idea that ERM is a process. Although some readers will likely hope that all tenets of risk management could be written down in a static, unchanging document, this is not the case.

The fact that ERM is a process and not a static set of rules arises from the dynamic nature of risk itself. Risks faced by organizations change with macroeconomic, country-specific, industry-specific, and firm-specific factors, to name a few. Since these risks are always changing, it is imperative that organizations view risk management as a process for which the components are reviewed and evaluated on a regular basis. This review and evaluation process should take place at all levels of the organization specified in the ERM definition, with collaboration between individuals of varying seniority and rank.

One of the great missteps taken by many boards of directors is their lack of interaction with people within the organization. Directors frequently hear from C-suite executives at their periodic meetings, but rarely—if ever—do they mingle with individuals high and low on the corporate ladder. Doing so allows directors to shatter what actors in a play call the "fourth wall": the invisible barrier that separates thespians from the audience. Without such action, directors mimic taciturn audience members who feel no connection to the actors themselves outside of the characters the actors play. Directors should be active participants in the "organizational theater."

Because ERM processes are implemented by people, it is important that directors understand who these people are, how they perceive information, and what their thoughts are on the organization's objectives. Effective ERM processes are predicated on a thorough comprehension of the "human element" by all participants in the process; ERM processes will not be effective if implemented in a robotic manner devoid of personal interaction.

Organizational Risks

Because organizations are composed of flesh-and-blood humans who possess feelings and make errors, risks to the organization will always exist. For that reason, the organization's appetite for risk should be an input into an ERM process. How much risk should the organization take? How can these risks be measured? Though we seek to answer the latter question in our subsequent chapters focused on quantitative control methodologies, the first question is one for an organization's senior management and board.

The appetite for risk is a central choice made by many decision makers. The idea is one that has been pondered by philosophers and economists alike. In finance, the Capital Asset Pricing Model (CAPM) states that expected returns should be linearly increasing in risk. However, CAPM defines risk as the variance in returns related to any particular security. Our definition of risk, covered in Chapter 2, is much different from that set forth in CAPM; however, the risk/return tradeoff nonetheless exists within organizations implementing ERM. The introduction of a new product for a venture capital-backed firm will undoubtedly cause the organization (and its investors) to bear a great deal of risk. However, this is a conscious decision made by management and the board with the estimation that the risk/return tradeoff is favorable. This decision is based on available output data from an ERM process.

An ERM process's purpose, then, is not the complete enumeration and subsequent attempted eradication of these risks. Rather, such a program should provide only reasonable assurance on mutually agreed risk management objectives. ERM cannot, for instance, prevent earthquakes in California or tsunamis off the coast of Thailand. What it can do is help organizations understand the known risks they face and help managers tailor their goals to the firm's appetite for risk.

The COSO-ERM Framework

The COSO-ERM Framework is typically outlined in a three-dimensional cube as shown in Exhibit 5.4.

The ERM cube comprises eight risk components, four risk management objectives, and entity and unit-level components. Although there are four such entity and unit-level components in Exhibit 5.4, this dimension of the COSO cube will vary by the size and type of business using the framework.

Risk Components

INTERNAL ENVIRONMENT   The *internal environment* occupies the top spot in the COSO-ERM cube—and for good reason. Arguably the most important

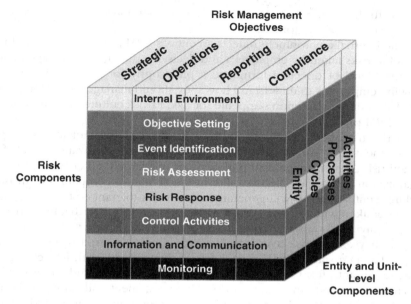

EXHIBIT 5.4 The COSO-ERM Framework

Source: © COSO. Reprinted with permission.

input to an ERM process is the internal environment in which the process is taking place. In the original COSO-IC Framework's cube, the Control Environment was placed at the bottom of the cube to symbolize its importance as the foundation of internal control. (See Exhibit 5.5 for more information.) COSO-ERM's authors, however, moved the environment to the top of the

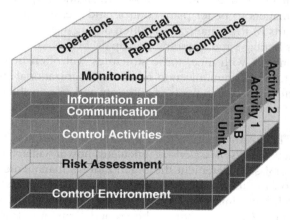

EXHIBIT 5.5 The Original COSO-IC Framework

Source: © COSO. Reprinted with permission.

cube to further enhance its importance and to symbolize that the environment is created by the tone at the top.

The internal environment reflects an entity's ERM philosophy and influences the risks taken by employees and decisions they make. Management and the board of directors formulate a philosophy for risk management, allowing employees to understand how they should manage risks. Doing so establishes the organization's appetite for risk, its risk culture, and the value of the ERM process.

A risk management philosophy is a set of beliefs promulgated by top management and the board of directors about an organization's belief-related risks. Risk management philosophies will largely differ based on an organization's strategic objectives. For instance, startup companies or those seeking venture capital will generally enjoy a risk-tolerant culture. Projects are undertaken with known, significant risks, but it is hoped that these risks will pay dividends at some point in the future. Other, more mature organizations may exhibit risk aversion. Some companies make a healthy profit by producing a stable product over a long time period, with few changes (e.g., restaurants, food service goods, soap manufacturers, and paper products manufacturers). An organization's risk management philosophy will not necessarily be written down on a piece of paper, but it is an attitude that is shared by employees at all levels of the organization. In tandem with an organization's risk management philosophy is its appetite for risk and its risk culture.

Another component of an organization's internal environment is its organizational structure. Although many different organizational structures (e.g., bureaucracy and matrix organizations) exist, they should each serve to facilitate communication within the organization. The organizational structure should also make clear delineations about roles and responsibilities. This will allow managers to better plan, control, and measure the performance of different parts of the organization. Often an organization's structure is a function of its heritage and founding principals' beliefs. As the organization grows—or shrinks—with time, these structures will often need to change to ensure that good communication remains. Organizational structure also provides a vehicle for assignments of authority and responsibility. This is an essential element of internal control highlighted in COSO's original work.

OBJECTIVE SETTING   An organization's *mission statement* sets forth what it hopes to achieve; its *vision statement* articulates how it will achieve that mission. From its mission statement the organization's management team and board work to formulate strategic objectives, operational goals, and related objectives, with the primary goal being value creation for shareholders.

The place of *objective setting* as the second element in the COSO-ERM cube highlights its importance in a proper ERM process. Objective setting allows managers and employees to understand the current state of the organization and to properly plan a future state through the enumeration of specific strategic objectives. COSO-ERM also suggests that organizations should define objectives in direct accordance with their mission statements; if these items are disparate, this situation should be remedied to ensure that all employees are in tune with a specific mission.

Many organizations today utilize some form of balanced scorecard approach when they are setting and evaluating objectives. This framework, popularized in the early 1990s by Robert S. Kaplan and David Norton, seeks to assist organizations in defining holistic objectives that will assist in value creation. Kaplan and Norton believed that too many organizations had focused their efforts exclusively on financial objectives and goal setting without placing a proper emphasis on other types of goals. They identified three additional types of objectives for managers to examine in evaluating performance: the customer, the internal business process, and learning and growth objectives. Examining these objectives, they argued, would allow managers to keep a better pulse on the organization, since financial indicators often lag behind the triumphs or tragedies businesses face.[10]

EVENT IDENTIFICATION   *Event identification* refers to management's ability to properly perceive risky events affecting the organization's ability to implement its strategy and achieve its objectives. Although it is certainly important for managers and employees to identify events with potential downside risks, it is also imperative that they identify upside cases as well. Events with potential downside risks should be mitigated through the organization's ERM process; those with potential upsides should be reviewed with respect to the organization's mission and vision statements as well as its appetite for risk.

In identifying events, practitioners should look to factors in the competitive environment, macroeconomic factors, and employee issues, not only at a static point in time but also with the aim of identifying any trends present in these variables. Doing so can afford the organization the ability to better plan for risks because the company can use its trend lines to forecast future events. It is also important that the organization keep a centralized database of information discussing impacts on the organization in the case that events occur. This will allow managers to quickly learn lessons from history as well as share these lessons with new employees and risk managers.

Events often overlooked by management include those internal to the organization. Frequently, departmental procedures will change, as will key personnel. These factors should be monitored to appropriately determine their impact on the organization before serious adverse effects can occur. Interviews and surveys with employees as well as an employee suggestion program can help the organization ensure that its internal procedures are running properly.

Events are described in COSO-ERM as being either favorable or adverse. SOX is only concerned with the adverse side—material weaknesses or errors in the financial reporting functions. The idea of risks that could be favorable is hard to fit into this context.

Favorable events are more appropriate to the broader COSO-ERM objectives of operations and strategy. COSO-ERM also describes them as opportunities. In practice, we have found that surprises of any type disturb management, who instead plan and implement strategies that they expect to earn predicted profits for the company and rewards to the stakeholders. Their ideal outcome is when everything works as planned.

Corporations are not in business to win a lottery. Sometimes, however, they make bets on the outcome of some venture. They want odds strongly in their favor, which requires an ability to estimate those risks and rewards.

Institutional investors use complex mathematical models to estimate the probability distribution of their returns, including the risk of losses. They can change that distribution by changing their credit criteria, type of investment instruments, or their investment sectors. This form of risk management is also known broadly as *financial engineering*, or *computational finance*. Many of the risk management issues discussed in the financial press, such as subprime mortgage derivatives, refer only to this environment.

COSO is composed of representatives predominantly from the accounting profession. Neither COSO-ERM nor the events considered by investment risk management provide the perspective for the enterprise risks of something like a financial enterprise.

RISK ASSESSMENT   *Risk assessment* describes an organization's ability to consider how potential events might affect the achievement of objectives. These risks are assessed along two dimensions, likelihood and impact, using a combination of qualitative and quantitative methods. With respect to any type of event, there exist numerous potential consequences. Managers should evaluate these consequences in developing an appropriate risk response.

Practitioners should assess risks along two dimensions: inherent and residual risks. We cover these terms in greater detail later on; here we offer brief definitions of these terms. *Inherent risks* are those that are inherent to the nature of an activity itself. For instance, the risks of errors in an organization's budget increase with the budget's size. Inherent risk is also a function of the tone set by management and the actions these individuals take, specifically with respect to their treatment of risks. *Residual risks* are risks that remain even after a risk management plan has identified and attempted to mitigate specified risks. These risks are always present in any organization.

RISK RESPONSE   Management identifies *risk response* options and considers their effect on event likelihood and impact in relation to risk tolerances and cost versus benefit. Responses include avoidance, reduction, sharing, and acceptance of risk. Assessment of risk responses and assurance that a risk response is selected and implemented are integral components of ERM; however, the particular response management selects is not. Effective ERM does not mean that the best response was chosen, only that the response selected is expected to bring the risk likelihood and impact within the entity's risk appetite.

CONTROL ACTIVITIES   *Control activities* are the policies and procedures that help ensure that appropriate risk responses are carried out. These control activities are present throughout an entity at all levels of the organization. Many of these controls with respect to financial reporting (e.g., separation of duties, audit trails, security and integrity, and documentation) are easy to identify and test for auditors and accountants because they were introduced in the original COSO-IC Framework. However, controls in the other three areas at the top of the ERM cube—strategic, operations, and compliance—might not be so easy to test. For instance, how can an organization's controls be related to its corporate strategy? Surely we can benefit from hindsight in such tests if we wait for a significant amount of time to pass; however, this is not our goal with an ERM process. We want to be able to test controls that will help ensure that the organization stays on top of strategy, adhering to its ordained mission and vision statements. The answer is, unfortunately, not simple. However, information and communication play a central role in the evaluation of controls for all parts of an ERM process.

INFORMATION AND COMMUNICATION   Information must be compiled from both internal and external sources, documented, and communicated in a timely manner to all stakeholders in an organization. This information must flow throughout the organization to all relevant parties, including customers, suppliers, and regulators.

Many organizations have a plethora of IT tools and communication methods. In many cases, the sheer quantity of these tools can overwhelm users with too much information. Consider the number of emails an executive receives on a daily basis. What was once seen as an electronic marvel has now become a nuisance for many. In communicating information, it is important that managers recognize this issue. If they communicate too much information to employees within too small a time period, employees might not read this information in its entirety, or it could be discarded.

Research has shown that the existence of strong communication tools within an organization is not enough to ensure adequate and proper communication. Instead, those firms that are able to leverage "intangible, complementary human and business resources such as flexible culture, strategic planning-IT integration, and supplier relationships" will best reap the benefits of good communication throughout the organization.[11]

MONITORING   ERM is a monitored process. *Monitoring* allows organizations to understand where they were before they began an initiative as well as the results of this initiative. It is also an essential part of an ERM process; without it there would be no way to identify the benefits of the ERM process. Monitoring also ensures that employees do not regard ERM as a "flavor-of-the-month" initiative. By monitoring an ERM program's activities, management is tacitly telling all stakeholders in the process that it values ERM and that it intends to maintain the program in the long run.

Monitoring can take many forms. As part of any ERM process, flowcharts should be developed to document the current state of the process as well as any desired future states. Evaluating competitors' ERM processes through benchmarking can also assist in the monitoring process. Some organizations are reluctant to divulge their own information; this scenario might be best exemplified by venture capital-backed portfolio companies of private equity (PE) firms. These firms participate in a high-risk environment. As such, it is imperative that the managers of firms under a given PE fund's umbrella continually assess risks and implement best risk management practices to mitigate these issues and achieve success.

Risk Management Objectives

The COSO-ERM cube details four risk management objectives: strategic, operations, reporting, and compliance. These elements share an equal, graphical depiction at the top of the cube, but the first two elements should arguably have the greatest importance in any ERM process. Without a sound organizational strategy and operations to produce and sell products and services, there exists no lasting need for financial reporting or compliance.

With respect to financial reporting, the COSO-ERM cube refers to reports generated for both internal and external purposes. In some instances, reports generated for internal purposes could require higher degrees of precision than those for external purposes. In the case of a fledgling company looking to introduce a completely new product, precise estimates of the potential market size and consumer demand are paramount to the business's success. Overestimation of the demand for a potential product could cause the organization to invest too much in research and development, creating a fierce cash burn that cannot be attenuated with subpar product sales.

Sound corporate strategy techniques and internal control procedures used in conjunction with risk management practices can help organizations mitigate such issues. It is the authors' belief that strong internal controls are the practitioner's best tool in developing a holistic ERM process. We detail these control procedures in the following chapters.

Summary

COSO's ERM framework is an important document that outlines a holistic risk management process for organizations. Many organizations use risk management; however, they frequently do so in a fragmented manner that does not allow interactions among risks to be examined and analyzed. The COSO-ERM Framework, however, in conjunction with the frameworks we introduce in subsequent chapters, will allow board members, operations managers, accountants, and all risk practitioners to understand, identify, analyze, and quantify risks their organizations face. At the heart of this risk assessment process is the concept of internal control.

Notes

1. "Bringing ERM Into Focus," *Internal Auditor*, June 1, 2003.
2. "Lay-Person's Guide to FCPA," www.usdoj.gov/criminal/fraud/docs/dojdocb.html.
3. Id.
4. Exact verbiage reprinted from the FCPA, available at www.usdoj.gov/criminal/fraud/docs/statute.html.
5. AICPA, Report of the National Commission on Fraudulent Financial Reporting (National Commission on Fraudulent Financial Reporting, 1987), *The Treadway Report*, 1987.
6. Committee of Sponsoring Organizations of the Treadway Commission, *Internal Control—Integrated Framework*, two-volume edition, 1994, consisting of "Executive Summary, Framework, Reporting to External Parties," September 1992; Addendum to "Reporting to External Parties," May 1994; and "Evaluation Tools," September 1992.
7. Id.
8. IT Governance Institute, CobiT 4.1, 2007. CobiT is the acronym for *Control Objectives for Information and related Technology*.

CHAPTER 6

Other Control Frameworks

Our previous chapter introduced both the COSO-IC and COSO-ERM frameworks; here we detail other control frameworks. These frameworks include those developed within the United States as well as abroad. We recommend that the reader begin a risk assessment with a thorough understanding of COSO's Internal Control and Enterprise Risk Management frameworks, but the use of other frameworks could be appropriate, given the type of risk assessment that is to be performed.

Professional Standards for CPAs

CPAs who render their professional opinion on a company registered with the SEC are regulated by the Public Company Accounting Oversight Board (PCAOB), while CPAs giving opinions on companies not registered are regulated by the professional association in which the CPAs are members, the American Institute of Certified Public Accountants (AICPA).

Professional standards for certified public accountants are published by the AICPA and set forth in Statements of Auditing Standards (SAS). Before SOX, these statements were the primary guidance for U.S. CPAs. Under SOX, the PCAOB was created and given authority to regulate public accountants who attest to the financial statements and financial controls of public companies in the United States, including their auditing standards. The PCAOB was created by SOX to replace self-regulation of CPAs by the AICPA. It applies only to CPAs who perform audits of public companies.[1]

PCAOB

Initially, the PCAOB adopted the AICPA's SAS standards as their Auditing Standard No. 1 (AS-1). Subsequently, the PCAOB issued Auditing Standard No. 2, *An Audit of Internal Control Over Financial Reporting Performed in*

Conjunction with An Audit of Financial Statements. This, the PCAOB's first piece of new material, dealt with a broad set of issues regarding internal control that were not addressed in AS-1, primarily because those auditing standards were focused on financial statements as a product, not a process. It was superseded by AS-5, discussed in a moment.

Auditing Standard No. 3, *Audit Documentation*, was comparatively brief and addressed procedural issues of external auditors.

Auditing Standard No. 4 establishes requirements and provides direction when a previously reported material weakness in internal control over financial reporting continues to exist.

Auditing Standard No. 5 (AS-5) replaced AS-2. This Auditing Standard is most relevant to this book. It retained most of AS-2, including its title, but includes a number of improvements and refinements. First and foremost, AS-5 is a principles-based standard, whereas AS-2 was a rules-based standard. AS-5 was issued in May 2007 and provides a greater risk-based approach to financial statement audits than its predecessor. Although AS-5 sets standards solely for outside auditors who review and certify financial statements of public companies, its rules also provide guidelines for internal personnel. The standard allows outside auditors to specifically assess management's ability to establish and document key internal controls.

The PCAOB's Auditing Standards apply only to auditors and audits of companies reporting to the SEC under SOX. Auditors of private companies, nonprofits, government entities, and other entities not registered with the SEC are still directed by the AICPA Standards. They are not subject to the PCAOB's Auditing Standards but sometimes are required by their board or regulators to mimic them. This usually includes application of the COSO Framework.

AICPA

Commencing with calendar year 2007, all entities receiving a CPA's opinion on their financial statements must also evaluate the control documentation and assess the internal controls over financial reporting. However, the testing required for an opinion on that internal control is not required. The AICPA promulgated 11 new Auditing Standards, numbers 103 through 114, setting forth detailed requirements to guide CPAs on this issue. All these standards, with associated rules and guidance, can be viewed on the AICPA web site, www.aicpa.org. Of all these professional standards, SAS No. 109 is most relevant to the issues discussed in this book.

SAS No. 109 is titled *Understanding the Entity and Its Environment and Assessing the Risks of Material Misstatement*. Although it is directed at CPAs performing audits of non-SEC regulated companies, its guidance is highly relevant to everyone performing risk assessments. Naturally, SAS

No. 109 recognizes the COSO Framework and all five components of internal control. It does, however, deviate from the literal text of the COSO Framework. For instance, SAS No. 109 states, "... the auditor's primary consideration is whether, and how, a specific control prevents, or detects and *corrects...*" (emphasis added). This is an important conceptual difference from the COSO Framework, and we agree with this change by the AICPA.

All auditing standards serve two clear purposes:

1. They give guidance for auditing procedures that are usually prudent and effective, when applicable. For example, after the McKesson-Robbins case[2] was exposed in 1938, auditing standards were changed to require CPAs to physically observe and test the existence of inventory. This procedure appears to have been generally effective against a repeat, but still did not keep Phar-Mor (a former Youngstown, Ohio, based chain of discount drug stores) from concealing an inventory fraud in 1992 using different methods.
2. They provide a defensive shield for auditors who missed a material misstatement to claim that it was not really their fault. Unfortunately, a good plaintiff's lawyer can usually find some obscure opportunity, prescribed somewhere within the voluminous and complex standards, where some simple test would have revealed the problem.

The only truly satisfactory audit standard is *results*: Find any material misstatements and weaknesses and fix them before the statements are made public. Furthermore, any audit failure that allows financial reports to be published with material misstatements will probably be followed by an investigation by the SEC's Enforcement Division and by civil lawsuits.

The ugly reality is that few business managers or CPAs were given the education to make them experts in assessing internal controls. A college program in accounting generally concentrates on accounting theory and practice, not on systems and controls. Even with that narrow focus on accounting, the subject is so complex that five years of accounting study are usually required to sit for the Uniform CPA Examination. Only one course in auditing is required by most jurisdictions to sit for this exam, although many business schools encourage a more generous study of controls and auditing. Even diligent study, passing the CPA exam, and designation as a CPA might not be sufficient for this particular task. Research published in *Scientific American* presents evidence that *10 years* of intensive experience is usually required to acquire real expertise in practically any complex subject.[3] Managers and CPAs are en route to accumulating this experience, but many are not there yet.

A partial solution to this apprenticeship is to have one's assessment carefully reviewed by an experienced expert. This review leverages the expert's knowledge. However, to do this we are back to requiring documentation that enables the review. How can the expert document the mental path he took to reach an intuitive conclusion? A matrix display of the control model can provide that reviewable document.

CobiT

Control Objectives for Information and Related Technology (CobiT) is the product of the IT Governance Institute, an educational foundation associated with the Information Systems Audit and Control Association (ISACA). ISACA has always appealed to both internal and external auditors, but the external audit firms historically provided the greater proportion of financial support and human resources. Naturally, then, these CPAs turned to CobiT when they found unanswered questions concerning IT in the COSO Framework.

In this approach, applications and facilities are classified as separate systems, with the facilities being one of the general infrastructure systems, together with technology. Data is a component of application systems. People fulfill a huge variety of roles, but in the context of resources they serve as part of systems and controls.

The CobiT Framework is quite elaborate, but restricted to the IT environment that usually supports most of the information needs of an organization. As such, it does not compete with the several frameworks, including COSO's, that address the entire enterprise.

The CobiT Framework covers five areas of internal controls, each focused on IT issues:

1. Strategic alignment

   IT operations should be aligned with all other "enterprise operations."

2. Value delivery

   Processes should ensure that an enterprise's IT function is delivering its "promised benefits against the strategy, concentrating on optimizing costs and proving the intrinsic value of IT."

3. Resource management

   IT investments should be made deliberately by management and support critical IT resources.

4. Risk management

   An enterprise's "appetite for risk" must be understood by senior corporate officers, who should also have an "understanding of compliance requirements, transparency about the significant risks to the enterprises and embedding of risk management responsibilities into the organization."

5. Performance measurement

Processes should track and monitor "strategy implementation, project completion, resource usage, process performance and service delivery, using, for example, balanced scorecards that translate strategy into action to achieve goals measurable beyond conventional accounting."

These areas of controls are obviously focused on IT, but they do provide general guidelines for practitioners setting up other control frameworks. Namely, a control framework should be strategically aligned with the organization's objectives; deliver organizational value in excess of its costs; be set up deliberately; reflect the organization's appetite for risk and reflect an understanding of any compliance requirements; and properly monitor an organization's performance with respect to control objectives.

Because the COSO Framework is extremely terse regarding the peculiar control issues in a computer environment, many practitioners adopt the CobiT methodology to fill the gap. In recognition that many of the CobiT objectives are not relevant to financial reporting, the IT Governance Institute issued a mapping of CobiT to SOX objectives.

We provide more extensive details and discussion of this framework in Chapter 16, General and Infrastructure Systems.

Other Control Principles and Frameworks

Note that although most contemporary control guidance refers to risks, these guides usually view risks only from the adverse viewpoint. True risk management also recognizes that risks can bring rewards or benefits. For example, investment risk measures usually include the volatility of market prices, specifically the statistical variance function. Market prices may bring gains as well as losses, and gains (in the years since the Great Depression) are actually more common.

The various security and control frameworks usually focus only on the negative aspect of risk.

Other than the COSO Framework, PCAOB AS-5, and AICPA–SASs 104 to 114, many of the pronouncements regarding risk assessment and internal control focus on security. Most of the other English-speaking countries have also published their own control framework documents as alternatives to the U.S. COSO Framework. A partial list of these includes:

- *CoCo.* Canadian internal control framework.
- *Turnbull Report.* U.K. internal control framework.

- *AS/NZS 4360:2004.* The internal control framework published jointly in Australia and New Zealand.
- *King Report.* South Africa internal control framework.
- *GASSP. Generally Accepted Security Standards,* by the International Information Security Foundation.
- *IFA. Managing Security of Information,* by the International Federation of Accountants.
- *OECD. Security of Information Systems,* by the Organization for Economic Cooperation and Development.
- *ISO 27002.* International Standards Organization.
- *BITS.* A private consortium of major U.S. banks and affiliated organizations.
- *SysTrust.* By the American Institute of Certified Public Accountants and the Canadian Institute of Chartered Accountants, based on CobiT.
- *Payment Card Industry Data Security Standards (PCI DSS).* This is a list of 12 guidelines that imposes strict regulations on all transactions taking place between the card company and the merchants it trades with. These standards have been in place since 2005 and focus on privacy and security of personal credit information.
- *HIPPA.* Privacy of personal health-care information.

CoCo (Canada)

Following the release of the COSO Framework in 1992, the Canadians published a report in 1995 entitled *Guidance on Control,* which presents a slightly different viewpoint and a control model referred to as *Criteria of Control* (CoCo). The Canadian economy is somewhat integrated with that of the United States, so many large Canadian corporations are also subject to the Sarbanes-Oxley Act and its endorsement of the COSO Framework. CoCo differs only slightly from the COSO Framework.

Canadian public companies are required to attest to their internal control over financial reporting under the Canadian Securities Administrators' Multilateral Instrument 52-111, *Reporting on Internal Control over Financial Reporting,* which is similar to SOX Section 404. The COSO Framework, the Canadian CoCo Framework, and the U.K.'s *Turnbull Report* are all deemed acceptable as frameworks for the assessment. CoCo's National Instrument 52-109 requires reporting similar to SOX Section 302.

The *Turnbull Report* (U.K.)

The *Turnbull Report* in the United Kingdom is similar to the COSO Framework. The original report was issued in September 1999 and was last revised in October 2005. Online materials may be accessed on the Internet at www.frc.org.uk/corporate/internalcontrol.cfm. The Financial Reporting Council also has published "The Turnbull guidance as an evaluation framework for the purposes of Section 404(a) of the Sarbanes-Oxley Act," available at the same site.

The *Turnbull Report* closely resembles the COSO Framework. It recognizes the same four objectives but includes internal financial reporting, together with external financial reporting. It also is risk based and recognizes the same five components of internal control. Only preventive and detective controls are recognized, but it does not explicitly exclude corrective. It also is silent regarding any significant differences related to information technology. Finally, it puts somewhat stronger emphasis on internal auditing as a monitoring control.

AS/NZS 4360:2004

The Australian/New Zealand (ANZ) Standard for Risk Management was first published in 1995 and was republished in 1999 and 2004. It describes and defines risk management in broad terms that may be applied generically in many contexts and is widely accepted internationally and praised for its clarity and brevity. It should be considered an alternative to the COSO Framework for Australian and New Zealand companies.

The ANZ Standard recommends nine steps in a program of risk management:

1. Senior management support
2. Risk management policy
3. Communicate the policy
4. Accountability and authority
5. Customize the risk management process
6. Identify and provide resources
7. Develop plan by organization unit
8. Manage risks
9. Monitor and review

The process involves:

1. Communicating and consulting with stakeholders
2. Establishing the context
3. Identifying risks
4. Analyzing risks qualitatively *and quantitatively* (emphasis added)
5. Evaluate the risks
6. Treat the risks
7. Monitor and review

Copies of these standards are available through www.riskmanagement. com.au.

Long ago, before the advent of computers, most texts addressing internal controls recommended lists of best practices generally applied in the practice of bookkeeping. They told people *how* to keep complete and accurate books and seldom explained *why* the prescribed procedures were prescribed. The advent of digital computers rendered many of the traditional practices impractical or ineffective.

Ever since Grace Hopper discovered the first bug crushed inside a computer relay,[4] various organizations have articulated principles for integrity and security of digital information. One of the best of these was *Computer Control Guidelines,* issued by the Canadian Institute of Chartered Accountants (CICA) in 1970.

IFA, GASSP, and OECD

Some of the accepted security principles include:

- Pervasive Principles of Generally Accepted Security Principles, by the International Information Security Foundation (GASSP)
- Core Principles for Managing Security of Information, by the International Federation of Accountants (IFA)
- Principles for Guidelines for the Security of Information Systems, by the Organization for Economic Cooperation and Development (OECD)

We group these principles together because their statements are nearly identical. Only slight differences exist in the number, sequence, and descriptions of the principles. In brief, they each state nine principles, as follows:

IFA	GASSP	OECD
Accountability	Accountability	Accountability
Awareness	Awareness	Awareness
Societal factors	Ethics	Ethics
Multidisciplinary	Multidisciplinary	Multidisciplinary
Cost effectiveness	Proportionality	Proportionality
Integration	Integration	Integration
Timeliness	Timeliness	Timeliness
Reassessment	Assessment	Reassessment
Societal factors	Equity	Democracy

Accountability addresses a control environment practice that identifies individual roles, actions, and responsibilities and facilitates discipline. It includes the concept of data ownership, which is a controversial subject in the context of personal privacy.

Accountability might also be viewed as a form of control, since it enables and anticipates discipline.

Awareness refers to security policies, procedures, and threats. It involves risk assessment, control compliance, and the control environment.

Ethics deals with the social standards for information use and privacy protection. It is concerned with what is being done with information more than how it is done.

Multidisciplinary recognizes the multiple concerns and viewpoints of customers, users, IT providers, and owners.

Proportionality, or *cost effectiveness*, calls for controls and costs to be proportionate to risks and values. It endorses cost/benefit considerations.

Integration calls for coordination of all controls. This is one of the important characteristics of the approach we illustrate in this book, particularly in the linkage of infrastructure consequences to application problems.

Timeliness recognizes that speed can be essential to effective security.

Assessment or *reassessment* recommends periodic review, consideration, and audit of risks and controls. This is a meta-control.

Equity, societal factors, and *democracy* are each slightly different ways of recognizing that society and individuals have rights and interests that may govern information systems. Some of these rights are redundant with the ethics principle, and others address intellectual property rights, information ownership, and the like.

There is little to debate within the three sets of security principles. At the same time, they give no hint as to how one might achieve them.

International Standard 27002

ISO 27002 is one of several recognized international standards. It carries a distinctive cachet in that it often is required by insurance companies to qualify for their reinsurance of IT casualty risks. This standard is specifically focused on security, but the separation between security and other objectives is indistinct. This and most other definitions of security include the need for integrity and availability. Integrity, in turn, encompasses many related objectives of financial reporting.

The outline of ISO 27002 is as follows:

1. Scope
2. Terms and definitions
3. Security policy
4. Security organization

5. Asset classification and control
6. Personnel security
7. Physical and environmental security
8. Communications and operations management
9. Access control
10. Systems development and maintenance
11. Business continuity and management
12. Compliance

Within these major topics the ISO lists more specific issues and concerns and even more specific control objectives (e.g., network routing control) and controls. The recommended controls generally appear to be appropriate and desirable, but such specificity could become outdated and inadequate in a relatively short time. Control techniques, particularly security control techniques, must evolve at least as fast as the threats.[5]

PCI DSS

Payment Card Industry (PCI) Data Security Standards (DSS) are 12 guidelines that impose strict requirements on all transactions taking place between a credit card company and merchants. The standards are enforced by the several major credit and debit card processors as a condition to acceptance of credit and debit card transactions from merchants. The strategy is to embed automated control features in the computer software used for accepting and transmitting the transactions. Accordingly, commercial software must be assessed and tested to obtain approved status. The objective is security that will prevent card fraud and identity theft. The summary of these standards is:

Build and Maintain a Secure Network

Requirement 1: Install and maintain a firewall configuration to protect cardholder data.
Requirement 2: Do not use vendor-supplied defaults for system passwords and other security parameters.

Protect Cardholder Data

Requirement 3: Protect stored cardholder data.
Requirement 4: Encrypt transmission of cardholder data across open, public networks.

Maintain a Vulnerability Management Program

Requirement 5: Use and regularly update antivirus software.
Requirement 6: Develop and maintain secure systems and applications.

Implement Strong Access Control Measures

> *Requirement 7:* Restrict access to cardholder data by each business's need to know.
>
> *Requirement 8:* Assign a unique ID to each person with computer access.
>
> *Requirement 9:* Restrict physical access to cardholder data.

Regularly Monitor and Test Networks

> *Requirement 10:* Track and monitor all access to network resources and cardholder data.
>
> *Requirement 11:* Regularly test security systems and processes.

Maintain an Information Security Policy

> *Requirement 12:* Maintain a policy that addresses information security.

More details are available at the web site www.pcisecuritystandards .org.

BITS

The BITS consortium was formed by several major U.S. banks and has added more banks and associated organizations. Among other things, BITS (not an acronym) publishes a standardized questionnaire, with corresponding test procedures, and a control assessment model of the results for use by any organization that is concerned with the IT *security* of its own operations or its service providers.

The BITS materials are available at www.bits.org and include a particularly good compendium of security threats and hazards.

SysTrust

SysTrust is a standard articulated by the AICPA and the Canadian Institute of Chartered Accountants (CICA) that contains 58 reliability criteria intended to accomplish four principles. These principles are:

1. *Availability* addresses the use and operation of a system. The AICPA and CICA would consider loss of availability a serious adverse consequence of problems.
2. *Security* protects access, which they would consider a major class of threats and problems.
3. *Integrity* deals with complete, accurate, timely, and authorized processing. Their structure would treat loss of integrity as another important

consequence of problems and incomplete, inaccurate, untimely, and unauthorized processing as separate problems.

4. *Maintainability* assures continuity and adaptability to change while retaining the first three principles. Their structure would classify this as still another important consequence of problems.

The first three principles are the same as those of ISO 17799, although SysTrust is not presented as *security* principles. This illustrates the difficulty in distinguishing security from more general control concerns.

The 58 reliability criteria contain a mixture of common threats, problems, and concerns, together with a number of generally desirable control environment factors and controls.

Although the primary functions of CPAs and CAs are financial in nature, nothing in SysTrust limits it to financial issues.[6]

COSO 1994 might be the preference of the SEC in applying SOX and Generally Accepted Auditing Standards, but we can still consider and borrow useful pieces from these other pronouncements.

Insurance Model Audit Law

Although companies in the insurance industry in the United States are regulated by the individual states of domicile, the National Association of Insurance Commissioners (NAIC) provides the states with model laws that it recommends for enactment by state legislatures. Because many insurance companies operate under licenses in multiple states, everyone's interest is served by keeping the laws and regulations fairly consistent. Most states do enact the model laws, although some might make minor or major changes.

The insurance Model Audit Law is less stringent than SOX. It does not require that management's assessment be audited and supported by a formal opinion from the external auditors. It does, however, require that those auditors review management's assessment and consider it in the planning of their annual statutory financial statement examination.

Other than that, the Model Audit Law requires that the internal controls over financial reporting be documented and that management puts in place procedures to monitor the performance of those controls. Complete documentation must be provided to the periodic statutory examinations. These requirements only apply to insurance companies with annual premiums over $500 million.

Many large insurance companies are already subject to SOX because they are also public companies and already receive formal opinions on their control over financial reporting. However, these activities represent reporting to public investors and the SEC in accordance with GAAP. Insurance regulators require application of a different set of accounting principles, known as *Statutory Accounting Principles* (SAP), which include entire accounts that do not exist under GAAP and accounting methods for accounts that do exist under GAAP that are quite different from GAAP. The assessment for the Model Audit Law must cover those additional systems and methods that are used for SAP but not GAAP.

Summary

We have provided the reader with a general overview of the numerous national and international frameworks that discuss the concept of internal control. In the United States, the most widely used framework is that developed and published by COSO in 1992 and amended in 1994. Each of these frameworks sets forth a definition of internal control and standards for analysis, but we use the COSO Framework as the basis for an expansion of quantitative risk management techniques. We feel that these techniques allow practitioners to better plan audits, understand areas of weakness in internal control systems, and test the accuracy of their evaluations of various processes within the business cycle.

Notes

1. All the PCAOB standards can be found on the organization's web site, www.PCAOB.org.
2. The McKesson & Robbins, Inc., scandal of 1938 was a major event in the financial world. McKesson & Robbins, today the largest healthcare corporation in the world, was taken over in 1925 by a convicted felon, Philip Musica. Using assumed names, Musica expanded both the company's legitimate and illegitimate business operations. Together with three of his brothers, Musica generated bogus sales documentation and paid commissions to a shell distribution company under McKesson's control. After 13 years of rule under Musica, McKesson's treasurer discovered that the shell company was bogus.
3. P.E. Ross, "The Expert Mind," *Scientific American*, August 2006, p. 64.
4. Hopper was a Rear Admiral in the United States Navy and one of the first programmers of the Harvard Mark I calculator. While working at Harvard, Hopper and her associates discovered and removed a moth in one of the computer relays. Her associates, using an accepted engineering term, noted that there was a "bug" in the relay. Some scholars credit this event with popularizing the terms *computer bug* and *debugging*.
5. All the ISO publications and standards are available at www.iso.org/iso/home.htm.
6. The web site for SysTrust is provided by the AICPA at http://infotech.aicpa.org/Resources/System+Security+and+Reliability/System+Reliability/Trust+Services/SysTrust/.

CHAPTER 7

Qualitative Control Concepts

B efore discussing our quantitative methodology, we introduce in this chapter qualitative control concepts. These concepts are most commonly used in business today. Many practitioners will be familiar with the key qualitative control concepts we present here, but this chapter will clarify the definitions and relationships of terms, phrases, and concepts used in this book. These will ensure that all readers (and authors) share common information about these concepts before progressing to quantitative model formulation.

Some of the terminology used by COSO in its Internal Control–Integrated Framework (COSO-IC) and Enterprise Risk Management–Integrated Framework (COSO-ERM) documents differs from that used in this book. We accept the authority of the COSO podium, but we also accept the Confucian concept that when a thing is called by its correct name, its proper place in the order of all things is made clear. We do not assert this rigor to be pedantic because we believe it assists in clarifying the role and contribution of the various problems, controls, consequences, and their relationships. We retain our terminology over that of COSO in those instances where we believe that our apparent meaning is clearer and the significance of the role is made more obvious.

Here is a translation of the specific quote by Confucius: "If names be not correct, language is not in accordance with the truth of things. If language be not in accordance with the truth of things, affairs cannot be carried on to success." *Confucian Analects*, translated by James Legge; Project Guttenberg, www.gutenberg.org/dirs/etext03/cnfnl10.txt.

We further believe that technical publications, such as this book, are clearer and better understood if each important word is used with one meaning only. Therefore, we narrow our use of "risk" (as specified in previous chapters) to mean only a probability. Uses of that word to allude to other definitions such as the nature of potential problems or their consequences tend to add confusion to a subject that already is complicated.

What Is Control?

In this book, *control* is anything that tends to cause the reduction of exposures. It is not necessarily an activity, as described by COSO. Adequate
control can accomplish this task by reducing the estimated risks associated
with exposures or by reducing the magnitude of the exposure. Recall our
definition of risk, problem, incident, and exposure from Chapter 1:

Risk = Probability that a problem occurs
Problem = an event or incident that would be harmful to objectives.
Incident, Event = Risk times the opportunities for occurrence, mitigated
    by the environment and control activities
Consequence = Expected harm or loss caused by an incident. The
    reverse of an objective.
Exposure = Incidents times the magnitude of the consequences (usually
    expressed in dollars)

Using these definitions, we have that controls can reduce exposures
by reducing the probability of occurrence of problems, the frequency of
occurrence, or the magnitude of the consequences caused by the problem.

Consequences

Controls are justified only if they serve a purpose. This purpose is the reduction of exposure. As stated in Chapter 1, an exposure is the magnitude of a
consequence (usually stated in dollars) times the number of incidents that
may occur. The term *exposure* is often misused to describe an event that has
occurred.

For example, fire itself is not an exposure. An exposure is the destruction
    that fire may can cause. Fire, itself, is a potential problem—a cause
    of the exposure.

Therefore, before we can begin to evaluate controls in any context, we
must identify the consequences that controls should prevent or detect and
correct. The following list includes 10 samples of the adverse consequences
an organization might encounter:

1. Erroneous record keeping
2. Unacceptable accounting
3. Loss or destruction of assets
4. Fraud and embezzlement
5. Statutory sanctions

6. Erroneous management decisions
7. Excessive costs/deficient revenues
8. Competitive disadvantage
9. Business interruption
10. Failure to meet business objectives

Erroneous record keeping is the recording of transactions contrary to established policies. The errors can involve the time of recognition, value, or classification. This is one of the primary issues of COSO's financial reporting objective.

Unacceptable accounting is the establishment or implementation of accounting policies that are not generally accepted or are inappropriate to the circumstances. This is another one of the primary issues of COSO's financial reporting objective. It could also lead to further consequences, such as statutory sanctions.

Loss or destruction of assets refers to the unintentional loss of physical assets, monies, claims to monies, or information assets. This is one of the primary issues of COSO's safeguarding assets objective.

Fraud and embezzlement may be perpetrated at different levels—against management or by management. Direct misappropriation of funds is only one ramification of fraud. Deliberately misinforming management or investors is also fraudulent, even if only to keep one's job. This is another one of the primary issues of COSO's safeguarding assets objective.

Statutory sanctions refer to any of the penalties that can be brought by judicial or regulatory authorities having jurisdiction over an organization's operations. This is the primary issue of COSO's compliance objective.

Erroneous management decisions are objectionable in themselves but can also lead to other consequences. Such decisions could arise due to misleading information, lack of information, or errors in judgment. This is one of the primary issues of COSO's operations objective.

Excessive costs include any expense of the business that could be readily avoided. A related consequence is loss of revenues to which the organization is fairly entitled. This is another of the primary issues of COSO's operations objective.

Competitive disadvantage relates to any inability of an organization to effectively remain abreast of the demands of the marketplace or to respond effectively to competitive challenges. This is another of the primary issues of COSO's operations objective.

Business interruption may include anything from a temporary suspension of operations to a permanent termination of the enterprise. This is another one of the primary issues of COSO's operations objective. At the extreme, such an interruption also affects the accounting principle regarding a "going concern."

Failure to meet business objectives is a consequence that also can be applicable to nonprofit organizations or government entities. Because such organizations often do not compete in a market, they measure their success by attainment of particular objectives. This is one of the primary issues of COSO's operations objective.

Obviously, these consequences are not all mutually exclusive. However, they do include many of the adverse effects that a business can encounter. We introduce these here because we refer to them repeatedly throughout the remainder of this book. Their purpose is to communicate in basic business terms, not to be philosophically elegant. To the extent that other terms may express a commonly recognized adverse business situation, such terms are also appropriate to describe consequences.

What Can Go Wrong: Causes of Exposures

Adverse consequences do not arise simply due to lack of controls. Consequences are caused by specific problems. The incidence or existence of a problem causes the consequences. Controls act to reduce or to eliminate these problems, but even without controls, the potential problems must actually occur before consequences result.

Problems are sometimes referred to as *risks, vulnerabilities, errors, incidents*, or other names. In this book, we refer to *risk* as the estimated probability of a problem happening, and we describe the nature of the risk as a *problem*.

COSO-IC refers to "risks/issues," which we call potential "problems" if they might occur, or "incidents" if they actually occur. In our view, and because we are espousing a probabilistic approach, *risk* is a word reserved for probability or likelihood, as in "... the risk of this problem occurring is. ... "

A problem can generate more than one type of consequence. No simple one-to-one relationship exists. Furthermore, the various consequences that may arise from a particular problem would not normally arise with equal probability.

> For example, in a bank, the loss of a check after it is partially processed would certainly cause erroneous record keeping because credit would have been given for the deposit but it could not be charged against the proper account. Excessive costs would also result because an extensive error-correction activity would be necessary. If very many items were lost, the bank might have to interrupt normal operations in an attempt to recover from the incident. The granting of credit for the deposit, without being able to deduct from

EXHIBIT 7.1 Estimated Qualitative Magnitude of Exposure for the Lost Check Example (H = High Likelihood, M = Moderate Likelihood, L = Low Likelihood, — = No Likelihood)

Magnitude of Exposure	Types of Consequences
H	Erroneous recordkeeping
—	Unacceptable accounting
L	Business interruption
—	Erroneous management decisions
—	Fraud and embezzlement
—	Statutory sanctions
M	Excessive costs
M	Loss or destruction of assets
M	Competitive disadvantage
—	Failed project objectives

the appropriate account, would constitute a loss of bank assets. Finally, the depositor's awareness that the bank was losing such transactions could cause him to place his business with a competitor.

The relationships between these enumerated consequences can be illustrated in tabular form. On a table, the potential problems can be listed across the top and the potential resulting consequences along the side. We can then place designations opposite each consequence and under each cause to indicate the probability that the cause would lead to the consequence.

Using this approach, the table that would result from our problem, losing a check, is illustrated in Exhibit 7.1.

In Exhibit 7.1, we estimate that the likelihood for erroneous record keeping is high in our lost check example. When such an incident occurs, it is almost certain that errors in record keeping will occur. We have also estimated as moderate the likelihood of excessive costs, loss or destruction of assets, and competitive disadvantage. If only one check has been lost and it was written for a small amount, this will decrease the likelihood of the two former consequences. If the incident is properly contained and handled by bank management, competitive disadvantage consequences can be minimized. A full-scale business interruption from such an incident is also unlikely.

Effects of Computers and Automation on Problems

The introduction of a computer or automated process for information processing does not directly affect the consequences that can harm a business. Rather, it changes the nature of the problems a business faces, as well as their relative frequency. Computers have gradually replaced humans for execution of both rudimentary and complicated procedures in large businesses over time, but small businesses continue to have a human element in many facets of their organizations.

For example, human errors in performing simple multiplication might be expected several times a day, whereas actual errors in such calculations by a computer are extremely rare.

The utilization of computers does not change any of the basic concepts of control. This is the reason that COSO has decided not to treat it as a separate dimension in its framework. Computers' effects on control are to change the nature and level of risk of what can go wrong, the effectiveness of different controls, and the medium in which they are implemented. Therefore, when a business task goes from human to computer, something very radical does occur in the surface appearance of the controls that are implemented in computerized systems. This occurs even though nothing fundamental has changed in the nature of controls themselves. When a task becomes automated:

- The extent of manual controls is abbreviated. Sources of data shift and are often independent of data users.
- Transaction trails are subject to gaps because there might no longer be a one-for-one correspondence between data entry and output.
- There is a migration in the location at which controls are implemented: from clerks and supervisors to systems analysts and computer software.
- Controls must be more explicit because many of the processing points that formerly presented opportunities for human judgment become abridged or eliminated.
- The quality of documentation is more critical because records that might have existed previously in hard-copy form are frequently embedded in computer files.
- Information file custody shifts. Responsibilities for custody of information assets become assigned to central data processing facilities.

For all these reasons, the structure and application of controls must be clear to all parties concerned.

The System of Internal Control

Although the "system of internal control" is discussed extensively in professional literature, rarely do companies actually use any discernibly systematic approach to the selection or structure of control features in their information systems. Rather, the system of internal control that is discussed usually refers instead to the internal controls within and around company systems.

Such internal controls can take an immense variety of forms, functions, and features, but they rarely form any system by themselves.

This situation was evidenced in two major studies of internal control. The researchers on the original 1976 *Systems Auditability and Control* (SAC) study[1] reported to the project advisory committee that they found no instance in which the controls in place had been engineered into their systems in any particularly analytic manner. Instead, systems designers explained that their selection had been based upon experience with other systems, published or verbal recommendations from others, and similar ad hoc approaches.

In 1980, the *Internal Control in U.S. Corporations* study[2] indicated essentially the same situation.

More recent studies, such as those described by Harvard Professor Michael Jensen, have demonstrated that internal control systems within companies have failed to accurately assess business operating environments and deal with industry-level shocks.[3]

A true system of internal control should provide a dynamic approach for continuously adapting internal control to a changing environment. Control features should be engineered into systems in the same way that buildings or bridges are engineered to resist the predictable stresses and burdens of their use.

Control problems are changing constantly due to changes in needs, technology, and practically everything else in the environment. A true system of internal control must anticipate, or at least respond to, the new and changed problems that arise. Such a system should incorporate the following capabilities:

- Direction, in the form of standards that set forth explicit levels of expected performance
- Reporting, which assists management in remaining aware of what systems and capabilities exist to be controlled
- Assessment, using control analysis of potential problems and risks
- Engineering of control into information systems in an analytic fashion, considering all relevant potential consequences and alternatives
- Implementation of rationally consistent and practical solutions, including retrofitting of existing systems that do not meet current standards

Management of the control function involves both control evaluation and monitoring of controls and potential consequences. This is often performed on periodic occasions but is obviously more effective if performed continuously. The worst situation exists when management never evaluates or monitors controls until serious consequences become obvious.

The effort required to evaluate and monitor controls grows as time passes since the prior such effort. Regular evaluation can require nothing more than fine tuning, whereas evaluation after a long period of unconcern could necessitate a major risk analysis project. Similarly, continuous monitoring can be designed as merely routine "controls over controls," whereas a long period of inattention could require a major audit. Management must make a business decision whether to expend a modest level of resources continuously or a high level of resources occasionally.

Control Assessment

Traditionally, texts dealing with control assessment have concentrated on the identification of controls. Certainly this task is essential, but it is far short of the full job.

After identifying controls, typical assessment literature indicates that the assessor subsequently evaluates the controls, usually without elaborating much further. In fact, the assessor customarily studies the detailed information that was gathered and then intuitively leaps to a conclusion. Such intuition is largely dependent on the skill and experience of the assessor. The quality of the decision becomes quite suspect when the system is highly complex.

Review of such conclusions is usually approached in one of two ways. A reviewer can simply accept the judgment of the assessor, or he could restudy the detailed information that has been gathered and reach his own independent, but also intuitive, conclusion. The first of these approaches requires a substantial amount of faith; the second requires a substantial amount of time and skill. Often neither approach is suitable or justifiable in the circumstances.

We believe that a third approach is feasible. The process of assessing controls can be made into a formal, rational, and reviewable process supported by documentation. The steps in this analysis are as follows:

- Understand the system.
- List the potential problems (event identification).
- Estimate the inherent risk of each problem (risk assessment).
- Segregate controls and fundamental activities subject to control.
- Classify the controls.
- Subjectively quantify the effectiveness of the purported controls over the various potential problems.
- Assess the adequacy with which each potential problem is controlled and estimate the remaining risk of its occurrence.
- Subjectively quantify the adverse consequences that would result from an uncorrected occurrence of problems that have a significant risk of occurring.

Understand the System

Control analysis is predicated on a reasonably thorough understanding of the system under review in the context of the control environment. The assessor must possess or obtain the minimum technical background to appreciate what the system really does, the problems that it must overcome, and the significance of the consequences if it fails. As a practical matter, this necessitates a certain "closeness" to the system. While remaining objective, the assessor should also have a sufficiently intimate acquaintance with the operation of the system to make informed judgments rather than merely rely on textbook guidelines. We offer many guidelines in this book, but the reader must still apply and tailor them before the results will be meaningful.

A fine balance must be struck between the effort expended in obtaining "closeness" and the production of meaningful analysis. The assessor need not be able to design or operate the system in question to adequately understand it. At the same time, however, some limited experience designing and operating similar systems is extremely beneficial. Some of this limited experience can be obtained by a "walk-through," processing a few transactions through the system.

Concerning computerized information systems, this means that the assessor need not be a professional programmer or computer operator but should have at least learned to program in some business-oriented language and run the results.

Understanding can be obtained most readily by studying the system's documentation. The format of appropriate systems documentation varies according to the nature of the system and the preferences of the designers, but documentation should fulfill the following objectives:

- Awareness that the system exists
- Capabilities in terms of the information the system retains, processes it performs, and results it produces
- Priorities and risks describing the tolerance for various adverse consequences, the problems that could cause them, and risks involved
- Assurances to management provided by the controls over the system
- Technical comprehension so that systems and programming personnel can efficiently investigate any problem or proposed redesign
- Recovery and complex maintenance so that the occurrence of problems with program logic or inputs, as well as complex enhancements, can be efficiently investigated
- New personnel and simple maintenance to instruct new staff due to turnover and design simple enhancements
- Technical support of system software and hardware used in processing
- Continued operations of existing systems without disruption

Because systems documentation is usually prepared by technicians during or after development (if at all), the items of documentation often emphasize the technical aspects of the system that are the focus of the technician's concerns and frequently disregard the concerns of management. Accordingly, an assessor will frequently experience considerable difficulty in obtaining an adequate understanding of capabilities, priorities, risks, and assurances. Therefore, the assessor is frequently forced to construct her own documentation summarizing more detailed documentation as well as information obtained through interview and observation.

List the Potential Problems

Problems were defined previously as the things that can go wrong to cause adverse consequences. They are adverse events or conditions that can be observed or measured.

Some organizations shy away from articulating problems. Somehow they view any anticipation of problems as negative thinking and contrary to the politically correct display of an optimistic, "can-do" corporate attitude. Some of this reflects cultural beliefs that good intentions will be rewarded and that effort can overcome any obstacles. Although laudable in moderation, too much corporate "happy-speak" can brush off issues that eventually will require attention and resources. Delaying that attention until real problems occur usually increases the damage and recovery effort, compared to objectively, or even pessimistically, anticipating these issues and dealing with them accordingly.

Problems are not equivalent to *scenarios*, which assume some motivation and sequence of events. The number of possible scenarios that a system could encounter is almost infinite. The motivations of people involved in the scenario can be difficult to determine, even by a jury. Therefore, analysis that is practical must address a more limited number of possibilities. Problems are a finite set of distinct situations that can be recognized without necessarily knowing the full reason they occurred or other situations that preceded or followed them.

Accordingly, various levels of problems could be considered in an analysis. This situation is illustrated by the old saying, "For want of a nail, the kingdom was lost." (Versions of the complete saying seems to date to the 14th century and goes, "For want of a nail, the shoe was lost; for want of the shoe, the horse was lost; for want of the horse, the rider was lost; for want of the rider, the battle was lost; for want of the battle, the kingdom was lost.")

Problems are best analyzed at the level of "messages" or "riders" as mentioned in the saying; problems that are as detailed as "nails" tend to be too numerous and obscure for practical analysis.

A complete list of potential problems at an appropriate level of detail is essential to a thorough control analysis. The evaluation methodology can compensate for most other omissions, but comprehensive identification of all potential problems is critical.

Problems can be listed for the entire system process or for each activity within the process. A listing by activity is more thorough but might not be necessary if only a few fundamental activities exist or if they all carry substantially the same problems.

Estimate the Inherent Risk of Each Problem

Potential problems will not necessarily occur at each opportunity, even in the total absence of control. The likelihood that problems will occur if they are not controlled is known as the *inherent risk*. Conversely, the likelihood that problems will *not* occur in spite of the absence of control is known as *inherent assurance*.

Inherent risk is dependent on the following:

- Nature of the system
- Nature of the transactions being processed
- Nature of the information
- Nature of the activity subject to control
- Consistency or rarity of the activity
- Value of the transactions
- Nature of the potential problem
- Appeal to theft or fraud
- Whether the occurrence will be obvious, even without controls

The inherent risk should be estimated in some general fashion to recognize the different priorities of controlling the potential problems. We discuss this estimate further later in this chapter.

COSO-IC's *risk factors* are *inherent risk factors* in this book, which is not much of a notational difference. Conversely, COSO-IC's *factors decreasing risk* are what we call *factors of the control environment*. COSO also addresses *control risk factors*, whereas we discuss *attributes* of various controls.

Segregate Controls and Fundamental Activities

If we intend to evaluate these things called *controls*, we should distinguish between them and the things they control. Surprisingly, even experienced assessors often have difficulty performing this task. However, logic dictates that this step is important because confusion over what is or is not a control will prohibit any lucid evaluation.

The proportion of controls to fundamental activities generally increases with the technological sophistication of a system. In a manual system, a person might perform one or two fundamental activities, then pass some document to another person who performs some control procedure. This frequent movement of documents, either for performing another fundamental activity or another control, is the reason that such systems frequently seem to incorporate so much paper shuffling.

Computer systems tend to reduce the number of fundamental activities, mostly by reducing the movement of documents, and increasing the number of controls. Therefore, a well-designed system using computers is usually better controlled than its predecessor manual system. However, it must be well designed to accomplish this task.

Accordingly, although in a manual system the proportion of fundamental activities to controls might be 50/50, the proportion of controls often exceeds 90 percent in an automated computer application.

The simplest way to document this task is to annotate a system flowchart or similar system description, with highlighting. The questions to address to each activity are: Does this activity provide control? and Could the system possibly function (albeit badly) without this activity?

On completion of this task, the assessor should list the activities and then separately list the controls. In addition, a tree chart or a flowchart of only the fundamental activities can be drawn to clarify identifying potential problems.

A comprehensive list of all existing controls is not necessary. All that is really needed is an understanding of sufficient effective controls to determine that all potential problems present a tolerably low risk.

Classify the Controls

Before we go into specific examples of various controls that are implemented over computer-related activities, let us delve into the fundamental nature of these controls to build a common foundation relating them with the controls with which we were familiar under manual systems.

Great varieties of control classification schemes are available. However, for purposes of control evaluation, the most useful seem to be these:

- System
- Hierarchy
- Function
- Discretion
- Objectivity

System

We can categorize controls according to the specific application or internal information system that incorporates them. Accordingly, we can have payroll controls, systems development controls, and so on. To the extent that systems are distinct, the controls embedded within them are distinctly members of that system. This classification method presents no serious difficulties in batch processing systems and systems that perform a clear-cut function. However, there is a growing tendency for integrated application systems in an enterprise resource planning (ERP) database environment to blend into an indistinguishable mass. Furthermore, the system of systems maintenance is often closely related to that of systems development.

Distinct computer systems controls include these:

- Application controls, which are unique to individual user systems.
- Systems development controls, which assure that the planning and development of systems are performed in a systematic manner.
- Systems maintenance controls, which limit access to existing application programs and assure the quality of program changes.
- Information-processing facility (IPF) controls, which apply to the physical processing location and to the way that most or all applications are processed within that facility. With current technology, a facility might look like a large closet with racks of servers connected to user workstations by Ethernet cables, or the connections might occur via an invisible wireless network connected to a local wireless router.

APPLICATION CONTROLS Application controls are specific to each information function and therefore are probably the most important in the entire EDP area in a review of overall control reliability. This is true for the following reasons:

- Controls over system development, systems maintenance, and IPF activities ultimately affect applications, problems, and inherent risks.
- Applications lend themselves best to audits by people familiar with business controls, providing them an opportunity to develop experience with the technical aspects of auditing computer systems.

SYSTEMS DEVELOPMENT CONTROLS Systems development consists of those functions that plan and develop application and IPF procedures. Evaluation of systems development should be done by people who are highly experienced in this area.

In evaluating systems management as a control factor, good performance results from the following:

- Using a consistent set of activities that is comfortable and acceptable to both users and systems analysts. These should be carried forward as standards from one project to another.
- Providing project direction. This is accomplished by establishing appropriate project objectives and scope, setting up realistic schedules that consist primarily of standard activities, and assigning responsibilities.
- Making sure that the results from each activity are documented, understood, and agreed to by those involved.
- Reviewing project progress at predetermined intervals for specified purposes.

The documentation referred to is one of the primary results of an adequate, strong systems management program. The presence or lack of adequate documentation in reviewing applications and IPF controls is, in itself, an evaluation of the effectiveness of systems development.

SYSTEMS MAINTENANCE CONTROLS Systems maintenance deals with ongoing maintenance and improvement of application systems after development is complete. Maintenance presents most of the same issues found in development, plus concerns over access. Maintenance also includes the installation of "patches" provided by software vendors to repair vulnerabilities and defects discovered belatedly in their products.

INFRASTRUCTURE CONTROLS In addition to controls for individual user applications, separate controls are applied to the IT infrastructure as a whole. This segregation of application and IT controls is aimed at making the best use of available resources. Application controls can be reviewed effectively by people with minimum computer expertise. IT controls, however, require a much higher degree of familiarity with computer systems and operations.

These areas and systems classifications of control are used as the framework for describing and evaluating controls throughout the remainder of this book.

Hierarchy

Development, maintenance, and processing facilities all serve to implement information applications systems. Accordingly, the quality and efficiency of applications systems will generally be affected by the quality and efficiency of development, maintenance, and processing. Therefore, we can designate controls over development, maintenance, and processing as *general controls* because they affect all applications in general,[1] whereas those controls within each application system are usually limited to that application.

We also find a hierarchy of control within specific systems. Often certain controls are considered so essential that other controls are provided to assure continued effective compliance with the essential control.

> For example, backup of current application master files and programs might be so important that elaborate security and management controls exist to assure availability.

Our analysis should evaluate the effectiveness of "essential" controls over potential problems. The existence of controls over essential controls will obviously increase our estimate of the reliability of the essential control.

Function

The most important classification of controls that we discuss in this chapter relates to whether a particular control technique functions to prevent a potential problem, detect the fact that the problem has already happened, or correct the effects of the problem after it has been detected.

Preventive controls are those that reduce the frequency with which problems occur. Detective controls do not keep problems from happening but rather detect them after the fact. The mere detection of a problem is not sufficient. When such situations are detected, a decision must be made as to what is appropriate corrective action, and then that action must be taken.

A *preventive control* acts as a guide to help things happen as they should. Often they are passive, involving no direct physical activity. Such controls often allow a significant percentage of violations. In Exhibit 7.2, we depict this concept as a funnel. One can liken it to a cattle chute that directs most of a herd of cows into a pen but that can be evaded by some of the mavericks. Preventive controls are often so subtly embedded within a process that people involved in the operation might not even be conscious of the controls' existence.

A *detective control* does not prevent a problem from happening; instead it triggers an alarm after the problem has happened. The detective control merely registers the occurrence. This "monitoring" function is often quite reliable. However, the detection that a problem has actually occurred is just that and nothing more. Detective controls will alert people involved in the process so that they will be conscious of the existence of a problem. This consciousness is mandatory if they are to take action to correct the effects of the cause.

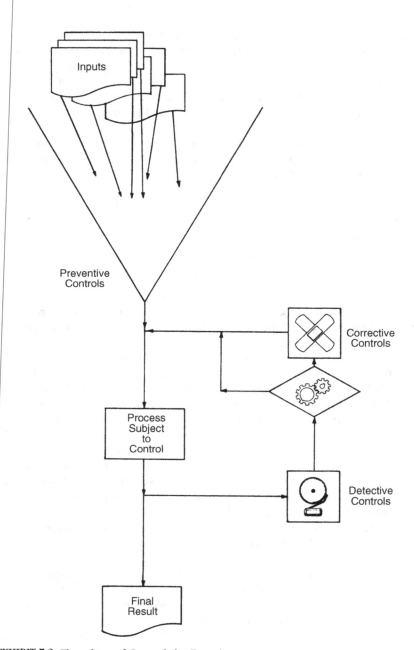

EXHIBIT 7.2 Flowchart of Controls by Function

The final type of control in this framework is *corrective control*. This type of control assists in the investigation and correction of problems that have been detected. Corrective action is always needed to resolve the problems that are detected. A decision might be made that corrective action is not worth the effort, but this decision must be made consciously and consistently, not by default. The alarm provided by a detective control is useless if no one is listening.

Because preventive controls are often passive (like the format of instructions on a screen), a detective control is usually needed to monitor that the preventive control is functioning. Even if it is certain that the preventive control is functioning, such controls are still needed to detect problems that occasionally evade the preventive control.

Furthermore, items that cause problems are often more difficult to handle than more normal ones; otherwise, the error would not have been made in the first place. Proper correction can also be difficult. Therefore, all items that are corrected must be subsequently processed through the same or even more stringent detective controls. Even when the correction is easy, it is likewise very easy to process it in the wrong direction so that something that should be subtracted is really added again. The pairing of detective and corrective controls embodies an old engineering concept, the *feedback loop*. Note in Exhibit 7.2 that after correction, the process returns to a point at which detection controls will be reapplied. This point applies just as well in information systems as it does in electronics. Detective controls over corrective controls are quite essential because error correction itself is a highly error-prone activity.

Functions of Controls

An analysis of controls according to their preventive, detective, or corrective characteristics clearly indicates that, for purposes of assessment, detective controls are the most important. They can measure the effectiveness of both preventive and corrective controls. This, then, provides the primary approach that we use in the succeeding materials to guide the evaluation and audit of controls.

Compound Controls

Some controls have two or more distinctly separate activities. The first activity is often performed by computer software to filter records and produce a report of those records that are included based on some criteria. The report is then to be reviewed by a person who must decide whether a problem has been detected. The first activity depends on correct programming and operation of the software; the second activity depends on the performance and judgment of a person. Both must operate effectively for the control to function properly. We consider this compound control to be a single control in our assessment analysis.

> For example, the accounts receivable application reports all sales invoices that are more than two standard deviations in excess of the customer's average sales invoice. The sales manager must then review the report and decide whether the invoice probably contains an error.

When Detective Controls Look Preventive

Some detective controls are linked to corrective controls that will immediately block further processing of the problem information. This is quite common with controls that detect whether data being entered fits the required format.

> For example, a database management system is programmed to require entry of a date in the format *mm/dd/yyyy*. It will display an error message asking for the correct format and will not record the date until it is entered in the required format.

Is this control preventive or detective and corrective? By the criteria used in this book, two controls are present; one is detective and another corrective.

An error has occurred; the date has been keyed in an unacceptable format. Nothing prevented the error from happening. Then a detective control recognized the error and a corrective control feature blocked it from being recorded. The detective control could have merely displayed a warning and allowed the incorrect date to be recorded, but it was deliberately programmed to block further processing until the acceptable format is entered. The person entering the date must be notified and recognize his error so that he can do whatever is necessary to correct it.

Discretion

The consistency of controls is a major concern in evaluating the expected level of compliance. Some controls are heavily subject to discretion in their use. Such discretion might be appropriate or unavoidable, but it also tends to reduce its reliability. Nondiscretionary controls can be more reliable, but they also are prone to be used when not appropriate.

For example, automobile seat belts are discretionary and can be ignored; airbags are nondiscretionary but can be dangerous to small children.

Objectivity

The objectivity of controls relates to their ability to clearly discriminate between real problems and routine anomalies. An objective control is one that functions decisively, such as balancing detail to a control total, whereas a subjective control is one requiring judgmental analysis, such as reconciliation.

The objectivity of a control should affect our appraisal of its effectiveness. Objective controls tend to be more effective than subjective ones. Furthermore, an objective control can be conclusively verified with a test of its compliance. However, mere compliance with a subjective control might not assure its effectiveness, so a substantive test might be more appropriate.

We can classify controls in numerous other ways. Each of the classifications tells us something different about the ways controls change—and change the assessor's viewpoint—in computerized information processing situations.

The reader should already be familiar with one or more approaches to classifying controls. The discussion in the next several pages explains the authors' viewpoint regarding a number of approaches and the reasons that we emphasize the "functional" approach.

Several other classifications might be useful. Some of the additional criteria that can be used to classify controls include:

- Objectives
- Location
- Organization
- Responsibilities
- Independence
- Familiarity
- Mode
- Durability
- Immediacy
- Cost

Objectives

A great deal of internal control literature addresses the subject of control objectives. Such objectives are variously presented at a general level (similar to the common "adverse consequences" in this book) or at a more specific level (similar to the "problems" discussed in this book). They can also be summarized at an intermediate level, such as integrity and security.

Integrity is the property of truthfulness. It is best exemplified by the courtroom oath "the truth, the whole truth, and nothing but the truth." Security deals with access and availability. It is primarily directed against computer abuse and catastrophic threats.

Control objectives have been stated by several professional societies, including:

- American Institute of Certified Public Accountants (AICPA), a member of COSO
- Canadian Institute of Chartered Accountants (CICA)
- Information Systems Audit and Control Association (ISACA)
- The Institute of Internal Auditors (IIA), a member of COSO

Naturally, because these objectives have been pronounced by different organizations at different times and with different goals in mind, they differ.

In this book, we generally consider objectives to be the reverse of consequences—that is, control objectives are the avoidance of adverse consequences. In practice, objectives tend to beg the question. Of course, everyone wants the balance sheet to be fairly presented. If everyone agrees, why would the balance sheet ever not be fairly presented? The answer is that a variety of things can go wrong. Those things are what we try to "prevent" or "detect and correct." These words would have no obvious meaning if we applied them to an objective, but they are the key attributes for control assessment.

However, both the general and the specific control objectives vary from organization to organization. Therefore, although general pronouncements have general applicability, particular objectives might not apply to particular organizations.

Location

AICPA literature also categorized controls by input, process, and output. This method of classifying controls according to location was expanded in the *Systems Auditability and Control Study* (SAC), which used the following categories of locations:

- Transaction origination
- Data processing transaction entry
- Data communications
- Computer processing

- Data storage and retrieval
- Output processing

However, the AICPA has noted that "it is often difficult to distinguish between controls over input and controls over the subsequent processing of that input."[4] Furthermore, the categorization of controls according to their location seems to provide relatively little assistance in the evaluation of those controls. Controls over input problems might be anywhere in the system, and an absence of controls among the input activities does not necessarily indicate any weakness.

The most significant aspect of the location of controls is probably the fact that the closer a control is located to the occurrence of a problem, the more immediately it is likely to deal with it. The location also must be known in order to test it.

Organization

Another way of classifying controls is to segregate controls that follow the vertical lines of authority of an organization chart and those that follow processing flows that cut across such lines.

> For example, supervisory controls are exercised upward along the vertical lines of the organization chart, whereas transmittals between departments might be diagrammed laterally between equal levels of the organization.

As indicated previously, the implementation of computers in many situations brings about an upward shift in the lowest level of common supervisory or line management control. This upward shift affects the nature of vertical controls because individuals having overall line authority over the processes are higher in the organization and have less time to provide detailed supervision. In addition, as additional departments (computer operations and systems development) become involved in a process in which only one department existed before, the need emerges for more lateral control. Accordingly, an organizational structure that provided adequate controls for a manual system will generally not provide an equal level of control for a system after the introduction of computers and ERP integrated application systems.

This is not to say that the vertical controls, such as supervision and segregation of duties, are no longer important to a computer system. However, their effectiveness and the related emphasis on them are reduced. This emphasis must be shifted more toward the lateral types of control such as transmittals, control totals, and edits.

This classification of control, vertical versus lateral, indicates that greater emphasis and concern must be placed on the lateral type than was the case in manual systems. Therefore, application controls can no longer be evaluated on a department-by-department basis. Effective control of computerized activities depends on the adequacy of controls during development, in computer operations, and within all user departments. An evaluation of any single department will omit highly relevant supplementary controls existing in other departments. Only in this way can the entire picture be seen and properly evaluated.

> For example, the reliable processing of a mortgage payment to a bank depends on controls exercised by the branch tellers, the mortgage department's staff, programs developed by the systems development department, and handling and security of files maintained by computer operations. This chain is only as strong as its weakest link.

Responsibilities

All the various departments and individuals involved in IT must understand their appropriate roles concerning control. Many of the so-called "computer" problems in businesses today stem from confusion as to who should do what.

RESPONSIBILITY OF USERS As an information system becomes increasingly centralized, the user gives up some direct involvement and the information processing facility acquires a greater degree of information file custody. In considering control responsibilities, it is important to recognize that there are marked differences between physical custody of media and hardware and control over accuracy and reliability of the data.

The computer user must still conduct himself as a prudent businessperson. The user must understand and specify what controls are necessary in the handling of transactions, the processing of data, and the availability of information output. The user must still understand the information processing system at a logical level. This is the level of detail that the user can compare with generally reasonable business practices. Although he should not be expected to become an expert in computer technology, he must retain the responsibility to operate and test controls.

IT RESPONSIBILITIES IT management, in turn, is responsible for all custodial processes associated with handling, processing, storing, and outputting data between receipt of input data and delivery of results to users. In meeting custodial responsibilities, data processing personnel should apply the same types and degrees of care expected of the organization's treasurer in the handling of cash and negotiable securities.

Additionally, the IT activity has central responsibilities in the area of technical design of systems. IT staff must determine that levels of service and control acceptable to users are specified and designed into systems. Trade-offs are made between manual and computerized systems based on economies, compensating controls to offset abridged manual procedures, and company policy.

Quality assurance is an important responsibility assumed by IT management with centralization of processing and file custody. IT is in a position to assure that control procedures meet defined requirements and is the primary entity that can assure quality in information processing.

WHO IS RESPONSIBLE? With the managers of systems development, systems maintenance, the information processing facility, and user departments involved and with top management, external auditors, and internal auditors also concerned, who is responsible for the controls of a particular operation? This question has frequently been debated, but it is usually resolved that the application users must be primarily responsible. Their performance is being affected by the computerized system; they have the most immediate knowledge of a computerized application; and they have the most to lose. However, where the user manager cannot reasonably be expected to have adequate technical comprehension to exercise total control responsibility, higher levels of management should provide necessary support to assure proper technical controls. This is often provided by a separate quality-assurance function.

Independence

Controls are usually expected to be independent—both of each other and of the activities subject to control. However, compliance with some controls can depend on compliance with other controls.

> For example, review of the accuracy and propriety of a transaction depends on the nature and integrity of the documentation available for review.

Controls that are independent of each other can serve to compensate for each other if one should fail.

> For example, if each of three controls over a single system is moderately reliable, the probability of them all failing simultaneously is much lower than the probability of any one failing.

The independence of control from the fundamental activities subject to control is sometimes confused with *segregation of duties*, which involves the separation of the ability to initiate transactions from the recording of them and from the custody of assets. The primary purpose is to prevent abuses; the secondary purpose is to promote efficiency.

The *independence of control* involves the separation of the actions providing control from the actions being controlled. The primary purpose is to provide objectivity.

The use of computers to implement controls can cause significant problems with independence. Controls can be embedded in the same computer programs as the activities they control and could be implemented by the same programmer. The exact effect of controls and activities being somewhat dependent is difficult to estimate, and the assessor should carefully consider the implications during evaluation.

Familiarity

Business-trained managers and assessors find that many controls in computerized systems include simple and obvious incorporations of business practices. Such controls are functional in nature. They can be implemented by either people or computers, without any significant change to their surface appearance.

> For example, supervisory approval of the work performed by a network administrator appears little different from supervisory approval provided over bookkeeping clerks.

There are also significant numbers of controls that are new and peculiar to the technology of computers.

> For example, parity controls are incorporated by the manufacturers of computer equipment to detect electronic failures in the transmittal or recording of binary-coded data. No parallel situation can be found in purely manual processing.

Particular controls would not normally be considered purely business or technical. Rather, controls over computer functions lie in a spectrum of relative technical complexity. Though the examples we've given are probably extremes, many other controls might be considered in gray areas between these extremes. This is not to say that there is anything unbusinesslike about technical controls, given an appreciation of the technical environment that brings rise to their use. Rather, this classification relates controls to the relative degree of technical education that is found among business managers and assessors.

Just as a businessperson without technical expertise in computer controls cannot design, implement, or evaluate a complete set of effective controls, neither can an IT technician who is lacking in business skills. Full understanding of controls requires a combination of business and computer expertise. Businesspeople and IT technicians must effectively merge their skills to guarantee the success of the resulting operations.

The specifications of controls for reliable processing of business applications depend primarily on knowledge that is already familiar to businesspeople. Some factors change, but once a businessperson acquires a moderate knowledge of this new technology, she will find that the IT environment is not so mysterious after all.

The development and implementation of new business applications on the computer require a greater degree of technical expertise. A business-trained individual can substantially increase his effectiveness by acquiring a limited knowledge of the activities that comprise the systems development process. Knowledge of file concepts, programming languages, hardware, and other technical elements are rarely essential for the businessperson who has adequate technical support.

Finally, the evaluation of the information processing facility (IPF) is the most heavily oriented toward computer technology, since it handles the functions of actually operating the computer and the machine-readable files. An individual with limited technical expertise could encounter difficulties in evaluating her findings and persuading technical management to follow her recommendations. At the same time, however, many activities of IPF operations, such as physical security, are still essentially business judgments. Effective evaluation of these activities lies well within the capabilities of an individual having only a moderate technical background. The more tangible nature of IPF operations, compared to application processing, further reduces the evaluation difficulties that could be encountered by a nontechnician.

The incorporation of various levels of technical expertise in controls over computer systems does not prohibit a manager or assessor who has a sound business background but limited technical knowledge from effectively designing, implementing, or evaluating the controls over computerized application processing or computer operations. However, a greater level of technical expertise will be required in dealing with controls over the systems development process or the technical aspects of computer operations.

Mode

Many analysts distinguish between controls that are implemented by actually using the computer versus those implemented by humans. However, only two important characteristics differ according to the mode of implementation: consistency and speed. In all other characteristics, the essential nature of controls is the same. Depending on the quality of their implementation, manual controls can be quite effective and reliable, and computer controls can be quite ineffective and unreliable. However, the computer controls will at least be consistent. In high-volume situations, however, one computer can be capable of implementing detailed control procedures over far more activities than could any single human.

Durability

The durability of controls addresses their capability to function under stress, such as very high transaction volumes, high inherent risks, or deliberate attack. Highly durable controls are also known as *robust* controls.

This characteristic is important to the effectiveness of controls that could encounter high stress. Robust controls are particularly important to prevent computer abuse.

Immediacy

The speed with which controls act has significant impact on their effectiveness. Preventive controls must function at least as fast as the activities they control or they will slow the entire process.

Detective controls should report a problem soon after its occurrence so that corrective action can commence promptly, while the original people involved are available and can recall the circumstances.

Corrective actions should proceed swiftly so that the effects of the problem do not persist and become the cause of additional problems.

For these reasons, detective controls that operate on a cyclical basis, such as an annual count or review, could allow the accumulation of problems until the consequences reach material dimensions and are substantially useless against major problems that require immediate correction.

> For example, an annual physical count of negotiable securities will not help much when the corporate treasurer has already flown to Brazil.

On the other hand, modern computer systems can provide substantial control improvements when properly designed. The speed and interactive capabilities of an online application system can subject transactions to extensive edits and reasonableness checks, all while the transaction is still in the process of being initiated and correction of any problems is at its easiest.

Cost

In information systems, as elsewhere, each control has a cost. No control should cost more than the potential problems it is established to prevent or detect and correct. The cost of investigating and correcting problems should not be overlooked in this cost/risk concern. To the extent that controls are poorly designed or excessive, they become burdensome and are under threat of being ignored. A review should be made to see whether the problems could be caught earlier in the processing system, minimizing:

- The control points required
- The damage that could be done to the file
- The necessary correction effort

The needs of management and the significance of any given error, as well as the evaluation of cost and risks, are effective balances. They help determine where and to what extent controls should be applied.

Preventive controls are generally the lowest in cost (in terms of both time and capital). Detective controls usually require some moderate operating expense. Corrective controls are almost always quite expensive. Three to ten times more effort might be required to correct something that occurs improperly than it takes to do it right the first time.

The design of optimum controls, therefore, requires a set of trade-offs. Preventive controls might be the cheapest to operate, but they are seldom adequate alone. Therefore, some detection and correction activity is always necessary. The cost/benefit balance must be struck between the cost of implementing further preventive controls and that of operating the correction activities. Elimination of detection controls is seldom an appropriate means of cost reduction. Without them, neither the effectiveness of preventive controls nor the resulting exposure can be measured.

Throughout the remainder of this book, we concentrate on the application of these classifications.

Having segregated and listed the available controls in a system, the assessor should classify their characteristics as illustrated in Exhibit 7.3.

Assess the Effectiveness of Controls

The assessor's appraisal of the effectiveness of particular controls is a subjective decision based on the varied characteristics of the control, the assessor's experience, and common sense.

A few controls are quite easy to evaluate. They usually are the ones that lie on one of the extremes, so they are obviously very reliable or

EXHIBIT 7.3 Classifications of Control Characteristics

- System
- Hierarchy
- Function
- Discretion
    - Objectivity
    - Cost
    - Independence
    - Immediacy
    - Durability
    - Responsibilities
    - Location
    - Objective
    - Organization
    - Familiarity
    - Mode
    - Purpose

obviously quite unreliable. Unfortunately, most controls lie somewhere in between. Very few scientific studies measure the absolute reliability of particular controls. Therefore, each assessor can only apply her best judgment and document her opinion so that it can be reviewed and considered.

The most important controls are usually the detective type. These might measure the effectiveness of preventive controls and exercise control over error corrections. Accordingly, the assessor should first review the detective controls as the most likely classification of controls that should be relied on.

At the same time, detective controls are not complete unless adequate provision is made for correction. Accordingly, the second most significant area for control evaluation is corrective controls.

Finally, some preventive controls over particular problems might be effective enough and sufficiently susceptible to testing to be reliable. Furthermore, the preventive controls will normally be the most important in recommending improvement, since they are the easiest to implement and are essential if exceptions are to be kept to a level that can be effectively corrected.

A control acts directly on a problem and thereby indirectly impacts the consequences. Therefore, although controls are intended to limit exposures, they really act on a problem. No simple one-to-one relationship exists between the list of controls and the list of problems. Various control techniques could affect a particular problem, and a particular problem could be controlled by various techniques.

EXHIBIT 7.4 The Relationship of Controls to Problems

Controls	Problem: Losing a Check
Training	L
Secure custody	M
Prenumbered form	H
Endorsement	L
Transmittal document	M
Amount control total	H
Document control count	H
Reconciliation	H
Discrepancy reports	M

Key to strength of controls:

H	Highly reliable
M	Moderately reliable
L	Low reliability
N	Negative contribution

All the controls that could be exercised over a particular problem need not be utilized—only those that are sufficient to effectively limit the consequences. Assessors are sometimes tempted to request that all the potential controls that are conceivable be implemented simultaneously over a particular process. This is particularly likely if the assessor is relying on some control checklist or questionnaire. This is not necessary (and is, in fact, wasteful) if the implemented controls are sufficient by themselves. This effect of one control serving instead of another is generally referred to as a *compensating control.*

We can also depict this relationship between controls and problems in a table. Again, we can list the problems across the top, but with the controls along the side. Furthermore, we can also insert designations in the intersecting squares to signify the order of magnitude with which the particular control will affect the particular problem. An illustration of such a table is provided in Exhibit 7.4.

Assess the Adequacy of Control Over Each Problem

The determination of when control is sufficient is subjective. It must be weighed in the light of the costs of implementing further controls and balanced against the potential consequences. However, for the preliminary evaluation, a simple rule of thumb can be adopted for an evaluation of whether control is adequate over a particular problem.

One highly reliable control over a particular problem should be adequate. Such controls are designated by the letter H on the control evaluation matrix. This does not mean that the control has to be perfectly reliable but rather that it would tolerate only an insignificant level of error.

Two or more controls of moderate strength (designated by the letter M) should be present if a strong control (H) does not exist. Although useful, such controls would not be deemed sufficiently reliable by themselves.

A very large number of useful but low effectiveness controls (designated by the letter L) would have to be available if there are not sufficient strong or moderately effective controls. At some point, probably no quantity of weak controls makes any particular difference. This does not mean that controls that are useful but not especially effective should be completely discouraged since they will often reduce the error rates to levels that are more readily dealt with by the other controls. At the same time, they will seldom be of sufficient use to merit reliance or testing.

Problems that fail to meet the control ratings described here should be considered insufficiently controlled. This means that a reasonable probability exists that the problem would not be prevented from occurring, not detected, or not corrected when it occurs. Whether this is a serious risk depends on the resulting consequences.

Appraise Adverse Resulting Consequences

If adequate controls exist over specific problems, the adverse consequences that remain should be negligible. The evaluation of adverse consequences applies primarily to those problems that are not effectively controlled.

The consequences listed on the control evaluation matrix should be tailored to suit the specific circumstances of the system under examination.

For example, if the application has no direct impact on accounting entries, the exposure to unacceptable accounting would not apply.

Finally, the magnitude of the consequence must be estimated. This involves appraising the maximum plausible exposure.

Obviously, specific estimates might be quite subjective and are often omitted in practice. Although the subjectivity should be recognized, it should not be an excuse to avoid any estimate.

These relationships can be combined into one *control evaluation matrix* by simply placing one over the other so that the potential problems are

EXHIBIT 7.5 The Control Evaluation Matrix

Problem Controls	Losing a Check	Key to Strength of Controls
Training	L	
Secure custody	M	H: Highly reliable
Prenumbered form	H	
Endorsement	L	L: Low reliability
Transmittal document	M	Blank: No significant use
Amount control total	H	N: Negative contribution
Document control count	H	
Reconciliation	H	
Discrepancy reports	M	
Consequences		
Key to Magnitude of Exposure	H	Erroneous record keeping
H: Highly likely		Unacceptable accounting
M: Moderate liklihood	L	Business interruption
L: Low probability		Erroneous management decisions
Blank: Very unlikely		Fraud and embezzlement
		Statutory sanctions
	M	Excessive costs
	H	Loss or destruction of assets
	M	Competitive disadvantage

aligned. We can then trace the three-element relationship of problem, control, and consequence to analyze the control quality. This is illustrated in Exhibit 7.5.

The Control Evaluation Matrix

A control evaluation matrix can be utilized as a tabular illustration of the control evaluation process. By documenting the evaluation process in this manner, the assessor's evaluation process is structured and the reviewer is provided a far greater capability to review and challenge that process.

Each potential problem is subject to four types of risk. The first type is the inherent risk that we have already discussed.

> For example, estimate that an inventory purchase transaction will be recorded inaccurately in the perpetual records in only a small proportion of the opportunities, even if no controls exist.

Second, only if a problem would actually occur do we need to be concerned with preventive controls. To the extent that preventive controls function effectively, the actual observable occurrence of a problem will be reduced. Therefore, we can designate the second level in our evaluation model as the prevention risk, and we can designate the product of the inherent and the prevention risks as the actual incident risk.

The actual incident risk is the first level of risk that we can actually measure. Inherent risk can never be observed and measured unless we actually find a situation in which no preventive controls exist. This is extremely rare. Consequently, we are unable to develop reliable statistics regarding the inherent risk of most potential problems because the actual occurrence of the problem is practically always reduced by some degree of preventive control.

> For example, if an inventory purchase would record the part number inaccurately in a small proportion of those cases where no controls at all exist, we might estimate that the use of a well-designed input form would reduce the incidence of errors but still fail to eliminate them in the majority of the opportunities. This would leave us with a moderately reduced occurrence risk.

Third, the effectiveness of detective controls is ascertainable only if events actually occur that they are intended to detect. (This presumes that the detective control does not report occurrences when, in fact, they have not occurred.) To whatever extent the detective controls are effective, they will measure the actual occurrence rate described previously. To the extent that detection controls fail, the problem will proceed to cause whatever consequences it will.

> For example, if the occurrence risk of an inaccurately recorded part number is significant and detective check digit controls are fairly effective in identifying the majority of those occurrences, the resulting risk of the wrong perpetual record being updated and going undetected is substantially reduced.

Finally, even if controls succeed in detecting an occurrence, it must be corrected before adverse consequences can be avoided. Corrective controls will only be utilized for those problems that are detected. Therefore, if preventive controls are extremely effective, we might never exercise our corrective controls simply because there is never any need. As noted previously, error correction is itself an extremely error-prone activity. A significant risk often exists that even if the occurrence of a problem is successfully detected, the corrective controls will fail to halt the consequences or restore the damage.

For example, if most of the transactions are detected when they have inaccurate part numbers, correction still requires an investigation as to what part number should have been recorded and either the reinitiation of a corrected transaction or the initiation of an error correction transaction. If the correction process fails in about half the cases, actual errors will be introduced into the perpetual records and proceed to cause their consequences at a noticeable rate.

The ultimate error rate, therefore, is a result of the inherent risk and the likelihood that preventive, detective, and corrective controls will fail to perform their functions.

For example, inherent risk is high, prevention risk is high, detection risk is moderate, and correction risk is moderate—then the resulting error rate is still too high.

We can illustrate this model graphically using the control evaluation matrix applied to the following five alternatives:

1. The problem does not happen to occur.
2. The problem would occur, but preventive controls stop it.

Preventive controls fail, and then:

3. Both detective and corrective controls function properly.
4. The detective controls function, but the corrective controls fail. Consequences result.
5. The detective controls fail and, therefore, the corrective controls are never applied. Consequences result.

In the first three alternatives, no problem actually persists, and no consequences result. The last two cases are where consequences will, in fact, result. Exhibit 7.6 illustrates the alternatives in the examples.

In practice, the assessor might want to categorize them by general levels such as *high, moderate,* or *low*. Detection and correction failures will be measurable only using highly effective testing techniques that can discover and evaluate the resulting consequences. Even then, the assessor might be uncertain as to which specific problem brought about the consequences revealed by the audit.

For example, a physical count of inventory will reliably reveal those items not accurately recorded within the perpetual inventory system, but even the most extensive investigation might not reveal

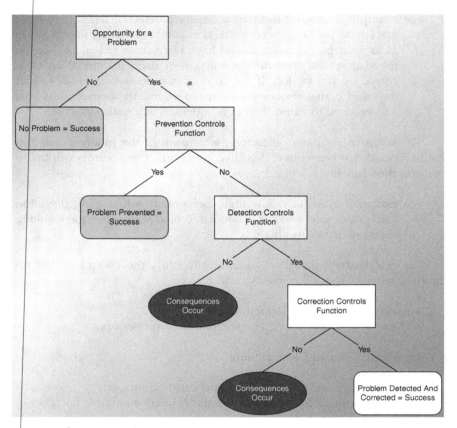

EXHIBIT 7.6 The Control Functional Decision Tree

what went wrong with particular transactions that resulted in the differences.

Therefore, although the risk estimates are highly subjective, this approach to control evaluation structures a rational approach to the primary characteristics of control that will ultimately determine the relevant adverse consequences. Furthermore, and perhaps even more important, the resulting matrix documentation facilitates a more effective review by breaking the evaluation process into its primary components and allowing the reviewer to concentrate on those key judgments that have the greatest impact on the net risk assessed.

This approach to control analysis has sometimes been characterized as a *risk analysis* or *risk-based approach* and has been contrasted with the

EXHIBIT 7.7 Shifts from Negative to Positive Terminology

Problem Consequences	Control Objectives	COSO Objectives
Erroneous record keeping	Complete and accurate records	Financial reporting
Unacceptable accounting	Proper accounting classification and disclosure	Financial reporting
Loss or destruction of assets	Safeguard assets	Safeguard assets
Fraud and embezzlement	Security	Safeguard assets
Statutory sanctions	Statutory compliance	Compliance
Business interruption	Continuity	Operating
Erroneous management decisions	Sound management decisions	Operating
Excessive costs	Minimize costs	Operating
Competitive disadvantage	Competitive advantage	Operating
Fail objectives	Achieve objectives	Operating

objectives approach. In fact, this approach to control analysis goes considerably further than the typical risk analysis and is not fundamentally different from an objectives approach. The adverse consequences that we described previously can be converted to objectives by a simple shift from negative to positive terminology, as shown in Exhibit 7.7.

This method also differs from risk analysis via the addition of the explicit evaluation of controls in relation to potential problems. Risk analysis by itself merely estimates exposures using an intuitive or statistical estimate of the likelihood of problems actually occurring in some general circumstances. This works well when directed to the analysis of exposures from threats such as tornadoes or fire, for which typical circumstances are discernable, but it becomes questionable if applied to problems that are peculiar to the specific system.

In contrast, the control evaluation matrix approach produces an analytic estimate of the risks of problems that is specifically tailored to the system under examination.

Though this process is subjective, it is quite workable and has been effectively implemented by numerous organizations since its origination in the mid-1970s. Furthermore, it requires only a moderate amount of training. Novice assessors can understand it quite quickly; however, experienced assessors sometimes have difficulty unlearning obsolete habits.

The method also seems to be universally applicable to any type of system and any level of technology. In this book, the same methods are repeatedly applied to general and application EDP systems. It can also be applied to non-IT as well as noninformation systems. In fact, it can, and has been, used to evaluate systems for performing financial audits.

How Much Control Is Enough or Too Much?

This is the ultimate decision that must be made by management and the board of directors. A control assessment can tell about nature and dimensions of the risks but not how much risk is acceptable.

Some risks might be high but the exposure low because the potential consequences simply do not amount to much. Other risks might be low, but the potential consequences are so totally unacceptable that even low risk is too much. Conversely, the risk might be so well controlled that the cost of control exceeds the alternative costs. The management decisions must be made from this information.

No formula or rule of thumb is available to help with these decisions, but some of the considerations should include the following:

- Criminal indictments
- Civil litigation
- Default on securities covenants
- Bankruptcy/liquidation
- Takeover by a competitor
- Material change in stock price

Test Selected Controls

The common term for controls to be tested is *key controls*, but most authoritative auditing literature does not use this term. Instead, it specifies that an opinion on the adequacy must be verified by testing those controls that are being relied on. This ambiguity is one of the reasons that the early opinions for Sarbanes-Oxley carried excessive testing and cost. Even after several years of experience, the costs have not declined to the levels originally predicted by the SEC.

In general, the selection of "key" controls to be tested should be based on the following considerations:

- We assume that the successful functioning of any one control will be effective in preventing or detecting the incidence of a problem. More than one correction control is often necessary. Which specific prevention control acts successfully in a particular instance can be difficult to determine. The identity of a successful detection control is usually more obvious, as are the identities of corrections controls that are activated.

- The selected controls should generally include one or more detective controls that are both highly effective and have high implementation. The number of such controls is based on the proportionate tolerance for errors. The smaller the tolerance, the more and stronger will be the controls selected. One strong control might be adequate if the tolerance for error is not too stringent. Additional controls will need to be selected if the tolerance is very small.
- Prevention controls will sometimes be selected as key, but not usually. Selection of detection controls will usually reveal whether the prevention controls are effective without further direct testing. Prevention controls might need to be selected if sufficient detection controls are not available.

Summary

Within this chapter we have discussed qualitative control methodologies. We have provided the reader with a framework for qualitative control assessments, and also discussed the economics of internal controls. We have also highlighted the difference between preventive, detective, and corrective controls, and discussed methods for evaluating each of these types of controls.

Notes

1. Institute of Internal Auditors, *Systems Auditability and Control,* 1976.
2. Research Foundation of Financial Executives Institute, *Internal Control in U.S. Corporations,* 1980.
3. M. Jensen. "The Modern Industrial Revolution, Exit, and the Failure of Internal Control Systems. *Journal of Finance.* Vol. 48, Issue 3, pp. 831–880, 1993.

CHAPTER 8

Quantitative Control Relationships

This chapter details a quantitative framework for assessing the complex relationships between internal controls. This framework can be
organized into a comprehensive structure that permits the modeling and
forecasting of the efficacy of internal control.

Traditionally, the assessment of internal control over systems has been
a largely intuitive process performed by experienced practitioners. There
are many guidelines that practitioners can reference in performing such
assessments, but much of the internal control assessment process is highly
subjective. However, there is no universally accepted formal process for the
design of internal controls in information systems. The quantitative methods
presented in this chapter serve to fill this gap.

We present the reader with a new approach to internal control evaluation. This methodology asks practitioners to take their evaluations one
step further from the often-used qualitative approach to one that quantifies
risks. Using this new method of quantitative control evaluation, assessors,
managers, and board members can better assess organizational risks, reducing the likelihood for material misstatements and areas of control weakness.
This framework can be naturally used to quantify financial reporting risks,
but it extends equally well to operational and strategic risks.

Moving from Qualitative to Quantitative

Many people who assess controls are accustomed to qualitatively classifying systemic risks. Examples of qualitative rankings for such risk include
scores such as *high*, *medium*, or *low* or a numerical scale from 1 to 5.
Though the latter scale might resemble a quantitative ranking method, these
numbers merely assign a numerical value to a qualitative ranking. Used in
practice, such a scale could easily be replaced by a descriptive scale, such
as *very low*, *low*, *medium*, *high*, and *very high*, without any adverse effect
on the ranking methodology. However, our discussion revolves around

quantitative methods as assessors to quantify for analysis of systematic risks.

In the context of risk factors, a high risk on a quantitative scale could equate to a 99 percent probability of occurrence. It could also symbolize lower probabilities, such as 85 percent. Low risk factors might, on the contrary, represent probabilities of occurrence anywhere from 1 percent to 60 percent. Medium risks, then, would be something in between, possibly 50, 66, or 80 percent. Although the precise meaning behind qualitative rankings will vary according to the nature of potential problems, their consequences, and the context within the organization, quantitative rankings permit users to better understand systematic risks and potential internal control modes of failure. They also allow users to better plan tests of control systems and better understand the sensitivity of material auditing misstatements to control factors and parameters.

At first, many practitioners who have experience with qualitative assessments are reluctant to quantify their ratings. They often feel that assigning a number implies a precision to which they cannot attest—at least not without more analysis and thought. In fact, our quantitative modeling structure is remarkably tolerant of imprecise estimates, and the person making a quantitative judgment should spend no more time or thought about quantitative precision than they did about qualitative precision.

Systems Control Functions

We can relate controls in a quantitative manner by concentrating on the following issues:

1. Potential problems (also called incidents or events)
2. Opportunities for the problems to occur
3. Inherent risk factors
4. The control environment
5. Prevention control design
6. Implementation of prescribed controls
7. Detection control design
8. Correction control design
9. Control costs
10. Consequences
11. Loss per occurrence

Each of these functions may be considered individually and in the context of their operation and relationship within the particular system. This consideration can be subjectively or objectively quantified. Subjective

quantification might not be measurable, but the overall effect on the outcome can be determined.

We now present mathematical formulae that express relationships
among these 11 parameters. In addition, we present a series of examples of
these formulae incorporated into an Excel model.

Input 1: Potential Problems (Incidents)

Problems describe the things that can go wrong in the system. They are
the causes of adverse consequences. They are also referred to as *incidents, threats, hazards, risks, vulnerabilities, undesirable events, challenges,
detailed control objectives,* and other synonyms or antonyms. A comprehensive awareness of what can go wrong is an essential prerequisite to
evaluating the control over a system, even if we elect not to model it further.
Omission of significant types of potential problems cannot be compensated
for elsewhere in the assessment.

Problems are *what* can go wrong, not *why* they go wrong. Focusing on
scenarios, motives, or minute details within problems tends to result in an
unworkable quantity of issues. For example, the occurrence of fraud might
be determined only after lengthy deliberation by a jury. Effective internal
controls cannot wait for such determination. They must operate with the
foreknowledge that potential problems might be deliberate, but they cannot
wait upon that determination.

Accordingly, a practical level of assessment concentrates on the 10 to 20
most significant potential problems in the particular system. If many more
than 20 problems deserve full assessment, the system should be divided into
subsystems.

Problems can be viewed as the inverse of detailed control objectives.
However, positive statements of control objectives often fail to communicate
the possibility that they might not always be achieved. For example, one
student asked, "If I design a system to do something, why wouldn't it?" Only
youth could hold such optimistic naïveté. We must assume some degree of
pessimism to be effective in modeling control.

Identification of problems is a key component of quantitative control
management and the first input in a control matrix. Problems within a system must first be identified for systemic risks to be appropriately quantified.
Accordingly, risk practitioners should first prepare a complete list of potential problems associated with a system. This list will later form the basis
for estimates made with respect to the control framework's effectiveness. It
is important to note that a practitioner should not yet attempt to quantify
the impact of these problems. The goal at this stage is purely qualitative
enumeration.

Input 2: Opportunities

Opportunities are the number of occasions that are presented for things to go wrong. Unlike the previously described qualitative problems, control practitioners must make quantitative estimates of the number of occasions on which a control-related incident could occur. These estimates must be formulated for each problem a practitioner has listed in his control matrix.

In an application system, this might be related to the number of transactions, program runs, or reports produced. In an infrastructure system such as a computer operations facility, it could be the annual possibility of an accidental fire. Typically, opportunities are quantified by year. Accordingly, if 100,000 transactions a year are submitted for processing, then 100,000 opportunities exist for various input problems. On the other hand, if the possibility exists continuously, such as for fire, we can consider the situation to be either one annual opportunity or 365 days of opportunities. The unit of measure used for opportunities is important only to the extent that it must be consistent with the inherent risk and other probability estimates used in the assessment.

Input 3: Inherent Risk Factors

Once problems and the number of opportunities for each of these problems have been identified, the inherent risks associated with a control system must be quantified. Inherent risk is the likelihood of problems in an environment without any controls and is determined by various inherent factors. Some of the factors that determine inherent risk include:

- Nature of the system
- Physical location
- Degree of automation
- Source and nature of the computer language
- Nature of the transactions
- Nature of the information
- Nature of the specific activity subject to control
- Rate of change in each of the preceding factors
- Appeal to theft, fraud, or vandalism
- Number of other systems and people to which the system is connected

The *nature of the system* (i.e., application, computer operations, or the like) determines the nature of potential problems that differ according to the system. For example, an application could lose an input transaction, whereas a power failure could shut down an entire processing facility.

The *physical location* changes the inherent risk of physical hazards such as flood or earthquake and might also influence data corruption.

The *degree of automation* addresses the relative reliance on computers versus people. Computers tend to be more consistent than humans; people can exercise independent judgments never contemplated in the computer system design.

The personal computer revolution of the 1990s expanded the potential market for purchased computer systems of all types. Systems developed and used by others are more likely to be thoroughly debugged than ones developed internally. The particular *computer programming language* used in software influences the complexity of the programs and the maintenance effort.

The *nature of the transactions* not only influences their volume, source, and complexity, it also defines their relationship to data elements in storage and relevance to ultimate control objectives.

The *nature of the information being processed and stored* can be indicative, quantitative, or objective. The problems arising with each can be quite different.

The *nature of the activities subject to control* also prescribes different potential problems. Examples of such activities include transcribing data and performing logical decisions.

The *rate of change in all the preceding factors* can have a great influence on their inherent risk. Usually, the more rapid the rate of change, the higher is the inherent risk.

Some information systems will have obviously greater *appeal to theft, fraud, or vandalism* than others. Systems that generate monetary payments clearly present greater attraction to theft than ones that archive news articles.

Finally, the *number and nature of other systems and persons to which the system is connected* bring proportionate risks. An isolated, standalone system carries much less risk than one that is connected to a network. A system constantly connected to the Internet is vulnerable to virtually everyone and everything in the world all the time. The Internet presents the greatest current challenge to control because substantially all modern computer systems are connectable, even when connection is not intended.

These various factors act in an additive manner for different types of problems. Because we are estimating the risk probability of the problem, the total probability cannot exceed 100 percent. The estimation of the quantities involved with these factors is highly subjective because substantially no experience is ever obtained under the total absence of any controls. Therefore, actual inherent risk situations are rarely, if ever, observed. However, the high degree of subjectivity should not inhibit the quantification of some estimate. Although the estimate might not be very precise, the use of a reasonable general magnitude will promote a better control assessment than simple intuition.

When quantifying inherent risk factors in the control system, a practitioner should try to estimate inherent risk factors that are mutually exclusive. In other words, the domain of each inherent risk does not overlap any other. This permits us to derive an estimate of the total inherent risk using the following equation:

$$\text{Total inherent risk} = \text{Inherent risk factor}_1 + \text{Inherent risk}$$

$$\text{factor}_2 + \ldots + \text{Inherent risk factor}_N$$

In this equation, the assessor sums each of N inherent risk factors to arrive at the total inherent risk for a given potential problem. This formula is used for each potential problem identified by a control assessor. If two types of inherent risk factors are related to each other, the assessor will need to make a judgment about the degree to which each factor influences the other. If the occurrence of both risk factors is perfectly correlated, their contribution to the total inherent risk of that problem should be no more than the contribution of each individually.

Recall that inherent risks are risks that are present when there is a lack of controls in a given system, and the estimates made by the practitioner of probabilities of occurrence should be made using this mentality.

Exhibit 8.1 is the first of a series of exhibits that we present in this chapter to illustrate not only each section of the model, but also the Excel coding for the calculations in each section. The shaded rows display the formulae, while the unshaded cells display the input data and the results of the calculations. We invite the reader to open a new Excel worksheet and transcribe these examples for later use.

	A	C
1	Quantitative Assurance Model Template	
2		Problem #1
3	Opportunities>	1000
4	Units of measure>	Transactions
5	Inherent Risk Factors	
6	Factor #1	0.03
7	Factor #2	0.02
8	Inherent Risk=	=(+C6+C7)
9	Inherent Risk=	0.05

EXHIBIT 8.1 Example Inherent Risk Calculation

Source: © Copyright William C. Mair, 2009. All rights reserved.

Input 4: Control Environment

The *control environment* is composed of a number of factors that mitigate the inherent risks and provide a supportive environment for the internal controls. The factors differ from preventive controls in that they are intangible and are more descriptive of attitudes than of actions. For instance, the tone set by management (often called the "tone at the top" in the COSO-IC Framework) is a part of the control environment. It is not a specific action taken by management but rather a philosophy that describes the manner in which the organization is run.

Controls should be susceptible to positive verification by management inspection, review, or audit tests. Factors and characteristics that tend to reduce problems but, by their nature, cannot readily be verified should be considered as components of the control environment. Some of these factors include:

- Nature of the business
- Management attitude; the "tone at the top"
- Involvement and oversight by the audit committee
- Plan of organization, including segregation of duties
- Definition of duties
- Existence and communication of formal standards
- Level of computer technology
- Personnel

The *nature of the business* has a very global impact on all the systems in the organization. From the perspective of a particular application, it determines the relevance of that application to the organization's operating goals and thereby influences the tolerance for many of the problems that the system may allow.

The *attitude of top management*, or the *tone at the top*, leads the operating personnel in their conscientiousness and tolerance for problems. Leadership is a very important element in attaining excellence in anything.

The Sarbanes-Oxley Act emphasizes the role of independent directors on the *audit committee* as the supervisors of top management. They must possess expertise in control over financial reporting. They also are given authority over the compensation, retention, or replacement of the independent accountants. The internal audit function might report directly to them.

The *plan of the organization* designates the relative roles of people and information systems in the overall management strategy. This includes such intangible control characteristics as segregation of duties and independence of controls.

The existence of various types of *formal standards* tends to reduce some types of problems by better communicating procedures, policies, and expectations and by promoting more predictable consistency.

Computer technology might well be part of the solution as well as part of the problem. The automation of an information system and the use of various aspects of computer technology change the nature of the potential problems and the likelihood of their occurrence.

Finally, the degree of *reliability of personnel* involved in the system can have a major impact on the actual occurrence rate of problems. In some cases, a system that is extremely weak in formal internal controls will operate satisfactorily simply because of the involvement of highly experienced and competent people. At the other extreme, very incompetent people will usually overwhelm an otherwise adequate system of internal control, so such systems rarely ever function satisfactorily.

Probabilities associated with each control environment factor should be estimated for each potential problem. These probabilistic estimates should express the fact that the control factors will reduce the inherent risk of a problem. Care must be exercised to consider these estimates only as factors separate from those already considered part of the inherent risks. For example, one should not place a high value on competent personnel by reducing inherent risks if the estimates of inherent risk already were heavily colored by that same awareness of personnel competence.

The combined effect of the control environment factors is the joint probability of all the individual factors simultaneously failing to avoid the inherent risk. A formula for this is the series:

$$\text{Total control environment risk} = (1 - p_1) \times (1 - p_2) \times \ldots \times (1 - p_N)$$

In this equation, p_1 through p_N represent the probabilities that control environment factors 1 through N will reduce inherent risks. Thus $(1 - p)$ denotes the complement of this probability, or the probability that the control environment factor will fail. Again, note that in using this equation, we are assuming that each control environment factor acts independently of the other. If two factors are interrelated, the equation must take into account the covariance between these factors.

In Exhibit 8.2, we have elaborated a set of control environment factors for our example. Multiplying the complements of each control environment risk factor together using our equation for the control environment risk, we calculate this value as 0.343.

If we feel that two factors are not independent, we must use conditional probability to express this relationship. For two dependent events A and B, we have that the probability of A occurring with B is given by:

$$P(AB) = P(A|B) P(B)$$

	A	C
1	**Quantitative Assurance Model Template**	
2		**Problem #1**
3	Opportunities>	1000
8	Inherent Risk=	=(+C6+C7)
9	Inherent Risk=	0.05
10	**Control Environment**	
11	Tone at the top	0.3
12	Reliability of personnel	0.3
13	Competence of personnel	0.3
14	Environment Risk=	=((1-C11)*(1-C12)(1-C13))
15	Environment Risk=	0.343
16	Preliminary Risk=	=+C8*C14
17	Preliminary Risk=	0.017
18	Potential Incidents=	=+C3*C16
19	Potential Incidents	17.2

EXHIBIT 8.2 Example of Control Environment Risk Calculations

Source: © Copyright William C. Mair, 2009. All rights reserved.

For instance, let us divide our last control factor, Personnel, into Reliability of Personnel and Competence of Personnel. These two factors are arguably related to one another. In this instance, we must use the preceding equation to calculate the joint probability that both controls will prevent inherent risks. Supposing that the probability the competence of personnel is an effective control is 0.2 and that the probability the reliability of personnel is effective, given that the competence of personnel is 0.7, we have that the total probability of both controls stop inherent risks as:

$$P\left(\text{Both Competent and Reliable}\right) = 0.7 \times 0.2 = 0.14$$

Preliminary Risk and Potential Incidents

Having just estimated the inherent and control environment risk probabilities, we can now derive an estimate of what we will call the "Preliminary Risk." This risk quantifies the riskiness of a system before any active controls are used to prevent, detect, or correct potential incidents. The formula for preliminary risk is given by:

Preliminary risk = Total inherent risk × Total control environment risk

In this example, our preliminary risk would be equivalent to 0.5 ×0.343 =0.017. This estimate would increase (decrease) if the probabilities associated with inherent risks or the control environment increased (decreased). If we multiply the preliminary risk by the number of transactions, we arrive at the expected number of incidents due to the preliminary risk:

$$E\left(\text{Incidents due to preliminary risk}\right) = 0.017 \times 1,000 = 17.2\,\text{Incidents}$$

Where E() denotes the expected value.

Input 5: Prevention Controls

Prevention controls are tangible elements of an information system that tend to prevent the actual occurrence of potential problems. Other names sometimes used for such controls include *safeguards* and *protections*. They can be either an activity involved in the system, such as a password verification routine, or a passive characteristic of the system, such as a user interface that is intuitively clear.

Access controls are a very important subset of prevention controls. Access controls filter systems and people to grant access to the system to only those who are authorized. Access can be further filtered to specified levels of information and functions.

> For example, a customer could be granted access to view his individual records but no other customer's records. The customer might be allowed to change his mailing address but not his balance owed. In contrast, a customer service employee might be allowed access to all accounts and be authorized to initiate adjustment transactions.

Access controls must be robust because they could be required to withstand multiple deliberate and malevolent acts of penetration. Once access is attained, however, the problems that can be introduced might appear as similar to those that might occur accidentally and by authorized users. Although system controls should be designed with some expectation of the deliberate introduction of problems to the system, the controls themselves rarely will be capable of discerning the underlying motivation that gives rise to a particular problem. Therefore, controls designed around various assumptions of motivation and scenarios will be no more effective, and could be less effective, than if the controls are simply designed to address themselves to *what* can happen rather than *why*. Further, access controls are not only preventive. As described later, detection and correction controls should also serve a role in security and control of access.

Access might be so important to the assessment of other prevention controls that the model might first estimate the failure rate of the access controls and then estimate the net effectiveness of the remaining prevention controls over potential problems with those queries and transactions that attain access.

The probability that a prevention control will successfully prevent the occurrence of a problem should be estimated for each control over each potential problem. Hence, the probability that a control will fail to prevent a problem is the complement, or one minus the estimated probability. Only one control has to function effectively to stop an incident from happening. The probability of all controls simultaneously failing to prevent the event's occurrence is the product of the complements of the reliability for each control. Two *independent* controls that are each 95 percent reliable would each fail $1.00 - 0.95 = 5$ percent of the time. In combination, the probability that they would both fail at the same time is $0.05 \times 0.05 = 0.0025$, or $1/4$ of 1 percent.

Returning again to our example, let us suppose that three independent preventive controls have been implemented, each with an estimated effectiveness of 50 percent. Then the joint probability that each of these controls fails is given by $(1 - 0.50)^3 = 12.5$ percent. Therefore, we have a chance of less than 13 in 100 that the control system will fail to prevent a potential event. Given that our previous estimate for the expected number of incidents system was roughly five per year (from both the inherent and control environment factors), we have that the expected number of incidents *after* these prevention controls have been implemented is $12.5\% \times 5 = 0.625$ events.

One common concern with this method focuses on overestimating the reliability of a control. This overestimation would seem to contaminate the entire assessment process. Contrary to intuition, our formulae show that the assessments of risk are *not* highly sensitive to errors in judgment of their reliability. Even if the failure of a control is underestimated by 100 percent (e.g., 5 percent rather than 10 percent), the resulting probability of failure should still be a small number. The reason for this is that most potential problems are addressed by multiple controls, applied in functional layers, and overlaid by monitoring and management. As the number of controls in the system increases, the impact of overestimation decreases commensurately. Generally, when more than five controls are present in the estimate of prevention, sensitivity to overestimation of any given control is rather insignificant. Consider Exhibit 8.3, where we have plotted the effect of overestimation on the number of incidents as a function of the number of controls. The degree of overestimation here is 50 percent for one control. Here we have assumed that each control has an estimated effectiveness of 75 percent and that there exist 1,000 potential incidents to prevent.

Notice that after five controls are present, the impact of overestimation of a single control is negligible.

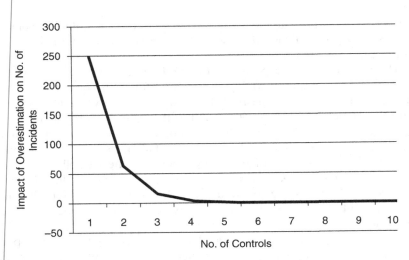

EXHIBIT 8.3 Impact of Overestimation by Number of Controls

In some cases, the utilization of a particular control to help prevent a particular problem can have counterproductive effects on some other problem. When this is the case, the estimated reliability should be considered a negative value and its net value should be the estimate of the percentage by which the problems will be increased. This is one instance in which the approach in this book differs from classic probability mathematics.

Input 6: Implementation of Controls

Of course, independent controls will be as effective as they are capable of being only if they are applied as appropriate. This issue of *control implementation* inserts another factor in the assessment of controls that distinguishes between the design of the controls and their actual effectiveness. One should estimate the frequency with which each control feature will be employed when an appropriate situation arises. The net effectiveness of that control then is recalculated as the product of the estimated effectiveness when correctly applied times the proportion of instances that it actually will be effectively applied.

Programmed and other automated controls can provide very high implementation rates. Humans, however, are prone to intermittent lapses and seldom should be relied on to deliver more than 95 percent implementation. Even automated controls should not be assumed to be 100 percent perfect. Unusual combinations of problems, power failures, deliberate override, faulty logic, program bugs, and other breakdowns can nullify the reliability of automation.

As each control is identified and its effectiveness is estimated, the assessor must also estimate the implementation rate using whatever additional information is available. In a surprising number of interviews, personnel will candidly admit that one or another control procedure is commonly ignored. Even when everyone claims 100 percent commitment and perfect compliance, the assessor should maintain a healthy skepticism. Actual control implementation can be measured by management reviews, audit tests, or other monitoring procedures following the preliminary control assessment.

In Exhibit 8.4 we have calculated the total prevention control effectiveness probability by multiplying the probability that a control prevents an incident by the compliance probability. This yields the effectiveness of each control. For instance, the effectiveness of Control #1 is $0.8 \times 0.9 = 72$ percent. The total prevention control failure risk when N convention controls exist is then given by:

$$\text{Prevention risk} = \left(1 - \left(\text{Implementation rate}_1 \times \text{Probability that prevention is effective}_1\right)\right) \times \left(1 - \left(\text{Implementation rate}_2 \times \text{Probability that prevention is effective}_2\right)\right) \times \ldots \times$$
$$\left(1 - \left(\text{Implementation rate}_N \times \text{Probability that prevention is effective}_N\right)\right)$$

This equation expresses the probability that each control—at its estimated level of effectiveness—fails to curtail risky events from occurring. As shown in Exhibit 8.4, the total prevention control risk is 12.2 percent.

	A	B	C
1	Quantitative Assurance Model Template		
2	Sensitivity Factor	1.0	*Problem #1*
18	Potential Incidents=		=+C3*C16
19	Potential Incidents		17.2
20	Prevention Controls	*Implementation*	Design Effectiveness
21	Control #1	0.9	0.8
22	Control #2	0.7	0.4
23	Control #3	0.4	0.99
24	Prevention Risk=		=(1-($B21*C21))*(1-($B22*C22))*(1-($B23*C23))*$B$2
25	Prevention Risk=		12.2%
26	Actual Incidents=		=C18*C24
27	Actual Incidents=		2.1

EXHIBIT 8.4 Prevention Control Risk

Output A: Forecast Actual Incidents

Up to this point, all the estimates of inherent factors, control environment factors, and prevention control reliability have been subjective judgments. If the assessment process were nothing more than the multiplication of various subjective estimates, it might well produce a result no more reliable than some traditional intuitive approach but with more effort. However, not only can the combined result of these initial judgments be calculated, it can also be compared to actual observations and experience with the system under assessment. This first checkpoint provides a major control over the assessment process itself and is a primary strength of the proposed model.

We can estimate expected incidence of problems within the assessed system, P, by multiplying the number of opportunities for failure within a system by the inherent risk probability by the probability that all the control environment factors will fail (what we call the *control environment risk probability*), times the probability that all the prevention controls will fail (the prevention control risk probability). A formula for this can be expressed as follows:

$$\text{Incidents} = \text{Opportunities} \times \text{Inherent risk probability} \times \text{Control}$$

$$\text{environment factors fail} \times \text{Prevention controls fail}$$

In our example, this equation would be computed as:

$$\text{Incidents} = 1000 \times 0.05 \times 0.343 \times 0.122 = 2.1 \, \text{Incidents per year}$$

This estimate from our example could then be checked against the actual number of errors detected within the department. From this estimate, we could anticipate roughly 2 errors would occur per year associated with this particular problem. If the estimate of expected incidents does not agree with what has been observed in practice, the practitioner should investigate further to uncover whether or not the model is in error or that incidents are not being properly reported. If the model is found to be in error, we first suggest that the practitioner revise her estimates of the inherent risk probabilities, since these estimates are the most difficult to observe in practice.

Input 7: Detection Controls

Detection controls are functions within a system that act to detect the fact that a problem might have occurred. Other names used for such control features include *edits, alarms, warnings, exceptions*, and so on.

As with preventive controls, we must estimate the likelihood that the design of each detective control will successfully detect each particular potential problem, should it occur. The complement of this estimate is the probability that it will fail to detect. Only one control has to function effectively to detect that an incident has happened. The overall risk that all the independent detection controls will fail with respect to a particular occurrence is the joint probability of each one of them failing. The mathematical formula for this is very similar to that described for preventive controls, namely:

$$\text{Detection risk} = (1 - \text{Probability that detection is effective}_1)$$
$$\times (1 - \text{Probability that detection is effective}_2) \times \ldots$$
$$\times (1 - \text{Probability that detection is effective}_N)$$

In addition, the anticipated implementation rate for each control must be estimated. Detection controls often are dependent on a human hearing or seeing the alarm, and this can limit their practical effectiveness. Combining the implementation rate into our previous expression, we have that the revised detection risk is given by:

$$\text{Detection risk} = (1 - (\text{Probability that detection is effective}_1 \times \text{Implementation}_1)) \times (1 - (\text{Probability that detection is} \text{ effective}_2 \times \text{Implementation}_2)) \times \ldots \times (1 - \text{Probability} \text{ that detection is effective}_N \times \text{Implementation}_N)$$

where Implementation_N denotes the probability that the Nth control has been implemented correctly.

Detection controls also can serve to measure the accuracy of the preceding forecast of actual incidents of problems. Each detected incident can be tabulated and then the summary can be compared to the calculated forecast. Where significantly different, the forecast should be reconsidered for errors in judgment or differences in circumstances.

Detection controls only detect problems. To the extent that they are effective, they still only inform us that a problem has occurred. They will not lessen the impact of the problem or remedy its consequences.

For the purposes of our example, let us suppose that three detection controls are implemented, with a probability of detection of 85, 60, and 80 percent respectively when implemented correctly. These controls have an implementation probability of 99, 90, and 95 percent respectively. Then we have that the overall detection control risk probability (that is, the probability that all our controls will fail to detect an incident) is 1.7 % (see Exhibit 8.5).

Output B: Forecast Detected Incidents

This second output provides a key monitor of both the model and the actual system. Every incident that is detected by the controls should be logged and

	A	B	C
1	Quantitative Assurance Model Template		
2	Sensitivity Factor	1.0	Problem #1
20	Prevention Controls	*Implementation*	Design Effectiveness
26	Actual Incidents=		=C18*C24
27	Actual Incidents=		2.1
28	Detection Controls		
29	Control #11	0.99	0.85
30	Control #12	0.9	0.6
31	Control #13	0.95	0.8
32	Detection Risk=		=(1-($B29*C29))*(1-($B30*C30))*(1-($B31*C31))*$B$2
33	Detection Risk=		1.7%
34	Detected Incidents=		=C26*(1-C32)
35	Detected Incidents=		2.1

EXHIBIT 8.5 Detection Control Risk

Source: © Copyright William C. Mair, 2009. All rights reserved.

monitored. Initially, this provides a checkpoint for the assessment model; once the model is found reasonably reliable, it provides an assurance that the system continues to function in the same manner. If a significant change or trend appears, it should trigger an investigation into whether some control factors have changed.

The formula for forecast detected incidents is given by:

$$\text{Forecast detected incidents} = (1 - \text{Detection risk})$$

$$\times \text{Forecast actual incidents}$$

In our example, our expected forecast of detected incidents would be equal to $(1 - 0.017) \times 2.1 = 2.1$ incidents. This accounts for substantially all the actual incidents, but not quite. Further, once they have been detected, the issue of fixing them remains.

Input 8: Correction Controls

Correction controls act once a problem has been detected, to quench its impact or remedy its consequences. This type of control can be called by a number of other names, including *mitigating, extinguishing, remedial, restorative, recovery, containment, repair, retrofit*, and so on. Detection controls are of limited value without adequate correction controls to accompany them, and correction controls cannot be used unless the specific need for their use can be detected.

Some control literature, including the original COSO, mentions only preventive and detective controls. The implication is that correction is a trivial task amounting to merely doing the job again correctly. This might have been partially accurate back when most transactions were processed on paper. Today, however, transactions are ephemeral and can vanish with a disconnected user. Adequate correction usually requires deliberate design and implementation of controls to capture all the details that might be used to diagnose and apply correction.

As with all the other types of controls, evaluation of correction controls requires an estimate of the probability that the design of each corrective control will successfully deal with each type of problem that might be detected as well as the possibility that they might not be implemented in accordance with their purpose. The likelihood that they will fail to do so is the complement of that estimate. The overall correction risk is that all the applicable correction controls will fail simultaneously. This is calculated as the joint probability of each one of them independently failing. The mathematical formula for this is, again, very similar to that described for preventive and detective controls:

$$\text{Correction risk} = \left(1 - \left(\text{Probability that correction is effective}_1 \times \text{Implementation}_1\right)\right) \times \left(1 - \left(\text{Probability that correction is effective}_2 \times \text{Implementation}_2\right)\right) \ldots \times \left(1 - \left(\text{Probability that correction is effective}_N \times \text{Implementation}_N\right)\right)$$

Returning to our example, let us suppose that we have two correction controls, with 90 and 60 percent effectiveness, and a 98 and 60 percent respective probabilities of correct implementation. Then the total correction control risk is 7.6 percent, as shown in Exhibit 8.6.

In some circumstances, more than one correction control might be required to fully correct a problem. This typically might occur when one

	A	B	C
1	Quantitative Assurance Model Template		
2	Sensitivity Factor	1.0	Problem #1
20		Implementation	Design Effectiveness
36	Correction Controls		
37	Control #21	0.98	0.9
38	Control #22	0.6	0.6
39	Control #23	0.7	
40	Correction Risk=		=(1-($B37*C37))*(1-($B38*C38))*(1-($B39*C39))*$B$2
41	Correction Risk=		7.6%

EXHIBIT 8.6 Correction Risk

Source: © Copyright William C. Mair, 2009. All rights reserved.

correction control acts to extinguish or stop an incident from producing further damage, but another correction control is still needed to reverse the damage that did occur. In those situations, we might segregate corrective controls that distinguish the further consequences of a problem from other corrective controls that remediate or reverse the consequences of the problem.

> For example, a fire extinguisher could halt a fire, but it will not repair any damage or even clean up the water it released. To recover from limited damage, a cleanup crew and carpenters are required.

To quantify this more complicated relationship, the model of correction control can be split into two independent sections.

Output C: Forecast Residual Incidents

The second major checkpoint in the assessment process comes with the calculation of expected *residual incidents*. Residual incident risk, R, is calculated as the probability of a problem occurring *in spite of prevention* controls and the likelihood that the detective and corrective controls will all fail to succeed in their functions. This relationship is shown by the following formula:

$$\text{Residual risk} = \text{Prevention risk} \times \left[\text{Detection risk} + \left((1 - \text{Detection risk})\right.\right.$$
$$\left.\left. \times \text{Correction risk}\right)\right] = 1.1\%$$

Note that within the brackets in this formula, we are calculating the joint probability that the detection control will work but that the correction control fails to work once this incident has been detected. This probability is given by $((1 - \text{Detection risk}) \times \text{Correction risk})$.

Forecast residual incidents can then be calculated by using the formula below:

$$\text{Residual incidents} = \text{Forecast Actual Incidents} \times \left[\text{Detection risk}\right.$$
$$\left. + \left((1 - \text{Detection risk}) \times \text{Correction risk}\right)\right]$$
$$= 0.2 \text{ problems that persist}$$

The actual incidence of uncorrected problems can be measured by audit tests and compared with the expected number determined by this model. If the actual and expected rates are significantly different, there is some flaw in the values or relationships in the model that must be reconsidered. This ability constitutes the third key checkpoint over the model.

Output D: Control Ratings

Together with a forecast of expected incidents, the model at this point could produce a useful management metric—a *control rating*. This rating is on a scale of 0 to 100 percent and summarizes the net control over each potential problem. Low ratings might result from general absence of applicable controls, ineffective design, or poor implementation. The summary rating can be substituted for the detailed estimates and calculations that generally would be too tedious for presentation to top management, the board of directors, or the audit committee (see Exhibit 8.7). The control rating can be calculated using the following formula:

Control Rating = 1 − (Forecast Residual Incidents/Potential
Incidents) = 99%

This model encompasses all inputs and outputs discussed through this point. An Excel-based model containing the file used to prepare this example is available for download at www.cca-advisors.com/quantitative_model.htm.

Input 9: Control Costs

Controls have a cost to install and a marginal cost to operate. Naturally, the cost of controls should not exceed the benefits they provide by reducing exposure. Too often, proposals to add particular control features are denied based on cost. The cost of an added control generally is easier to determine

	A	B	C
1	Quantitative Assurance Model Template		
2	Sensitivity Factor	1.0	Problem #1
18	Potential Incidents=	=+C5*C18	
19	Potential Incidents		17.2
20			Design Effectiveness
24	Prevention Risk=	=(1-($B21*C21))*(1-($B22*C22))*(1-($B23*C23))*$B$2	
25	Prevention Risk=		12.2%
26	Actual Incidents=	=C18*C24	
27	Actual Incidents=		2.1
32	Detection Risk=	=(1-($B29*C29))*(1-($B30*C30))*(1-($B31*C31))*$B$2	
33	Detection Risk=		1.7%
40	Correction Risk=	=(1-($B37*C37))*(1-($B38*C38))*(1-($B39*C39))*$B$2	
41	Correction Risk=		7.6%
42	Residual Risk=	=(C24*(C32+((1-C32)*C40)))	
43	Residual Risk=		1.1%
44	Residual Problems=	=(C26*(C32+((1-C32)*C40)))	
45	Residual Problems=		0.2
46	Control Rating	=1-(C44/C18)	
47	Control Rating		0.99

EXHIBIT 8.7 Residual Risk

than its benefits and thus can present a bias against control. The control model can include marginal or full absorption cost estimates for comparison to benefits. The sum of these costs can be compared to the exposure value and "what-if" scenarios.

Input 10: Consequences

The next set of relationships is those between the problems and the consequences they produce. Other names used for consequences include major *control objectives, assertions, harm, losses,* and *consequential losses.*

Consequences are defined here as the adverse effects caused by problems. The nature of the consequences will vary, depending first on whether the system is an application or an infrastructure system. The primary consequences of infrastructure problems are application problems. This key relationship provides the linkage between models of infrastructure and applications. Additionally, infrastructure systems also can have direct adverse consequences of the same types as are produced by problems in application systems. The most obvious example of this is excessive costs.

For each type of problem, we must estimate the correlation or likelihood that, if it actually occurs and remains uncorrected, it will cause any of the potential consequences. Then these relationships are multiplied by the forecast of uncorrected problems to forecast instances of consequences. When the consequences that will result from each problem are determined, they can be summed to produce an estimate for each type of consequence (see Exhibit 8.8).

	A	C
1	**Quantitative Assurance Model Template**	
2		**Problem #1**
44	Residual Problems=	=(C26*(C32+((1-C32)*C40)))
45	Residual Problems=	0.2
48	**Consequences:**	**Correlation**
49	Erroneous record keeping	0.99
50		=+C$44*C49
51	Unacceptable accounting	0.05
52		=+C$44*C51
53	Loss/destruction of assets	0.01
54		=+C$44*C53

EXHIBIT 8.8 Consequences of Residual Problems

Here, as we have only analyzed one issue within our system, we only have a single column of consequences. For this example, we have enumerated three possible consequences, "Erroneous record keeping," "Unacceptable accounting," and "Loss/destruction of assets." We have assigned a likelihood of 99 percent, 5 percent, and 1 percent to each of these consequences, calculating the forecast number of consequences beneath each probability. For instance, we anticipate 0.19 incidents, or one approximately every 5 years, associated with erroneous record keeping. This estimate was calculated by multiplying the forecast number of residual problems, 0.2 by 99 percent.

Input 11: Loss Value per Incident

Most consequences can be associated with a likely monetary value. Often a range of possible values could result in various instances, and sometimes the value is quite ambiguous. For example, a fire could range from trivial to devastating but would present a clear value of the losses after the occurrence. In contrast, damage to the organization's reputation might be quite hard to identify specifically amid the other effects of the marketplace, product development, and other factors.

Loss per incident is the most difficult and uncertain estimate in the entire model. Some incidents, by their nature, only result in errors of a fraction of the transaction value (e.g., wrong sales tax rate). Other incidents that are not detected and corrected might cause progressive damages that lie in the upper range of normal activity. Ideally, the range and likelihood of losses per incident would be expressed as a probability distribution. Usually, however, no one has enough information to construct such a function. In lieu of this, conservative estimates should be set toward the higher end of the possible range. As experience grows, detected incidents can provide a floor for estimating the consequences of those incidents that are undetected.

Output E: Exposure

Either a range or a most likely value associated with each type of consequence can be accumulated. We refer to this value as the *exposure*. Another common synonym is *annual loss exposure* (ALE).[1] Exposures are very useful for the purpose of cost/benefit decisions and considering alternate risk management strategies, such as insurance (see Exhibit 8.9).

In this example, we have estimated that the loss value per incident associated with "Erroneous record keeping" is $200 thousand per incident, $400 thousand per incident for "Unacceptable accounting," and $2 million for "Loss/destruction of assets." The total exposure associated with these consequences is just under $7 million.

	A	C	D	E	F	G
1	Quantitative Assurance Model Template					*3×3 Example*
2		Problem #1	Problem #2	Problem #3		
3	Opportunities>	1000	1000	260		
4	Units of measure>	Transactions	Transactions	Days		
46	Residual Problems =	=(C28*(C34+((1-C34)*C42)))	=(D28*(D34+((1-D34)*D42)))	=(E28*(E34+((1-E34)*E42)))		Value
47	Residual Problems =	0.2	11.5	4.9		Loss
50	Consequences:		Correlation			Loss Value per Incident
51	Erroneous record keeping	0.99	0.6	0.05		200
52		=+C$46*C51	=+D$46*D51	=+E$46*E51	=SUM(C52:E52)	
53		0.19	6.93	0.24	7.36	
54	Unaccept accounting	0.05	0.05	0.05		400
55		=+C$46*C54	=+D$46*D54	=+E$46*E54	=SUM(C55:E55)	
56		0.01	0.58	0.24	0.83	
57	Loss/Destruction of assets	0.01	0.2	0.05		2000
58		=+C$46*C57	=+D$46*D57	=+E$46*E57	=SUM(C58:E58)	
59		0.002	2.31	0.24	2.56	
60				Exposure =		=(F52*G51)+(F55*G54)+(F58*G57)
61				Exposure =		$6,915

EXHIBIT 8.9 Example of Exposure Calculations

Source: © Copyright William C. Mair, 2009. All rights reserved.

CONSTRAINTS AND LIMITATIONS   Although this approach to control assessment provides a facility to predict actual incidents, it still cannot predict everything that one would like to know.

PROBABILITY DISTRIBUTION OF CONSEQUENCES   The magnitude of the consequences is not only a function of risks and controls but also of the time that passes until those controls detect the problem and bring corrective controls to bear.

>For example, consider a fire as an illustration. At its start, a fire will smolder, giving little indication of its existence and causing little harm. Then it will break into open flame and consume fuel more rapidly. The flames then expand at an accelerating rate, raising the general temperature and transforming its environment into a raging inferno. This process can continue only as long as the fire can reach more and more fuel. As the available fuel is consumed, the fire will start to burn out. Eventually, it will return to smoldering over the area it engulfed. A graph of the destruction looks like this:

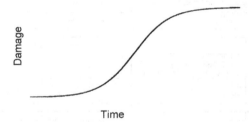

This *S*-shaped damage curve is typical of many kinds of consequences. For example, it is seen in the spread of a computer virus among vulnerable systems in a network.

Sensitive detection controls can provide warning while the problem is still in its early, limited phase. Robust correction controls can quickly extinguish the problem and remediate the minor damage. Time is of the essence, but this model does not predict the time between the trigger and the response.

Anyone Can Build A Model . . .

... but not everyone can build a model that works. Exhibit 8.10 provides a simplified example drawing together the pieces that we have discussed above. As in the exhibits in this chapter, the shaded rows show the Excel coding for each calculation, with the actual results of the calculation

	A	B	C	D	E	F	G
1	Quantitative Assurance Model Template						*3X3 Example*
2	Sensitivity Factor	1	*Problem #1*	*Problem #2*	*Problem #3*		
3	Opportunities>		1000	1000	260		
4	Units of Measure>		Transactions	Transactions	Days		
5	Inherent Risk Factors						
6	Factor #1		0.03	0.05	0.01		
7	Factor #2		0.02	0.2	0.05		
8	Inherent Risk =		=(+C6+C7)				
9	Inherent Risk=		0.05	0.25	0.06		
10	Control Environment						
11	Tone at the Top		0.3	0.2	0.1		
12	Reliability of personnel		0.3	0.1	0.4		
13	Competence of personnel		0.3	0.4	0.2		
14	Environment Risk =		={(1-C11)*(1-C12)*(1-C13)}				
15	Enviornment Risk =		3.343	0.432	0.432		
16	Preliminary Risk=		=+C8*C14				
17	Preliminary Risk=		0.017	0.108	0.026		
18	Potential Incidents =		=+C3*C16				
19	Potential Incidents		17.2	108	6.7		
20	Prevention Controls		*Implementation* Design Effectiveness				
21	Control #1	0.9	0.8	0.5	0.2		
22	Control #2	0.7	0.4	0.5			
23	Control #3	0.4	0.99	0.5			
24	Prevention Risk =		=(1-($B21*C21))*(1-($B22*C22))*(1-($B23*C23))				
25	Prevention Risk=		0.1217664	0.286	0.82		
28	Actual Incidents=		=(C18*C24)				
29	Actual Incident=		2.1	30.9	5.5		
30	Detection Controls						
31	Control #11	0.99	0.85	0.4			
32	Control #12	0.9	0.6	0.6	0.6		
33	Control #13	0.95	0.8	0.1			
34	Detection Risk=		=(1-($B31*C31))*(1-($B32*C32))*(1-($B33*C33))				
35	Detection Risk=		0.017	0.251	0.46		
36	Detected Incident=		=C28*(1-C34)			Monitor	
37	Detected Incident =		2.1	23.1	3	*Monitor*	
38	Correction Controls						
39	Control #21	0.98	0.9	0.7			
40	Control #22	0.6	0.6	0.8			
41	Control #23	0.7					
42	Correction Risk=		=(1-($B39*C39))*(1-($B40*C40))*(1-($B41*C41))				
43	Correction Risk=		0.076	0.163	0.79		
44	Residual Risk=		=(C24*(C34+((1-C34)*C42)))				
45	Residual Risk		0.011	0.107	0.727		
46	Residual Problems=		=(C28*(C34+((1-C34)*C42)))				
47	Residual Problems=		−0.21	11 5	4.9		Loss
48	Control Rating		=1-(C46/C18)				
49	Control Rating		0.99	0.89	0.27		Value
50	Consequences:		Correlation				per Occurrence
51	Erroneous record keeping		0.99	0.6	0.05		200
52			=+C$46*C51	=+D$46*D51	=+E$46*E51	=SUM (C52:E52)	
53			0.19	6.93	0.24	7.36	
54	Unaccept accounting		0.05	0.05	0.05		400
55			=+C$46*C51	=+D$46*D54	=+E$46*E54	=SUM (C55:E55)	
56			0.01	0.58	0.24	0.83	
57	Loss/destruction of assets		0.01	0.2	0.05		2000
58			=+ C$46*C57	=+ D46*D57	=+ E$46*E57	=SUM (C58:E58)	
59			0.0019	2.31	0.24	2.5553	
60					Exposure =		=(F52*G51)+(F55*G54)+(F58*G57)
61					Exposure =		$6.915

EXHIBIT 8.10 Example of a Simple Model

Source: © Copyright William C. Mair, 2009. All rights reserved.

immediately below the formula. Using this, readers should be able to set up their own risk models.

Additional rows should be inserted to accommodate all of the factors and controls applicable to the assessment, and the formulae must be revised to include all of the rows. Column C should be copied and pasted to create as many columns as needed for the potential problems under study. We provide more complete and realistic examples in later chapters regarding several types of systems and objectives.

The two real tests of any model are:

1. Can it be "proven" by back-solving recent incidents based on the conditions known to precede those incidents?
2. Can it consistently predict incidents at the rate at which they are currently observed?

Most initial models using this or any other design should not be expected to work well on the first try. Initial tests usually reveal something that was overlooked or poorly estimated. This should be no cause to abandon the model, however, but rather guidance to revise it to incorporate the omissions and better estimates.

The most common misestimates occur in overestimating the level of implementation. Controls that would be effective, if implemented, frequently can be skipped or performed in such a perfunctory manner that they really are not applied.

> For example, an approval signature on a document should be evidence that the document was checked for accuracy and considered for reasonableness. If the approving person has too little time to deal with all the documents that are presented for approval, the signature might be inscribed with scarcely a glance at the supporting information.

Note: Although the authors provide formulae and illustrative models with algorithms, they cannot accept any responsibility for the suitability of these tools for application to any specific system or situation. Readers must determine that any models they build, including the algorithms coded into those models, fit the nature of the risks, controls, and circumstances. For additional guidance, readers must study Chapter 12, The Process for Assessing Internal Control.

Precision of Results

At best, the various results predicted by this type of model are the "maximum likelihood" value along a range of probable outcomes—a probability distribution. Because estimates are made only for what is probable, actual incidents within any designated time span will approximate the predicted rates. The model does not compute the range or standard deviation of the probable results. This would be extremely desirable, but reliable input values usually are not available, and the shape of the probability distribution usually is not known. It generally is not a symmetrical bell-shaped "normal distribution." We can speculate that it is likely to be a skewed distribution shaped like one of those illustrated here:

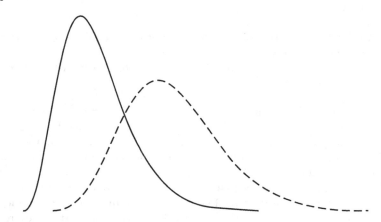

This type of frequency distribution is very common in populations of financial data. Its colloquial description is the 80/20 Rule. This means that about 80 percent of the total value is provided by about 20 percent of the sources.

For example, commonly, about 80 percent of sales are provided by about 20 percent of an organization's customers.

Of course, the 80/20 Rule is no more a rule than Murphy's Law is a law. These patterns are merely common observations and will not apply in some circumstances.

Sensitivity of Results

One of the many advantages of a quantitative model is that it can be tested for its sensitivity to its various components. The easiest way to test sensitivity to the various controls without altering the formulae in the model is to enter a zero (0) into the implementation cell for the control, then look at the effect on the residual problems and total exposure value. Inherent risk factors and environment factors do not involve implementation factors, so they must be zeroed directly to test their importance.

Another sensitivity test of control design effectiveness can be provided by creating one cell as a master sensitivity factor, then referencing that cell as a multiplier for all the risk calculations. When that cell is set to the value 2, for example, all the effectiveness calculations will be doubled and the control risks and exposure should decline. When the cell is set to 0.5, the effectiveness calculations will be halved and the control risks and exposure should increase. The effects on the forecasts of residual problems and the exposure will depend on the number of cells with nonzero values, the implementation estimates, and the estimates of consequences.

These "what-if" questions can be used to identify key controls, consider potential cost reductions, or plan alternative control approaches.

Summary

This quantitative approach to control assessment and risk management is a significant improvement over the solely qualitative approaches because its validity can be tested and demonstrated. Alternative opinions can be settled with factual observations.

The examples shown in this book are restricted in size to fit the constraints of the page format. A full-scale example is available for free download from www.cca-advisors.com. The quantitative model that we describe is an *open* model, meaning that we invite practitioners to modify it to fit their circumstances. The language we use to illustrate it is Microsoft's Excel, one of the most widely available systems in the world. Any decision to rely on the assessment produced by a model is solely the responsibility of the management of the modeled organization.

Note

1. Our definition of *exposure* is substantially identical to that of *annual loss exposure* (ALE), as used in Federal Information Processing Standards Publication 31, FIPs PUB 65, and elsewhere.

CHAPTER 9

Excel Applications

The Environment

In Chapter 8, we illustrated in detail our quantitative risk assessment model. Before we proceed to discuss other facets of the model (including interdependent systems) in subsequent chapters, we would first like to highlight common issues the reader may incur in constructing our quantitative models in Excel.

Computer applications based on the ubiquitous software package known as Excel present some of the least appreciated information risks. Modeling errors, including those found in user-made spreadsheets, are so common that there are now web sites devoted to compiling stories of such errors.[1] Errors have always existed in accountants' calculations, even before spreadsheet software was devised. Nonetheless, some practitioners confuse the neatness of today's spreadsheets with accuracy. This is not always the case.

The introduction of VisiCalc in 1979 brought accountants into the computer age in full force. Whereas previously many accountants were content with their columnar pads and 10-key adding machines, VisiCalc put their columnar worksheets onto their new personal computers and improved their efficiency. VisiCalc was a "killer application" that helped propel the personal computer boom of the 1980s.

Accountants quickly recognized this new capability. Now an accountant could develop his own computer application and not have to put up with the bureaucracy, arrogance, and delays of the IT department. Ad hoc computer applications sprang up all over the organization.

The genie is out of the bottle. No accounting department can live without Excel software, even if they found someone who still had a stock of those old green columnar pads. Excel files are so ubiquitous that most people now think of them as the current manual approach. People can create new Excel applications as readily, but more efficiently, as they used to with paper and pencil. Every trade and profession has its own jargon. The jargon of accounting naturally differs from the jargon of computing. Accountants can set up Excel applications without having to try to translate their needs into a foreign tongue, and failing. Put more simply, Excel software allows accountants to develop their own simple computer applications that fit their needs better and faster than explaining what they want to someone else.

Most accountants reuse their Excel files month after month for many years. They take the prior month's Excel file and add or replace the prior month's data with the current month's data. Each month, however, they might add or change it slightly to add another feature, function, situation, or idea. Sometimes they do not bother renaming their files and just overwrite the prior sheet, effectively destroying it. The Excel files can evolve over the months into something different and better, or worse.

Every Excel application contains embedded functions to sum columns of numbers, and multiply and divide various cells. What's more, they do these functions instantly and accurately while the values are being entered. These embedded functions provide a large productivity improvement and reduce the inherent risk of many types of arithmetic errors.

Using email, accountants can transport their Excel files to users in seconds. Associates can work on one Excel application as a group and users can incorporate the Excel files into their subsequent work. Many Excel files are never printed on paper and move through organizations electronically.

Beyond merely replacing the old columnar sheets, modern Excel software can attain dimensions never contemplated with paper. Over time, monthly data can accumulate and provide a larger picture. A single worksheet can contain tens of thousands of rows and hundreds of columns. Multiple Excel pages can form a *workbook*, which might take dozens of megabytes of storage.

Excel applications are also not restricted to accountants. Investment personnel, actuaries, engineers, and almost anyone else who works with numbers will use Excel software at least occasionally.

Advanced users also can program their own routines, known as *macros*, and add them into the Excel software. Commercial add-ins are also available for a variety of specialties.

Applications of Excel Worksheets

Excel applications are often used to support accounting and financial reporting in the following ways:

- Assemble data in the preparation of journal entries
- Directly prepare financial statements not included with general ledger software, such as changes in equity or cash flows

- Correct or adjust results of applications having limitations, constraints, or known errors
- As primary system accounting for financial areas having small quantities of data
- Analyses and "working papers" performing some control functions

More and more financial applications have direct feeds into the general ledger application system, but many application systems still produce separate reports that people must use to prepare journal entries that are then entered manually into the general ledger system. Excel files are generally used to assemble the applicable numbers taken from reports and documents to prepare and support general ledger journal entries.

No application system does everything perfectly. Requirements change and new transaction types can arise. Program maintenance changes to the application can often wait months, but accounting requirements cannot. Error reports might also require elaborate analysis to produce a correct answer. As workarounds or documentation of error correction, Excel applications are often used to adjust or recalculate the results from formal application reports.

Some small applications are maintained solely with Excel software. Excel files can hold substantial amounts of data and make complex calculations. In many ways, they constitute simple database systems. Applications such as long-term debt typically involve large numbers but small files and simple calculations. Companies often do not elect to invest in the cost of a formal application system for such needs.

Many controls involve analyses and documentation that are well suited to traditional working papers. Excel software is the modern replacement.

The purpose of this book is to enable quantification of risk and control assessments, not to provide a cookbook for control of any particular system. Therefore, the problems, risk factors, controls, and consequences used to illustrate quantitative assessment are not presumed to be comprehensive or applicable to any particular instance of a Excel file. Readers and others involved in such an assessment must identify and consider those problems, risk factors, controls, and consequences specific to the system they are assessing.

What Can Go Wrong with Excel Applications?

The error rate for Excel applications is enormous. Repeated studies have revealed errors at the rate of 80 percent or more. Part of the problem might be that Excel software gives an illusion of reliability. Any computer printout appears more authoritative than handwritten calculations. People are inclined to accept Excel reports with more confidence than those reports deserve.

Data Entry Errors

The easiest and most common error is simply miskeying a number. Nothing about this is unique to Excel; it happens with data entry in all forms, but formal application systems usually are designed to control input errors, while informal Excel applications are not.

Embedded Amounts

The cells on an Excel page can hold numeric data in various formats: as text data, formulae, advanced functions, and links to other cells. To avoid confusion and enhance the feasibility of review, these many uses should not be combined. This is especially true of variable amounts, which should not be combined with a formula unless the amount is an inherent constant for the formula.

> For example, the formula for the area of a circle is $A = \pi R^2$. The value of pi may be embedded, but the value of R should be displayed in a separate cell.

Figures Entered in Incorrect Formats

A figure entered in text format will be ignored or treated as zero by most Excel formulae and functions. Although a user is unlikely to manually enter an amount in text format by accident, he or she can easily do so using copy and paste or by transcribing data from another computer file.

Many Excel users familiar with the "Paste Special" function might be accustomed to copying and pasting "values" of cells without preserving their format. This can cause numerous issues if the "Paste Special" function pastes values in cells as text rather than numbers. However, when this is the case, Excel generally displays an error message next to the cell asking the user if he would like the cell converted to a numerical format.

Hardcoded Values

Users of spreadsheet software may hardcode values that would otherwise be calculated using formulas. Whenever this is the vase, the spreadsheet's designer should highlight these cells to remind a user that these values—unlike others in the spreadsheet—are not automatically updated. Better yet, hardcoded cells should be coded to point to reference a specific section in the spreadsheet where all hardcoded values can be entered (as opposed to entering these values in different locations throughout the spreadsheet).

Formulae Look to Wrong Cells

The easiest error to make in a Excel application is to reference a formula to an incomplete or incorrect range of cells. This error is especially easy to make if a new row or column of cells is inserted after the function was embedded.

> For example, the summation function can easily omit the first or last cell in a column of numbers that should be totaled, after inserting an additional row of cells.

> Copying and pasting cells in a spreadsheet can also errantly shift cell references if the user is not careful.

Formulas Reference Blank Cells

A cell might be appropriate but contain no data. This usually causes the calculation to treat the cell's value as zero, but it can have other consequences if it is involved in a logical test.

Appearance of Formal Development

Because most Excel applications are effectively just automated versions of traditional accountants' schedules on paper, each Excel file should be treated as an individual work product of one person. No formal system development process, with its trained staff and controls, typically produces Excel applications. They do not inherently differ from work papers prepared manually, except for making the staff more productive and providing print that is much clearer than most handwriting. Reliance cannot be put on consistency or program testing of Excel applications, because not only can they change, they usually do. A similar Excel file prepared for the next period should be viewed as another, independent product. As a rule, trust a Excel report or file about as much as you would if it was penciled on the back of an envelope.

Incomprehensible Design

The design of an Excel application usually is unique to the individual who originated it. A new employee assigned to the task will often have difficulty following the logic and properly updating a Excel file developed by a predecessor. Over time, even the creator could lose track of some of the paths and connections.

Self-Reliance

Individuals preparing Excel applications tend to excessive reliance on their own skills and do not code in functions to check or edit their own work. Although self-reliance might be a virtue as a lifestyle, it usually is not so appropriate in a business organization.

> For example, although Excel contains functions to perform data validation, few Excel preparers use them. Programmers designing formal application systems universally are trained to include such controls.

Mistaken Carryover of Data

In updating an Excel file used in a previous period, one can very easily lose track of which data has been revised and which remains from the previous version. The result can be a mixture of old and new data, which produces an incorrect result.

Logic Errors

A formula might be used incorrectly, leading to an incorrect result. This is particularly a risk when "if, then" functions are used. Another version is misapplying an advanced f_x function.

Copy-and-Paste Errors

One of the time-saving features of Excel software is the copy-and-paste function. In copying one formula cell to many cells, the copy will generally not be a literal copy but rather will advance the cell references. This is a particularly error-prone function. It can inadvertently look to or reference inappropriate cells.

Macrocode Errors

Macrocode really is computer programming code. Excel uses a language known as Visual Basic for Applications (VBA). All the logic errors that might be incorporated by a trained programmer are even more likely to be made by a Excel user untrained in programming. One study of programming error rates found a typical rate of 5 percent. Perhaps fortunately, few preparers use macros.

Misdirected Alterations

Excel files that are transferred to users in their electronic form can be altered or revised without the knowledge or agreement of the original preparer. This might be appropriate in case an error needs correction, but it could be harmful if someone accidentally or deliberately makes an inappropriate change.

Excel Controls

The following controls are commonly available to manage problems with Excel applications. We have sorted them according to their function.

Prevention Controls

TRAINING Excel skills have become a common prerequisite for hiring. Some employers administer a simple test to verify an applicant's claims, but the skill level tested might not meet the real needs of the job. At the same time, few employers provide training in good Excel practices. Excel software evolves with each new version. Commercial training is available from community education organizations, commercial trainers, and software products.

GUIDELINES AND STANDARDS Ad hoc development is a recipe for generating problems. Each company should establish standards and guidelines for user development of Excel applications. At the same time, these standards cannot be too bureaucratic or people will put up so much resistance that the standards will not be effective.

LOCK OR USE THE "TOOLS | PROTECTION" FUNCTION Excel and most other similar systems allow the preparer to lock out access to cells, pages, or the entire file. A password might be required to reopen assess. This option on the Tools menu can be used to prevent accidental or unauthorized changes to cells that hold formulas or other data that should not change with each version.

Detection Controls

REVIEW RESULTS The simplest control is for another person to review the Excel data and the reasonableness of the results, in the same manner as someone would review a similar schedule prepared with pencil and paper. At a minimum, this means looking carefully at the answers being produced and asking oneself whether they are consistent with other information on the subject.

For example, if the sales department is trumpeting higher results, accounting sales should display significant increases.

MANUALLY RECHECK SUMS AND CALCULATIONS Additional assurance can be obtained by another person manually recomputing summations and calculations in the Excel application. That person can use the same tool used for years before Excel software: a calculating machine. Obviously, this can quickly become very time consuming and might even take more time than the original preparation, so it would only be expected in simple cases.

PROGRAM TRADITIONAL BOOKKEEPING CHECKS Traditional techniques used by bookkeepers preparing paper reports can be employed in the computer versions, too, using basic Excel functions.

For example, when tables of numbers are added, the total can be checked by both totaling and cross-totaling (traditionally known as *footing* and *cross-footing*).

DISPLAY FORMULAS FOR REVIEW The normal view of an Excel file is simply the numbers entered in the cells and the numeric results of any functions. A reviewer cannot readily distinguish the numbers that were entered from the numbers that were calculated. For review purposes, the Excel page can be printed with all cells set entirely as text. This will display functions, formulas, and data.

USE THE "DATA | VALIDATION" FUNCTION Excel includes a Data Validation function to validate the entry to a cell. It can require numbers, text, or other formats and can specify sizes, ranges, and other attributes in the same manner as customarily used in formal computer programming.

USE THE "TOOLS | AUDITING" FUNCTION Excel includes some tools to assist in verifying the data cells used by a function and in tracing the source of errors. These tools can be used by the preparer or a reviewer.

INDEPENDENT EXCEL AUDIT SOFTWARE Independent software packages exist that can "audit" an entire Excel file and search for various common types of errors.

Correction Controls

ANNOTATE RESPONSIBILITY   Every Excel file and every report from that file should identify the individual who created it and the date on which it was generated. This puts employees on notice that they are personally accountable for the quality of their work and allows recipients to know who to contact with questions or corrections. Header and footer commands can be used that will indicate the current date automatically every time the Excel software is used.

REVISE EXCEL   The obvious, trivial solution to any Excel file and application error is to go back and correct the Excel file. Of course, one must know or be able to determine the origin of that Excel file, particularly if the problem is recognized in some printed report far from the source. Correcting the immediate error, however, might not reduce the risk of recurrence. When making a correction, the user should also consider adding some of the prevention and detection controls we've described.

CONVERT TO FORMAL APPLICATION   At some point, an overly elaborate Excel application should be converted to a formally designed application system. Because Excel files can have many characteristics of a database, conversion to a database application is the most common direction. A well-designed application system can readily avoid or control many of the problems typical to ad hoc Excel applications.

An Excel Model

Excel software is an immensely successful productivity tool for accountants and many others working with quantitative information. Unfortunately, Excel applications are less reliable than the person preparing them, since even very competent people can overlook errors as the Excel files evolve through generations of updates and changes.

Inasmuch as the models described throughout this book have been illustrated using Excel, readers who apply these concepts to model internal controls must be vigilant and exercise care to control the very Excel models they are using to assess control.

Exhibit 9.1 shows a sample control risk model associated with Excel applications. We will not delve into the specific risk calculations we've previously discussed; however, if further elaboration of the calculation methodology is needed, refer to Chapter 8 for more detail.

Spreadsheet	Documentation Reference	Wrong Data	Wrong Formula	Wrong Cells	Formal Appearance	Incomprehensible	Self-Reliance	Carryover Old Data	Macro Code Errors	Misdirected Alterations	Control Cost
Opportunities>		12	12	12	12	12	12	12	12	12	
Units of Measure>		Months	Months	Months	Months	Months	Months	Months	Months	Months	
Inherent Risk Factors											
Nature of use		0.05	0.05	0.1	0.4	0.2		0.2	0.2	0.2	
Independent development				0.2	0.5	0.5	0.1	0.1	0.1		
Inherent Risk=		5.0%	5.0%	10.0%	60.0%	70.0%	50.0%	30.0%	30.0%	30.0%	
Control Environment											
Tone at the top			0.1		0.1		0.3				
Reliability of personnel		0.3	0.1	0.4		0.1	0.2	0.2	0.1	0.1	
Competence of personnel		0.1	0.4	0.2	0.6	0.3	0.1	0.2	0.3	0.1	
Segregation of duties						0.1					
Environment Risk=		63.0%	48.6%	48.0%	36.0%	56.7%	50.4%	64.0%	63.0%	81.0%	
Preliminary Risk=		3.15%	2.43%	4.80%	21.60%	39.69%	25.20%	19.20%	18.90%	24.30%	
Potential Incidents=		0.378	0.2916	0.576	2.592	4.7628	3.024	2.304	2.268	2.916	
Prevention Controls (Implementation)											
Lock/protect tools	0.5			0.6	0.6	0.3		0.2		0.3	04
Training	0.05						0.4	0.7			
Prevention Risk=		100.00%	70.00%	70.00%	85.00%	98.00%	86.85%	100.00%	85.00%	80.00%	
Actual Incidents		0.4	0.2	0.4	2.2	4.7	2.6	2.3	1.9	2.3	
Detection Controls											
Review inputs	0.8	0.7						0.8			
Review results	0.95	0.3	0.6	0.6		0.7		0.3	0.5	0.5	
Recheck	0.5	0.85	0.8	0.9		0.5		0.9			
Traditional checks	0.9	0.7	0.4	0.5		0.7			0.5		
Display formulas	0.95	0.6	0.7	0.8		0.8			0.7		
Data validation	0.99	0.6									
Audit tools	0.8	0.6	0.7			0.5					
Detection Risk=		1.17%	2.88%	1.37%	100.00%	1.34%	100.00%	14.16%	9.67%	52.50%	
Detected Incidents		0.0	0.0	0.0	2.6	0.1	3.0	0.3	0.2	1.5	
Correction Controls											
Change spreadsheet	0.98	0.8	0.7	0.8		0.4		0.9	0.8	0.7	
Convert to application	0.1	0.9	0.95	0.95	0.95	0.8	0.9	0.9	0.95	0.95	
Annotation of creator	0.95	0.9	0.9	0.9	0.7		0.9	0.9			
Correction Risk=		2.85%	4.12%	2.83%	30.32%	55.94%	13.20%	1.56%	19.55%	28.42%	
Residual Risk=		3.985%	4.815%	2.918%	85.000%	55.395%	86.850%	15.494%	23.231%	52.798%	
Residual Problems=		0.02	0.01	0.02	2.20	2.64	2.63	0.36	0.53	1.54	Loss
Control Rating		0.96	0.95	0.97	0.15	0.45	0.13	0.85	0.77	0.47	Value
Consequences:											per Occur
Erroneous records		0.99	0.9	0.9	0.5	0.1	0.5	0.9	0.9	0.8	$2,000
Unacceptable accounting		0.05	0.6	0.05	0.2	0.5			0.7		400
Loss/Destruction of assets		0.01	0.05	0.05		0.1		0.01	0.05		2000
										Exposure=	$4,088

EXHIBIT 9.1 An Excel Assessment Model

Source: © Copyright William C. Mair, 2009. All rights reserved.

Summary

Defective Excel applications can cause far more damage than their appearance would threaten. Some major public financial restatements have been attributed to a simple error in some not-so-simple Excel file. At the same time, Excel files are so ubiquitous that corralling and taming them is a formidable challenge.

Excel applications are not under the effective control of the professional IT department, and users are prone to mistakes that professional IT personnel are trained to avoid. We can't turn every Excel user into a professional programmer, but we can educate the organization to apply and use controls that will dramatically reduce the risk of material misstatements and other costly errors.

Note

1. L. Pryor, "Spreadsheet Error Rates," www.louisepryor.com/showTopic.do?topic=31, accessed 2009.

CHAPTER 10

Interdependent Systems

Interdependencies

Organizational managers are reliant on numerous systems in making decisions. Information needs to be assimilated, synthesized, and distributed to managers in order for the decision-making process to take place. More importantly, a necessary condition for the decision-making process is information integrity. Even if a plethora of data is gathered, it is essential that this data be gathered and processed in a manner that preserves its integrity.

Information processing, as well as other essential processes within an organization, usually involves a large number of contributing interdependent systems. An organizational "system" is a structure that is designed to fulfill a certain goal within the organization. Systems can be viewed from a very high level or, conversely, a detailed level. The organization is itself a system; its goal is to achieve its mission statement. At a detailed level, one might deem something as menial as a copier a system: It exists to duplicate papers at the request of employees. According to our definition, departments within an organization could be effectively labeled systems if they are organized in a manner that encourages their employees to work toward a single goal. For example, within an accounts receivable department are multiple systems designed to collect payments from customers. Systems within the receivables department must track when invoices are mailed, contacts made to customers requesting payment, deficient accounts, dunning procedures, and the processing of cash to name but a few functions. Our definition of systems also includes multiple business applications, infrastructure systems that support the applications, and systems designed and operated by trusted service providers.

Viewed in the aggregate, a comprehensive risk assessment of a large department or organizational system would prove an insurmountable task. So many systems and processes would need to be evaluated with respect to their inherent, control environment, prevention, detection, and correction risk that the analysis would likely be stale by the time it were completed. The "curse of dimensionality" would undermine the risk management procedure to the point that it would become nearly useless.

In order to deal with these issues of dimensionality, we introduce within this chapter a framework for parsing a large system-wide risk assessment into a series of smaller assessments we call "interdependent systems." Interdependent systems are those systems that function together to achieve a unified, system-wide goal. Examples of these goals include collections from customers, financial reporting, internal information for management, or the actual products and services that are the reason for the enterprise's existence. Each of these goals is typically associated with one or multiple departments within an organization.

Viewed piecemeal, an assessment of these many systems can present a very confusing collection of functions, activities, and concerns to anyone who is trying to assess the overall reliability of the ultimate goal. What is the relevance of security? What is the relevance of patches to vendor software? What is the relevance of the computer language used five years ago to program an application? How essential is a particular control? The answers to these questions, and many others, must be organized to permit a comprehensive assessment. A piecemeal approach will only produce confusion, arguments, frustration, and excessive costs.

Dependence on IT Infrastructure

Information technology plays a central role in nearly every organizational system. One may find that an assessment of an IT system plays a central part in a system-wide assessment. As such, we offer some advice for those tasked with assessing such a system. Contrary to the pronouncements of COSO, the authors believe that the employment of information technology does have some fundamental and significant effects on internal control relationships. It might not be a whole other dimension to COSO's cube, but it sure does add depth to it.

One of the major effects is the migration of what formerly were application-level controls to various infrastructure IT systems. In the process of migrating, the applications become dependent on those IT infrastructure systems. Some of these systems include:

- Server computers
- Server operating system
- Database management systems
- Network (e.g., RAID)
- Email agents

- Host computers
- Host operating systems

In addition, the nature and likelihood of potential problems changes. Some of the problems are similar to earlier technologies, but others are unique to the new technology.

Of course, IT is not the only portion of the business infrastructure that can cause problems. More familiar support systems, such as telephones, heating and air conditioning, building security, and electric power, can fail or cause less obvious problems.

For example, fluctuations in the voltage of the electrical supply can cause failures of delicate electronic devices.

Many of the consequences of problems with the infrastructure are seen as problems in the dependent applications.

For example, in January 1999, an insurance company experienced repeated failures of its term life insurance issuance system. The problem appeared to be a value of –1 being entered for the date of issue. This problem should have been caught immediately by input editing controls, but the data was being recorded in spite of them. After exhaustive searching, programmers found a module that added 1 to the current year, input simply as 99, did some other calculations, and then subtracted 1 to restore the date as entered. Of course, the computer did not calculate "00" minus "1" as "99" but as –"1." The company had encountered its first Y2K bug, a year before it was expected.

Other consequences of problems with infrastructure are the sort of ultimate consequences that are seen from many problems, such as excessive costs or business interruption.

Because COSO is silent regarding any special implications of information technology, most persons responsible for assessments turn to the CobiT framework, published by the IT Governance Institute. CobiT sets out a tautology of IT control, but it does not show how to tie everything together, especially when something is deficient or lacking.

Auditors have lengthy experience assessing control over individual systems and locations. However, Sarbanes-Oxley mandates that all systems that contribute to the consolidated financial reports be assessed for the overall reliability of those reports. The enterprise risk management philosophy espoused by COSO in 2002 carries this task even further—to a comprehensive risk of the entire organization. No one has much experience in a formal and comprehensive assessment involving so many components. If experience and intuition can be sufficient to assess a single system, might they break down when applied on a large scale? This chapter describes a method for viewing and integrating the risks and controls of multiple systems.

Before delving into the interdependent systems framework, we wish to warn the reader about the nature of such assessments. The incredible interdependency of modern systems and software has made truly comprehensive knowledge of any functional information system by a single person nearly impossible. Realistic assessment of risks and consequences must draw upon a team having diverse viewpoints and knowledge. The network administrator may have scant knowledge of the applications being processed on the network, while the financial systems specialist may have limited awareness of the tricks hackers might use to penetrate sensitive files. We have seen this common situation effectively addressed by an initial team meeting which occurs prior to the start of the assessment. In this meeting, the control relationships and framework are set forth in detail so that all participants understand the evaluation framework and terminology.

Consequences Spread as Problems

The key concept we offer in this chapter is that *the consequences of problems in one support system will usually appear as the incidence of problems in dependent systems*. Their interdependent relationships can be modeled by carrying over forecast application problems from an infrastructure model to an application model and inserting them as occurrences that have bypassed inherent risk and prevention controls. We now explain the model shown in Exhibit 10.1 in detail.

Let us return to our quantitative model presented in a previous chapter for our example of a dependent system. Recall that our model requires estimation of inherent, control environment, prevention, detection, and correction risks. We present a sample model above with estimates for these risks pertaining to three problems within a given supporting system. We have labeled these problems "Problem A," "Problem B," and "Problem C." Once the model is complete, we can calculate a value for the residual problems in the supporting system.

The residual problems in the supporting system can produce some consequences in the form of dependent system problems. Exhibit 10.1 we see these as amounting to 34.09 incidents of Problem #1 and 2.64 incidents of Problem #2 in a dependent system. Some cost-related consequences also remain in the local supporting system without adding to downstream incidents. The problems that do not emerge downstream add to the incidents of similar problems that can originate at the dependent system level.

Quantitative Assurance Model Template		Supporting	System			*3 × 3 Example*	
		Problem A	Problem B	Problem C			
Sensitivity factor	1						
Opportunities>		520	520	260			
Units of measure>		Transactions	Transactions	Days			
Residual risk=		0.011	0.107	0.727			
Residual Problems=		**20**	**23**	**9.8**		Loss	
Control rating		0.99	0.89	0.27		Value	
Consequences:		**Correlation**				**Sum**	per Occurrence
Application Problem #1		0.99	0.6	0.05			
		=+C$45*C48	=+D$45*D48	=+E$45*E48	SUM(C49:E49)		
		19.8	13.8	0.49	34.09		
Application Problem #2		0.05	0.05	0.05			
		=+C$45*C51	=+D$45*D51	=+E$45*E51	SUM(C52:E52)		
		1	1.15	0.49	2.64		
Loss/Destruction of assets		0.01	0.2	0.05		$4,000	
		=+C$45*C54	=+D$45*D54	=+E$45*E54	SUM(C55:E55)		
		0.2	4.6	0.49	5.29		
					Exposure=	=(F49*G48)+(F52*G51)+(F55*G54)	
©Copyright William C. Mair, 2009. All rights reserved					Exposure=	$21,160	

Quantitative Assurance Model Template			Dependent	System		Problem #3	
			Problem #1	Problem #2			
Sensitivity factor	1						
Opportunities>			1000	1000		260	
Units of measure>			Transactions	Transactions		Days	
Inherent risk factors							
Factor #1			0.03	0.05		0.01	
Factor #2			0.02	0.2		0.05	
Inherent risk=			=(+C6+C7)	=(+D6+D7)		=(+E6+E7)	
Inherent risk=			0.05	0.25		0.06	
Control Enviornment							
Tone at the Top			0.3	0.2		0.1	
Reliability of personnel			0.3	0.1		0.4	
Competence of personnel			0.3	0.4		0.2	
Enviornment risk=			=((1-C11)*(1-C12)*(1-C13))	=((1-D11)*(1-D12)*(1-D13))		=((1-E11)*(1-E12)*(1-E13))	
Enviornment risk=			0.343	0.432		0.432	
Preliminary Risk=			=+C8*C14	=+D8*D14		=+E8*E14	
Preliminary Risk=			0.017	0.108		0.026	
Potential Incidents=			=+C3*C16	=+D3*D16		=+E3*E16	
Potential Incidents			17.2	108		6.7	
Prevention controls		Implementation	Design			Effectiveness	
Control #1		0.9	0.8	0.5		0.2	
Control #2		0.7	0.4	0.5			
Control #3		0.4	0.9	0.5			
Prevention risk=			=(1-($B21*C21))(1-($B22*C22))(1-($B23*C23))	=(1-($B21*D21))*(1-($B22*D22))*(1-($B23*D23))		=1-($B21*E21))*(1-($B22*E22))*(1-($B23*E23))	
Prevention risk=			0.217664	0.285		0.32	
Support system incidents			=Supporting!F49	=Supporting!F52		=Supporting!F55	
Support system incidents			34.09	2.64		5.29	
Actual Incidents=			=(C18*C24)+C26	=(D18*D24)+D26		=(E18*E24)+E26	
Actual Incidents=			36.2	33.5		5.5	

EXHIBIT 10.1 Linked Supporting and Dependent Systems

Source: ©Copyright William C. Mair, 2009. All rights reserved.

A dependent system usually cannot prevent a problem that has already happened in a supporting system. If the accounts payable system produces garbage, the general ledger system is going to get it. Detection controls in the general ledger system should catch the problems, and they will have to be corrected by adjustments in the short term, and by fixes to the A/P system in the long term.

Notice in Exhibit 10.1 that our dependent system problems have not changed from those illustrated in the model in Chapter 8—we are still evaluating the impact of Problems A, B, and C, but now we consider that this system is dependent on some supporting system. Notice that the units of measure for opportunities associated with each problem must be consistent from our example in Exhibit 10.1, or our units of potential incidents will not agree. However, while the opportunities must remain consistent interdependent systems, our estimates of inherent and control environment risk need not stay static. These risks may clearly differ depending on the nature of the interdependent system.

An example of two interdependent systems may include evaluations of general ledger and accounts payable system. If a problem in the accounts payable system incorrectly records the payables liability, the general ledger system may not properly record any debits or credits to the payables and expense accounts. We now discuss the notion of interdependent systems in greater depth, focusing on a key area of assessment that generally contains numerous interdependent systems: information systems.

Quantitative information systems (IS) risk assessments will often contain many assessments of interdependent systems due to the nature of data transmission.

> For example, interruption of a data transmission over a network because of a malfunction might appear to a receiving application as incomplete data for the processing of a current transaction. The application might not distinguish between incomplete data due to network problems and incomplete source data being provided from the source. Application controls might detect the missing data elements, but correction still depends on fixing the network. The application detection controls might be required to notify the network administrator.

Some consequences in IS might not extend beyond the source infrastructure system. An example of such consequences might be excessive operating costs. However, most consequences fall onto some dependent system.

Controls also can operate at various levels within a system. For example, certain data elements could be subject to specific edits and others to different edits. Some controls might apply to certain transaction types, whereas other transaction types might be subjected to different controls. Still other controls could apply broadly to many transactions or records. Accordingly, controls might need to be modeled at successive levels and then integrated to appraise overall problems and consequences. Enterprisewide database systems that share data among a variety of users and applications (such as ERP systems) can result in applications with such nebulous boundaries that the models might best be developed by transaction types or classes.

Controls at the level of data elements should be evaluated separately because many application control features are applied at this level. Such control features include most edits, reasonableness tests, and control totals. Once these are separately evaluated, the summarized risk can be in a higher-level model as a summary control or problem row.

SYSTEM AND DATA SECURITY   Security is important for protection of valuable assets and for assurance that only authorized people are entering and accessing company records. The related concern for personal privacy is often a statutory concern as well.

Although security unarguably is important, some have asked exactly how it is essential to the assessment of financial reporting to investors. The reasons are several:

- Security helps assure that the people maintaining the "books and records" are those people that are authorized to do so because of work assignment, competence, and honesty.
- Security can help identify the source of changes to the financial records that can assist in making corrections, if necessary.
- Security helps maintain segregation between incompatible duties (e.g., initiation, custody, accountability, independent control).
- Safeguarding assets is one of the objectives required by COSO 1994 and Sarbanes-Oxley.
- Most security assessments include the objective of integrity. This is also a very high-priority concern of financial reporting.

APPLICATIONS   An application supports a business function or accounting cycle, such as payroll, inventory, sales, or similar activity. A business function often uses more than one application, and integrated enterprise resource planning (ERP) systems can support multiple business functions. The general ledger system and the methods used to actually prepare the financial reports also are application systems.

TRANSACTIONS   Transactions record the financial events that constitute accounting transactions, as well as other events that might be vital to the operation of the organization. For example, although they are not recognized in the financial statements, sales orders represent a vital component of a business. The monetary values of transactions cause changes to the total value of financial balances as well as to essential administrative records.

DATA FIELDS AND ELEMENTS   Data elements are the finest details subject to financial control assessment. The current collection of data constitutes real assets or liabilities in many industries.

Hierarchy of Systems

Ultimately, all information systems control objectives are directed toward the product of the information system—that is, the *information*. Information normally is the direct product of what typically is referred to as an *application system*. Various infrastructure systems support such application systems. These are the ancillary systems and functions that develop, maintain, operate, connect, or otherwise support all or most of an organization's application systems. Therefore, the first fundamental relationship of concern in an assessment is that between infrastructure and application systems.

   Applications contain control features that are a part of and unique to the specific information application system. Application controls generally have no effect on other separate applications systems and are customarily viewed as activities or characteristics of the application being controlled. Typical application controls include edits of input data, reconciliation, and transaction trails.

   General controls are those internal controls that are part of the various infrastructure systems and that therefore have broad coverage over the applications systems they support. All the infrastructure systems provide an indirect impact on the activities and controls of all the various applications that use them.

   Typical *infrastructure controls* include security, project management, source code library software, and programmed controls in nonapplication software. However, specific infrastructure systems might apply to only one or a few applications or their components.

   For example, regardless of its size or function, every computer uses an operating system. The version and configuration of these operating systems will usually differ from machine to machine, so one might not assume that a control provided in one particular operating system installation will be found in a similar machine, even in the same department.

One of the distinctive trends during the evolution of digital computers has been the migration of functions and controls from the application level to the general infrastructure. In each new generation, more control functions have been assumed by some supporting layer of software, firmware, or hardware. For example, early application systems performed substantially all data validation, but this control function is now usually assumed by database management software.

Interrelated Control Models

Acknowledging that application systems are dependent on infrastructure systems leaves us with the questions of *how much* are they dependent, and when are the general controls enough?

We can relate control models to each other by linking the consequences of upstream models to the occurrence of problems in downstream models.

> For example, a consequence of a password being broken might be the addition of bogus employees through the data network into the payroll system. The potential for bogus employees is one of the problems we assess within the payroll application. However, bogus employees might originate by means other than breaking a password.

We must provide prevention controls to deal with other sources, but we cannot expect those controls to prevent those bogus employees already entered under the broken password. Accordingly, we link the consequences of the failed network controls after we calculate the occurrences of problems at the application level. These problems are still subject to the application's detection and correction controls. A simple example of this linkage is illustrated in Exhibit 10.2.

Security consequences can be very broad—an incident can effect many otherwise unrelated internal systems.

The consequences of problems in *systems development* will mostly be seen as errors, omissions, and inefficiencies in developed applications. Inefficient maintenance also could be a consequence of the programming language or database used. Applications purchased from or designed by third parties can be subject to these same defects. Although one might expect rigorous vendor testing, perfection is very elusive. In addition, without access to source code, a user can have a difficult time locating a source of problems.

System maintenance also subjects the affected applications with the consequences of maintenance problems. In fact, maintenance is more likely than original development to cause application problems, because it usu-

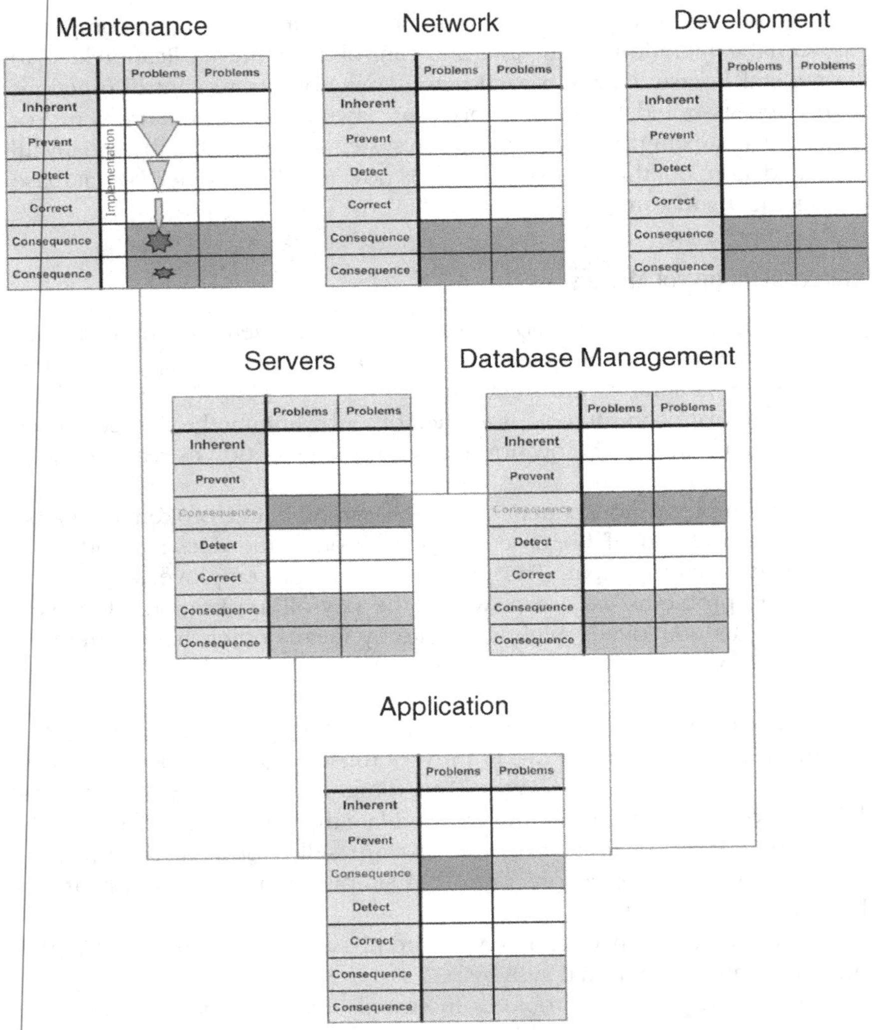

EXHIBIT 10.2 Cascading Linkage Example

Source:

ally receives less rigorous testing. From the application viewpoint, however, it might not be apparent which source caused the problem.

Maintenance by third-party software providers is often distributed as a *patch* to the software suite. Some patches are required by a change in requirements; others are in response to the discovery of a security vulnerability. Failure to install a patch can continue inappropriate processing or allow a security incident.

Another important set of related systems are the *server, database,* and *network.* Data or software can reside on either a host computer or a database, from which it is provided through a server connected via a network. Important data, including data that constitutes accounting records, can be better shared and protected in a central database. Modern computer systems can be arranged in practically infinite variations, but the component systems are limited to a few competing products.

The Internet is a transorganizational network. No single organization manages or controls it. Therefore, no user can fully rely on features that could be effectively implemented by unknown parties or be certain whether they are implemented at all. Most of them cannot be reached to test. An appropriate strategy is to assume the worst and provide compensating internal controls.

As noted previously, many important data validation controls reside in the database management system rather than in the application software that processes the data. Accordingly, the adequacy of the database controls will decide much of what problems occur with data during that application processing.

Many organizations have been surprised at the extent of their dependency on the proper functioning of third-party systems acquired from trusted providers. In addition, reliance on the Internet places a large dependence on the network components external to each organization. The complexity of evaluating modern information systems is partially driven by the migration of functions and controls from the application systems to various levels of infrastructure. Data capture can be accomplished using external sources and systems acquired from independent vendors.

Summary

Although the quantitative assessment models described in Chapter 8 have been the subject of extensive experiments and practice since the early 1980s, the concept of assembling and connecting multiple system models described in this chapter is much newer. The primary notion we introduce is that of interdependent systems. Within such systems, we demonstrate how consequences of problems in one system become incidents of problems in an interdependent system. We have also discussed the importance of interdependent systems in information technology systems with a specific emphasis on data integrity.

CHAPTER 11

Documentation

Documentation Objectives

Documentation must provide the information needed to comprehensively assess control features and test those internal control features selected as "key" to those risks that are relevant to the objectives. Documentation must identify, describe, and locate those controls. Descriptions must be sufficient for an assessor to comprehend the controls' purpose, operation, and likely effectiveness in terms of both design and implementation. For documentation to be adequate to that task, it should be predicated on some specified control framework and assessment methodology. For this reason, documentation created for purposes other than assessment will never be entirely suitable.

Some authoritative pronouncements and texts state that documentation is so important that a major lack of it should constitute a material weakness. On the other hand, other pronouncements and texts concede that adequate internal control might exist with little or no documentation. In either case, management and the external auditors will have an impossible time trying to assess internal control if nothing is documented.

Where documentation for the purpose of assessment is incomplete, management must upgrade the existing materials through interviewing knowledgeable employees, obtaining copies of audit background documentation from auditors, consolidating and summarizing detailed documentation, and generating documents tailored to the new purpose.

Documentation commonly is produced for the following purposes, other than for assessing or testing internal control:

- Systems design
- Systems maintenance
- Staff training
- Staff reference

- Error interpretation
- Error correction
- Tax compliance
- Legal compliance
- Regulatory compliance
- Financial statement support

Internal control of one kind or another can be relevant to several of these documentation objectives, but none of these objectives focuses on internal control as distinguished from other issues. One might hope, certainly, that explicit consideration of problems and controls might be an important design issue, but systems designers have yet to emphasize any special documentation of these characteristics. Efficient documentation for assessing internal control will differ from that intended for any of these other purposes.

The issue of documenting effective control is not that of documenting that particular controls are effective. The task is to determine whether all significant and relevant potential problems are addressed by controls that are sufficient to reduce the residual risks to tolerable levels. All controls will lack 100 percent effectiveness and will fail under some circumstances. In a well-controlled system, other controls will compensate for occasional lapses. This is the relationship that must be documented.

The issue is not so much whether documentation is needed; it is. Rather, the issue is what efficient documentation for assessing controls should look like.

Elements of Control Documentation

Management must document each control feature that provides significant contribution to preventing, detecting, or correcting any potential problem. For each such control, they need the following information:

- Identification of the control feature
- Location
- Accountability
- Activity subject to control
- Description
- Illustration or example
- Relationships

Identification

For reference and filing purposes, each control feature must have some unique identifier. This ID will organize and condense references and allow retrieval. In addition to an ID code, documentation often applies a short name or description as a caption or in a flowchart symbol.

Location

Each control activity has a defined location in each system. We must know where each control is in order to be able to go and find it, observe it, and test it. It might be an edit within a computer program or a manual activity within a department. To have locations, a *map* of each system is usually required. This might be an organization chart, a system flowchart, or a diagram of program modules.

Location also reveals some of the scope of the control. A control in a single branch operation will only address problems at that branch. Problems occurring before or after reaching the branch in question, or entirely at another branch, will not fall within the scope of the example control.

Accountability

Accountability is closely related to location. A control located in a computer program might dictate that a certain maintenance programmer is accountable for its proper functioning. A control location within a department might indicate that a certain person on that staff is accountable for its operation.

Activity Subject to Control

All activities within a system are either controls or activities subject to control. The activities subject to control should be the primary business functions of the system. The user department or assessor should document what activity is subject to the control that is being documented.

For example, the activity of transmitting customer purchase data from the point of sale needs to be controlled because transmissions could be lost, distorted, duplicated, or altered. Every activity is subject to potential problems. We use controls over the activity of transmitting sales data to alleviate the risks.

Typical transaction activities subject to control include these:

- Initiate
- Record
- Transmit
- Transcribe
- Store
- Calculate
- Sort

- Summarize
- Update/replace
- Merge
- Display
- Print

Many of these activities can also be applied as a part of a control. The distinguishing difference is whether the activity provides some component of business information or whether it acts to provide some assurance of the quality of that information. Activities, whether subject to control or providing control, are commonly documented using a flowchart.

Description

Describe the control in words, tables, charts, diagrams, or whatever formats suit the subject matter. Most commonly, the description is simply text written and stored in any word processing system or spreadsheet software.

Illustration or Example

Verbal descriptions should be supplemented by an illustration or an actual example. A page from a report or a screen capture image is often appropriate.

Relationships

Tables or charts can be used to document the relationship of the control to other elements. Some of the important relationships include:

- Which objective is served?
- Responsible/accountable person or department.
- Financial transaction types under its control.
- Problems and risks addressed.
- Whether the control prevents, detects, or corrects problems.
- Specific data elements subject to the control; that is, what value is edited, balanced, or reconciled?
- Where is it used by software modules, people, or business units?
- When is it used? What will trigger the activity?
- Recording media: How and where are transactions and files stored?

Common Documentation Formats

Tree Chart

A tree chart is really more like an outline of the various levels of processing. The highest level is often called a business cycle, which is then divided into

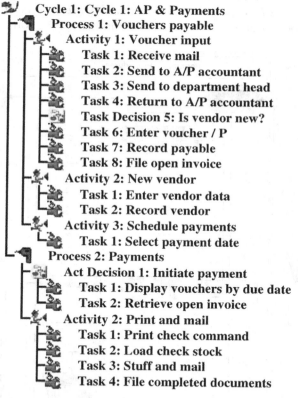

Cycle 1: Cycle 1: AP & Payments
 Process 1: Vouchers payable
  Activity 1: Voucher input
   Task 1: Receive mail
   Task 2: Send to A/P accountant
   Task 3: Send to department head
   Task 4: Return to A/P accountant
   Task Decision 5: Is vendor new?
   Task 6: Enter voucher / P
   Task 7: Record payable
   Task 8: File open invoice
  Activity 2: New vendor
   Task 1: Enter vendor data
   Task 2: Record vendor
  Activity 3: Schedule payments
   Task 1: Select payment date
 Process 2: Payments
  Act Decision 1: Initiate payment
   Task 1: Display vouchers by due date
   Task 2: Retrieve open invoice
  Activity 2: Print and mail
   Task 1: Print check command
   Task 2: Load check stock
   Task 3: Stuff and mail
   Task 4: File completed documents

EXHIBIT 11.1 Tree Chart

processes, then into activities, then into tasks. The activities and tasks are essentially the activities subject to control. An example of a tree chart is shown in Exhibit 11.1.

 Risks, controls, and other components are associated with the activities and tasks. They are viewed in other formats.

Flowcharts

Flowcharts are common and popular tools for documenting the sequence of activities in an information process. They take several formats. For manual activities, one of the most useful is known as a *swim lane* or *analytic* flowchart (see Exhibit 11.2). This type of flowchart documents the sequence of activities, recording media, decisions, and controls as well as the department or individual performing the activity. It might be prepared so as to delineate separation of duties. The origin of this format can be found in a 1966 text, *Analytical Auditing*, by Skinner and Anderson.[1]

A flowchart of an activity programmed into computer software is usually known as a *logic flowchart*. This format focuses on the functioning of program modules and instructions in a computer application.

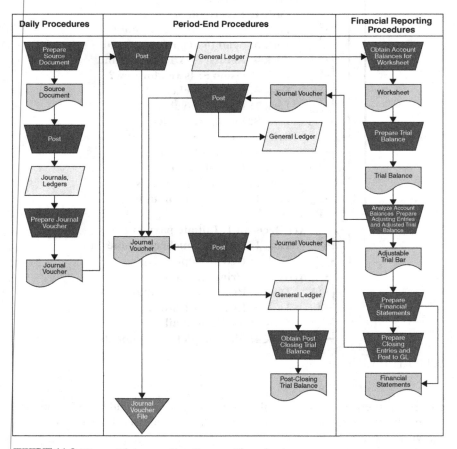

EXHIBIT 11.2 Financial Accounting Process Flowchart

Narrative Descriptions

A major portion of control documentation is usually in the form of narrative description. Word processing software is normally employed to facilitate maintenance of the documentation as changes occur in the design of the system and controls.

Edit Matrices

A flowchart is not very useful for displaying some of the important control activities within the database or application software: the data edits. A simple matrix format can be useful for this purpose, as illustrated in Exhibit 11.3.

Risk/Control Matrices

A risk/control table or matrix is often used to concentrate the important relationships between controls and problem risks. This tool is commonly used for qualitative assessments and is also a useful way to display quantitative models.

Several different formats of control matrix exist. Most of these are passive tabular listings of the risk and control attributes. One of the first of these passive matrices was published by Jerry Fitzgerald in 1978.[2] Another passive format is presented in *COSO—Monitoring*, Volume III, Appendix D (see Exhibit 11.4). The format used in our spreadsheet models in this book are active formats, where cell values act on the problems.

| Accounts payable vouchers | | | | | | | |
Data element / edit matrix	Input Present	Date Format	Date Range	Number Format	Number Range	Valid Code	Internal
Date	Y	mm/dd/yyyy	+/–30 days				
Acctg period		nn	open +1				
Vendor code						On file	
Vendor short name							Per code
G/L account	Y					On file	
Amount	Y			2 decimals	$10 million		
Discount terms						List	
Date due		mm/dd/yyyy	+ 30 days				
Date to pay	Y	mm/dd/yyyy	+ 25 days				
Approved by	Y					On file	
Budget category						On file	
Pmt check number							Generated

EXHIBIT 11.3 Accounts Payable Vouchers

Field Operations Fiscal Year 20X3 Risk Matrices

Heat Map Category	Objective Type	Domain/ Interviewee	Objective/ category	Objective	Risks	Impact		Probability	Mitigating Controls Discussed	Notes Regarding Significant Changes from Prior Year
					Maintaining qualified staff	H	5	L	1 Employee training; SOX testing, remediation and reporting to Audit Committee; Effective Audit Committee oversight over financial reporting	Rating for probability reduced from M - additional resources
					Inaccuracy of data from IT systems that impact financial reporting (i.e., staffing, inventory tracking, and financial)	H	5	L	1 Automated interface; Account reconciliations	
					Inaccurate accruals (tax reserve, worker's compensation, litigation, payables, vacation accruals)	H	5	M/L	2 SOX quarterly testing to monitor controls in place; In-house expertise, outside vendor analysis	Rating for probability reduced from M - additional resources
SEC Filing & Non-GAAP reporting	Financial/ Compliance	VP Legal & Compliance	Conduct timely and accurate SEC filing and reporting (i.e., 8-K, press releases, non-GAAP disclosures)	Lack of knowledge of required SEC reporting disclosures	M	3	L	1 Disclosure committee review; Audit Committee review; Certification process; Review by outside counsel	Rating for probability reduced from M - additional resources
8 FAS 109 Compliance										
FAS 109-FIN 48	Financial/ Compliance	CFO and VP Taxation & Compliance	Comply with FAS 109 and FIN 48	Lack of knowledge/understanding of accounting pronouncements; tax laws, and their impact on the sustainability of tax positions	H	5	M	3 More experienced, knowledgeable, tenured tax personnel; Subscription to tax research services; Use of outside tax consultants as appropriate	
					Lack of support and documentation of tax positions	H	5	M/H	4 Increased focus on documentation throughout the tax department	
9 General Accounting										
Inventory Management	Operational	Manager Inventory Management	Ensure timely and accurate payment of vendor invoices for inventory purchased for resale in the facilities	Facility not acknowledging receipt of merchandise in inventory-tracking system in a timely manner (i.e., within 24 hours of delivery)	M	3	M	3 Follow up with the facilities for items not yet received in inventory-tracking system; Proof of delivery obtained from vendor by the home office	Rating was H & H - audit results and the quantity involved versus the total population
					Improper 3-way match (wrong PO to invoice), invoice price and PO price not matching or duplicate payments	L	1	L	1 System restrictions in inventory-tracking system; Follow-up by merchandising with vendor on PO and invoice price differences; System warnings in inventory-tracking system	

EXHIBIT 11.4 Field Operations Fiscal Year 20X3 Risk Matrices

Source: © COSO. Reprinted with permission.

Documentation Tools

The most common tools used to prepare risk management and control documentation are found in Microsoft's Office Suite, particularly Word, Excel, and Visio. Word is commonly used to prepare the narrative descriptions as well as the various reports on risks and control. Excel is widely used to prepare tabular and matrix analyses, including the models we describe in this book. Visio is used for flowcharts, organization charts, and other diagrams of relationships. We cite Microsoft products because they hold such a major market share, but other vendors and products are available and compete via lower prices, more features, or easier use. Although these tools hold many advantages over paper and pencil, they still are labor intensive to prepare and maintain.

Specialized software that integrates the functions of word processing, spreadsheets, and charts is also available, with the added important benefit of easing the maintenance of the documentation as the organization and systems change. The interrelationships of the numerous processing systems and controls are elaborately intertwined. Only a relational database structure can track all the branches affected when a change in the processes or controls is made.

Case Example: Disbursements

Payments for materials and services are a financial function within every organization, so they can serve as a universal and familiar example.

Assume that a small business provides some kind of service. Most of the expenditures are for services as well, including utilities, advertising, subcontractors, and repairs. The company does not carry any inventory but rents a building and purchases equipment used to deliver the company's service. The firm has an installment loan with a local bank that is collateralized by some of the equipment it owns. The company keeps its accounting records on an accrual basis and provides the bank with quarterly unaudited financial statements (see the flowchart in Exhibit 11.5).

Purchases, accounts payable, and disbursements start with the receipt of an invoice. The company does not issue purchase orders because it has no receiving function and most of its bills recur monthly with the same vendors.

A few obligations, such as rent, recur monthly in the same amount and are not invoiced. For these, the company's accounting software is set up to make an automatic entry.

When accounting personnel receive an invoice, they record the obligation using the date they received the service or supplies. They also record the accounting category as well as the vendor, amount, and due date. Permanent information on each vendor is kept in the computer database. This includes the proper name for payment, the mailing address, a tax ID if appropriate,

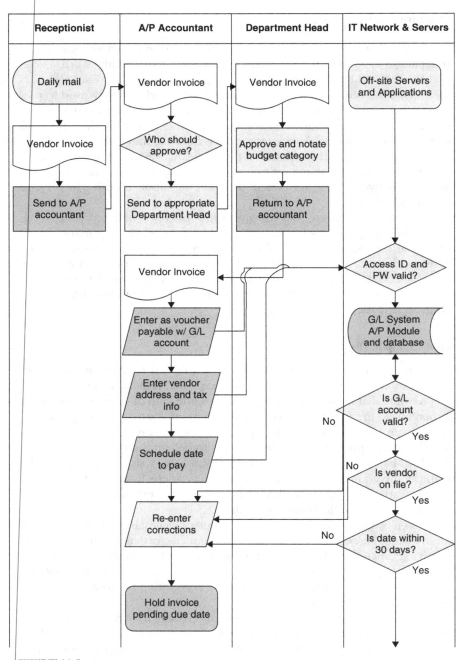

EXHIBIT 11.5 Flowchart of Disbursements System

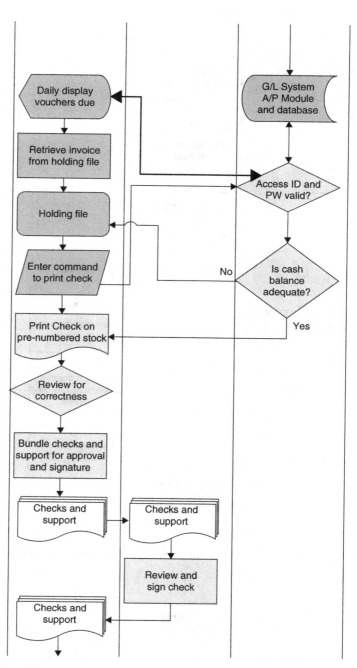

EXHIBIT 11.5 (*Continued*)

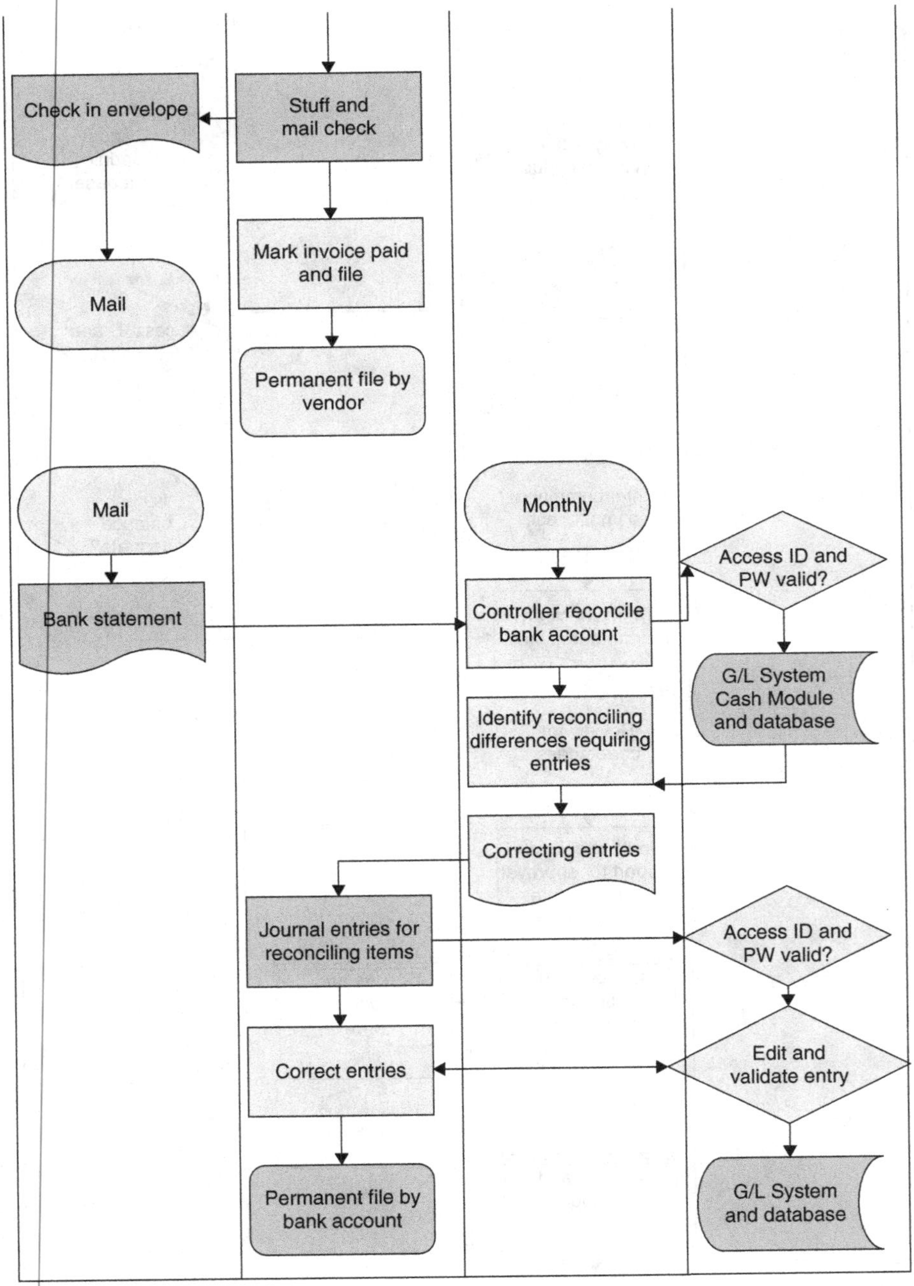

EXHIBIT 11.5 (*Continued*)

and other contact information. The accounting software is set up to remind personnel when the due date is close. Then they generate a payment and print a check.

At any time, accounting personnel can see the current total of their recorded accounts payable, but they do not know their real total liability until they receive all the invoices from the period. This might take a few weeks.

The accounting transactions are the following:

A. Record invoices payable for goods or services, including assets or expense accounts
B. Automatic payables for recurring obligations, such as a lease
C. Miscellaneous credits and adjustments to previous invoices
D. Payments of cash when payables are due

Outputs include:

1. Aged listing of accounts payable
2. Checks
3. Bank reconciliation
4. Vendor listing

What can go wrong with these transactions?

■ Invoice:

1. Never recorded
2. Recorded in duplicate
3. Wrong vendor recorded
4. Wrong accounting category recorded
5. Wrong amount recorded
6. Wrong date recorded
7. Debits not equal to credits

■ Automatic payable:

8. Wrong amount when change occurs
9. Otherwise same problems as an invoice

■ Credits and adjustments

10. Same problems as an invoice

■ Payment

11. Not recorded
12. Recorded in duplicate
13. Wrong payee/vendor
14. Wrong address for payee
15. Wrong accounting category
16. Wrong amount paid
17. Wrong date recorded
18. Wrong check number
19. Debits not equal to credits

■ Other

20. Management override
21. Access of private information by unauthorized persons
22. Fraud or theft

Potential problems can be documented in simple lists such as above, accompanied by whatever additional explanation and supporting documentation as is needed to make the issue clear. The inherent risks can accompany the problem lists and describe what factors support the estimated risk. The risk itself should be expressed as a probability.

Controls can also be documented descriptively in text, also supplemented by supporting documentation as is needed to make the control function clear.

■ When an invoice is recorded from a vendor, the system will recall the accounting category and amount from the last previous transaction. This generally reduces the risk of entering the wrong category, but it requires that the preliminary entry be changed for the correct date and amount as well as any change to the account category.
■ Automatic transactions will continue with the programmed date, amount, and category, even if the amount or other conditions change.
■ The risk of recording the wrong category for a payment is low because the system automatically applies the same debit of accounts payable and credit to the bank balance.
■ The system is designed to automatically produce debits equal to the credits in each transaction.
■ Vendors must be stored in a vendor list, which can include the address to send payment to as well as required tax reporting data. Vouchers to new vendors will be rejected until the required information is entered.
■ Only one person customarily enters all the transactions into the system; this might be the same person who installed the system and set up the programmed options.

- The system integrates the payables and disbursements records with its general ledger and financial reporting. Separate journal entries are not required to enter these transactions in the financial reports.

What internal controls exist in this environment?

- Provides programmed edits of the format of dates and amounts.
- Provides reconciliation tools for bank accounts and vendor account statements (see example).
- Checks are signed by a person other than the person who operates the system.
- An aged vendor payables listing is produced monthly in support of the balance and as a check on payment processing.

Summary

Documentation is the means for communicating the control components that are to be found in a particular system. The documentation must be sufficient to communicate all essential attributes, but concise enough to be digestible and maintainable. Very scant documentation might be considered a material weakness, but excessive documentation can defy comprehension. Documentation designed for some other purpose than assessing control will often be ill-suited for risk and control assessment. Eventually, the potential problems, risks, controls, and consequences must be tied together in a relational manner.

Notes

1. R. M. Skinner and R. J. Anderson, *Analytical Auditing: An Outline of the Flow Chart Approach to Audits,* Canada: Sir Isaac Pitman Ltd., 1966.
2. J. Fitzgerald, *Internal Controls for Computerized Systems*, San Leandro, CA: E. M. Underwood, 1978.

CHAPTER 12

The Process for Assessing Internal Control

Any assessment of internal control by external consultants brings some anxiety to staff employees responsible for the control functions. They might harbor concerns about being disciplined for failing to perform their jobs perfectly, laid off because they really do not work very much, or simply have a general fear of the unknown. Part of the consultant's task is to minimize such concerns so that candid information can be obtained.

Some of the assurances to employees from consultants might include:

- We are doing this to comply with a federal law, the Sarbanes-Oxley Act, not because of any complaints.
- We need to find any problems so that they can be fixed before the law requires public disclosure.
- No one is going to be blamed for any problems you tell us about or that we find.
- No one's job is at stake.
- We will focus on the financial statements; other issues will be noted but deferred.

Assurances to employees from management might include:

- Consultants are lending assistance because they have done it before.
- Consultants are being asked to help because everyone is already working hard at their regular jobs.

Of course, it is best if all these assurances are true.

How Does This Fit into COSO?

Most companies have a set of standard journal entries that they prepare and feed into the general ledger system. That system is used to store and summarize everything and then to produce the balance sheet and statement of operations. It almost never produces the complete set of financial statements. The statement of cash flows, the statement of changes in equity, and many of the schedules that are included in the notes usually are developed offline, possibly using the general ledger system but with other sources and adjustments.

Many modern general ledger systems are integrated with one or more application systems, and the journal entries automatically feed from the detail system into the summary. Many general ledger systems include accounts payable and check printing, invoices and accounts receivable, and other common application routines. At the extreme, an enterprise resource planning (ERP) system has almost everything integrated in one consolidated database and suite of application modules.

We have yet to see any general ledger software that can generate statements ready for public release. A "system" also must be applied to the preparation of financial reports. Many variations can occur, and the first step in assessing internal controls over financial reporting is to sort out these variations and their pieces.

Some contributing systems might be outside the company. The payroll system is the most common outside system, but outsourcing of many varieties of systems to application service providers (ASPs) is a popular alternative to in-house development and maintenance of common business functions.

The proper functioning of internal systems and their controls also relies on an infrastructure that provides computer hardware, systems acquisition and development, systems updates and changes, internal networks, and external networks. They also provide basic office functions, such as building services, building security, telephones, and email. Some of these functions might have little connection to the financial statements, but that has to be determined, not presumed.

Once this phase is done, the following steps generally should be repeated for each system that plays a significant role in the contents or preparation of financial reports. Following the assessment of each system, the controls leading to each general ledger journal entry must be tracked through the chain of processing and assessed.

System Assessment Steps

The process of assessing internal control over financial reporting involves 23 steps, including those designed to iteratively test the effectiveness of the process.

Step 1. Identify and Locate Documented Procedures and Attributes

System documentation can provide a useful starting point for control assessment. However, existing documentation usually is directed toward a different purpose than evaluating control, such as design, maintenance, operation, or reference. As a result, we should not expect that system documentation will cover all relevant details needed in a control study, and we certainly should not expect that the materials will be organized to show the control relationships in an effective manner.

Step 2. Prepare Documentation of System Features

Some of the formats that provide useful documentation of system features that require or provide controls include:

- Analytic flowcharts
- Database schema and record layouts
- Transaction and menu listings
- Examples of input forms, menus, and screen layouts
- Transaction/data element relationship matrix
- Examples of discrepancy reports
- Examples of reports used to prepare journal entries

Analytic flowcharts portray the movements of information through a system. Flowcharts gave a more complete picture before computer systems became as integrated as they are today, but flowcharts still provide useful information by indicating the participants in the system and their locations of entry.

The contents of the system *database* largely define the functions of the system. Inputs and outputs are constrained by what the database is designed to accept and store. Most database systems can readily display the organization and contents of the database. The technical name for this is *schema*.

A comprehensive list of *transactions* differentiates between processes initiated outside the system, such as a sales order, and processes initiated from within, such as depreciation expense. A complete list might be difficult to assemble, because most operating instructions are organized according to tasks and often omit what happens after. Drop-down menus can contain many of the transactions but not necessarily all. All that is required are those transactions that are eventually included in the financial statements.

> For example, purchase orders often are used to initiate the purchase of goods and materials, but GAAP does not record purchases until the goods or materials actually pass to the control of the purchaser.

As applicable, forms, screen layouts, and related menus can provide important information regarding inputs, transactions, processes, and results.

Other reports can document various types of controls, such as listings of unusual or questionable input data. Most modern systems, however, respond immediately to the submitter of questionable data, and listings might not exist.

Step 3. List Potential Problems

A comprehensive list of potential problems is the most essential item in the assessment process. At this stage, list all the potential problems that can be conceived, and plan to focus later on those that fall under Sarbanes-Oxley, financial reporting, or other objectives.

Step 4. Consider Inherent Risks in the Control Environment

The factors that influence inherent risks and the factors that support control in the particular environment are hard to separate. Inherent risk factors start with the very nature or purpose of the system. A disbursements application that records invoices and prints checks will have substantially different inherent risks than one that calculates depreciation of real estate.

The nature of the processing also has a major effect. A system using spreadsheet software on personal computers will have different levels of risk from one using commercial software and sharing a large computer network. Inherent risk factors usually add to the total inherent risk.

The control environment works the opposite way. Control environment factors can be very similar to prevention controls except that they are not susceptible to testing. The plan of organization, segregation of duties, and qualifications of the personnel are all part of the control environment that can tend to lessen risks. A very highly controlled system can still produce lots of problems if the people are incompetent. Conversely, good people can make a weak system work acceptably. Most control environment factors should never be given high effectiveness ratings (over 40 percent effectiveness). The nature of these factors generally does not deliver highly effective prevention, plus the inability to test them makes them impossible to rely on.

Segregation of duties is often used as an example of an internal control. It should provide two major benefits. First, dividing duties allows for specialization and makes it easier to attain competency at a particular task. Second, dividing incompatible duties should make it difficult for one person to abuse their position and deliberately alter records or bypass controls. Because its reliability is so difficult to test, we consider segregation of duties a factor of the control environment, not a control that can be relied on.

Step 5. Relate Control Objectives to Potential Consequences of Problems

The control objectives specified by SOX compliance refer to the COSO Framework but are not the same. The COSO 1994 Framework defines three primary objectives of internal control from the original 1992 work, plus another from a 1994 appendix. These objectives are:

- Operations
- Compliance
- Financial reporting
- Safeguard assets (added in 1994)

The SEC rules specify that financial reporting is the primary concern of SOX but also includes compliance with SOX itself and safeguarding of assets as objectives.

Only those problems that would cause material omissions or misstatements to be reported on the financial statements need to be considered beyond this step. Many serious problems only affect operations. These, in turn, might have serious effects on the numbers in the financial statements but not cause misstatements.

> For example, serious problems with the recording of sales orders would probably cause sales to decrease and might also allow inventory to deteriorate. As long as the financial statements disclose the sales really delivered and adjust inventory for actual deterioration, the problems do not harm financial reporting and are not relevant to Sarbanes-Oxley.

Furthermore, serious operating risk factors do not necessarily increase financial reporting risks.

> For example, reliance on the Internet can be viewed as increasing risk of operating disruptions. Denial-of-service attacks, attacks perpetrated with the intent of halting the firm's Internet servers, can be directed against the company from outside the company's systems, making online sales and customer communications temporarily impossible. The inability to receive sales orders for a few days could cost the company sales and lose some customers, but the process of financial reporting is not affected as long as the statements report sales that really were completed.

Step 6. Consider the Significance of Potential Consequences

The number and size of the opportunities for problems, the inherent risk level, the control environment, and the effects of the consequences of problems all combine to predict a level of potential consequences. This level can range from massive to trivial. SOX is expressly concerned with significant deficiencies and material weaknesses. Quantitative estimates will help decide the level of controls that the potential problem merits.

Many problems could affect a transaction in a way that would not affect financial reporting. These are not our priority if the mission is to render an assessment for SOX. Remember that only three data elements are usually required for a proper financial entry: date, accounting classifications, and amounts.

Step 7. Identify and Evaluate Prevention Control Activities

The first question is, what keeps this kind of problem from actually happening? The second is, how does it do it? Most employees involved in systems design or operations do not clearly distinguish what we call a control from the activities subject to control. Controls are the features of the system that prevent or detect and correct potential problems; but we do not need to spend time explaining this to personnel describing the control features. "What" and "how" questions will do quite well.

Prevention controls only keep problems from happening. Usually they cannot be relied on to be 100 percent effective. However, prevention controls can provide good value by not costing too much in the first place and by reducing the cost of corrective controls triggered by detective controls.

Although COSO speaks of control activities, not all controls involve any discernable action. Features as passive as the layout of a paper form or a computer screen can provide some control. Many other controls that are implemented by computer software only involve "activities" by momentary electric currents within the machine. These might be activities in some sense, but they are not visible to anyone, and they can vanish without a trace.

Access might be a sufficiently major issue that it should be considered separately as a special class of prevention control. Systems that are open to the Internet are good examples. Although the system might be intended to allow open access to anyone, security and privacy of the information that is entered usually is essential. Orders should be accepted from anywhere, but an Internet sales system must guard against fraudulent credit cards and protect customer credit card information from theft.

Once identified, the next question is, how effective is the control as it is designed? In a qualitative assessment, the answer might be high or medium or low. In a quantitative assessment, we follow on with the question, what or how much do you mean by that? Some people might consider 80 percent effective to be high in the particular context. Others might think of it as 95 percent. A quantitative assessment distinguishes between these.

This quantification should not require a lot of time to contemplate. The estimate that comes to mind in the first few seconds is probably close enough. Plenty of chances will be available to change an estimate after the complete model is assembled and reviewed. Instead, keep focused on the relevant data elements and potential problems as they would affect financial reporting or whatever other objectives might be at issue.

Step 8. Identify and Evaluate Detection Control Activities

The same basic question follows evaluation of prevention controls: How do you know if this kind of problem has happened in spite of efforts to prevent it? Many common accounting controls are detective in nature. These include edits, balancing, reconciliations, aging, matching of orders and receipts, and many more. Then how effective is the control as it is designed? This question is followed by, how much do you mean by that?

Step 9. Identify and Evaluate Corrective Control Activities

Next, we ask a similar question: What do you do to fix things when you know you have this kind of problem? Correction controls provide the system resources necessary to investigate and make corrections. Then again, how effective is the control as it is designed? This question is followed by, how much do you mean by that?

Correction controls can be subdivided into extinguishing, remedial, palliative, and compensating, depending on the degree to which they reduce the damage and restore the records to the state in which they should have been. Not all correction controls necessarily fix things completely or without a combination of computer and human involvement.

CONTROL IMPLEMENTATION   The controls identified so far are those designed into the information system. In reality, some might have not yet been implemented, might have been removed, or might simply be ignored.

Some controls are performed only by humans; others are entirely automated in computer software. Automated controls are usually the most dependable. Once they are programmed into a system, they will continue to function unless someone changes the program. However, not all programmed controls function automatically. Many must be triggered by a human decision.

The controls performed by humans are vulnerable to human errors and inconsistencies, but human intelligence can adapt them to unanticipated situations. A human control might be something very specific or something as general as "supervision" or "review." What does the person actually do? At best, an attentive person can detect many irregular or suspicious situations. At worst, the person might be doing nothing much at all. Even if the person is conscientious, what happens when she is out of the office for some reason?

A person might be given a list of transactions for his review and approval. To be effective, such lists must be short enough that the responsible person can have the time to study each item sufficiently to consider its validity. The list also must include sufficient detail that the review can make an informed decision whether to reject or investigate it. A thick report of thousands of items will receive a very doubtful review.

Still other controls involve a combination of computer and human involvement. The computer might identify and report a list of transactions that fall outside some defined range, and then the human reviews the list for patterns and unusual issues. The reliability of the control depends first on the computer reporting everything that it is supposed to and then on the judgment of the human to decide whether it needs further action.

> For example, a branch manager of Union Dime Savings Bank covered up embezzled funds by kiting customer check deposits. A computer report listed the manager's activities along with many other items. After the fraud was discovered, the person whose job was to review the report was asked why she didn't notice the unusual transactions. She replied that they were not unusual; they had been happening since she started in the job.

The reliability of a control involving multiple activities and media must be evaluated as one control. The estimated reliability must consider both the effectiveness and reliability of the programmed operations as well as those of the human elements.

In many cases, the system functions and controls that are described are the way things are going to be done after some further components are upgraded. This is useful information, but the system still must be assessed as it is, not as it might be some day.

In addition to the estimated effectiveness of each control over each potential problem, the assessor must estimate the level of current implementation. For automated tasks, this should not be 100 percent, because some risk always exists that some routine maintenance or operating error will interrupt the control. Perhaps some automated controls deserve a rating of 99 percent or even higher, but never 100 percent. Similarly, manual tasks must be viewed in recognition that people are absent due to sickness, vacations, and other reasons. If the control is performed by an alternate person, if at all, is it performed with the same level of skill and insight? Initialing a document to indicate that it has been reviewed and approved is evidence that the reviewer at least touched it, but it is not definitive evidence that she really exercised the control. Very few manual controls should be assigned implementation ratings much over 95 percent, even if they appear to be well implemented.

WALKTHROUGH The PCAOB and AICPA professional standards both call for a so-called "walkthrough" of the system and controls following the study of all the descriptive documentation. The purposes of this walkthrough are to:

- Help relate the abstract descriptions with the concrete reality of transactions and processing, and
- Provide some initial assurance that the descriptions are complete, realistic, and current.

"Walkthrough" is a rather archaic term that was originally coined when information processing systems were manual and could be observed as paper passed from desk to desk. A person assessing a system could literally walk through a room and follow transactions as they were processed by people. This environment is extinct, but the terminology lives on.

The obvious constraint is that most of the processing now is inside a computer network that is quite invisible to human eyes. A limited walkthrough can still be achieved by observing the activities of people using workstations to enter data and commands into various program screens. Although the benefits are limited by the electronic environment, observing whatever is visible is still a valuable learning tool. It will very often change some of the initial estimates of control effectiveness and implementation.

Step 10. Make a Preliminary Forecast and Back Test

After we have identified and substantially evaluated all the available preventive, detective, and corrective controls, we integrated them to estimate their combined effectiveness over each significant potential problem. A template of a standard control model will have the required mathematical functions already programmed, but changes might be necessary to accommodate unusual relationships. The model's software is "open" and can be changed by the user to adapt to unusual situations.

Several intermediate forecasts can be obtained from the model, including the probable number of problem occurrences actually detected by detection controls before correction. These measurements should be compared to discrepancy reports and similar information from past periods to validate the judgments and estimates incorporated into the models. This is known as *cross-validation* or *proving the model*. Initially, it usually will reveal at least some differences that must then be reconsidered and the model adjusted. If representative reports are not available for all types of problems, at least the intermediate forecasts should be review by experienced personnel for their opinions. No model should be relied on until it has been "proven" by some method or another.

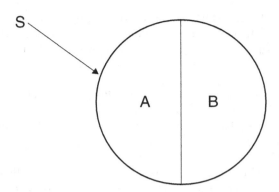

EXHIBIT 12.1 Set S Is Partitioned into Subsets A and B

To apply cross-validation, let us assume that we have a set S that contains a sample of data. Cross-validation requires that we partition S into subsets for future use. For example, say that we partition S into A and B, as shown in Exhibit 12.1. Here, S denotes the set contained within the complete outer circle, whereas A and B each comprise no overlapping portions of S. Cross-validation techniques allow us to perform our analysis on a subset of our total data (e.g., the subset A) and validate our results using a separate subset (e.g., the subset B).

Step 11. Rate the Level of Control

A byproduct of the integration of the control evaluations provides a measurement of their combined effectiveness—a control rating. This measurement also should be reviewed for reasonableness by people who are experienced with the system. Although we strongly believe that quantitative assessment is more reliable than qualitative assessment, we still agree that informed judgments must temper any conclusions.

Step 12. Recalculate Consequences and Exposure

Earlier in the assessment process, we calculated estimates of the consequences and exposure of the potential problems without any controls. Now we use the model to calculate the consequences and exposures in view of our identification and evaluation of existing controls.

Step 13. Link the Consequences of This System to Systems That Rely on It

The consequences of problems in one system might be incidents of problems in another information system. This is particularly likely if the first system falls into the category of "general" or "infrastructure" systems. It also is applicable when one or more application systems feed into the general ledger system.

The quantity of predicted problems are linked and inserted following the evaluation of prevention controls in the downstream system. By definition, problems occurring in one system already exist and therefore cannot be prevented when they are passed to another system. Instead, they must be detected and dealt with.

Step 14. Consider Costs and Benefits

The control models provide assessments with both qualitative and quantitative measures. In some cases, the qualitative nature of the consequences dictates that strong control must operate without regard to the quantitative effects on the financial statements. In other situations, the model can assist in cost/benefit analysis.

Step 15. Test Sensitivity

At any point after effectiveness estimates have been completed, the assessor may test the sensitivity of the model. The joint probability calculations may be modified to assist in this task. Simply insert an additional variable into the function representing each cell and link that variable to a single master cell. Then set the sensitivity master cell to 1. The model's results should be unchanged. However, if the sensitivity master cell is changed to 0.5, all the risk estimates will be reduced by half. If the sensitivity cell is set to 2.0, all the risk estimates will be doubled. In each scenario, the assessor can observe the effects on incidents, control rating, and exposure.

Step 16. Consider Potential Improvements

Although the assessment of internal control over financial reporting is prescribed as being the actual facts at a point in time, this does not prevent management from using the assessment models to assist them in adjusting controls in anticipation of the future. The models are very useful in "what-if" exercises that attempt to optimize the balance of controls, costs, consequences, and exposures.

Step 17. Prepare a Report

The final product of the assessment process is a report by management to the audit committee of significant discrepancies in any of the components of the overall system of internal control over financial reporting. Of course, the report must also include any material weaknesses that were found, but hopefully there will be none (see Exhibit 12.2).

Program for Assessment of Internal Controls
Over:_____System or function

	Procedure	Completed	Time
1	Identify and locate documented procedures		1 hr
2	Using existing documentation, interviews, and other available materials:		
2a	– Document reports used in developing financial entries		1
2b	– Document data elements stored by the system		1
2c	– Document inputs to the system and the actions they cause		3
2d	– Obtain approximate counts and values of annual transactions		1
3	Prepare a list of potential problems in the system		2
4	Assess inherent risk factors and their likely effects on potential problems:		1
4a	– Assess control environment factors and their likely effectiveness in reducing potential problems		1
4b	– Estimate inherent exposures, considering inherent risks and control environment for each potential problem		0.5
5	List potential consequences related to financial statement control objectives		0.1
6	For each potential problem, estimate the likelihood that its occurrence would lead to each consequence:		1
6a	– Calculate the overall likelihood of each consequence		0.1
6b	– Estimate the upper range of value of each consequence		0.5
6c	– Calculate the potential exposure of each consequence		0.1

EXHIBIT 12.2 Program for Assessment of Internal Controls

6d	– Identify those problems and consequences with material exposures to financial statement objectives		0.5
7	Identify functions and characteristics that may prevent problems:		3
7a	– Assemble documentation of control features		3
7b	– Estimate the likely effectiveness of each preventive control on each problem		1
7c	– Estimate the likely compliance with each control		1
7d	– Calculate an estimate of probable occurrences of each problem		0.1
7e	– If available, compare this estimate with known problem rates		1
8	Identify functions and characteristics that may detect problems:		3
8a	– Estimate the likely effectiveness of each detection control on each problem		1
8b	– Estimate the likely compliance with each detection control		1
8c	– Calculate an estimate of probable detected occurrences of each problem		0.1
8d	– If available, compare this estimate with known problem rates		1
9	Identify functions and characteristics that may correct problems:		3
9a	– Estimate the likely effectiveness of each correction control on each problem		1
9b	– Estimate the likely compliance with each correction control		1
9c	– Calculate an estimate of probable uncorrected occurrences of each problem		0.1
10	If available, compare this estimate with known problem rates		1

EXHIBIT 12.2 *(Continued)*

	Procedure	Completed	Time
11	Calculate a rating of the combined controls over each problem		0.1
12	Recalculate probable consequences and exposures based on estimate of probable uncorrected occurrences of problems		0.1
13	Link probable consequences to downstream systems and functions		1
14	Determine whether cost/benefit analysis is appropriate based on the nature of the consequences and exposures:		0.1
14a	– If cost/benefit analysis is appropriate, then obtain or estimate actual operating costs of each control		2
14b	– Calculate overall control costs based on estimated occurrences of control uses.		0.5
15	Compare costs and exposure values, considering "what-if" controls were added, deleted, changed, compliance improved, etc.		2
16	Prepare a memorandum of conclusions and recommendations		1

Reviewed and approved by_____ Date: _____

VERIFICATION BY TESTING   SOX and SEC rules require that assessments of the design of internal controls be further supported by evidence that the controls actually operate effectively. This point relates primarily to the question of actual compliance with the controls, but it also might indicate differences between expected and actual effectiveness of the control design.

Step 18. Selection of Key Controls for Testing

Not all controls identified in the assessment need to be tested—only enough of them to verify that sufficient controls are effective to reduce the exposures to unacceptable accounting and other control objectives to an immaterial level. The issue driving compliance with SOX is possible existence of material weaknesses, either individually or as an aggregation of significant discrepancies. Testing need not prove that internal control is actually as effective as management intends it. Operating objectives often require a higher level of control than do financial objectives.

We also find that some potential problems are over-controlled. This might arise from some intuitive design in response to some serious concern, or it might evolve over changes in management or the environment. For example, custody of cash is usually a serious control concern. Controls over cash custody often exceed what is essential for either financial reporting or safeguarding assets, or it could involve more cost than their likely benefits.

Key controls are those control features that will provide the minimum assurance to comply with SOX. Using the model, one can "turn off" controls by setting their implementation rates to 0, then turn them back on individually until the resulting exposure drops below a material level. Key controls need not all be highly effective, but controls with low inherent effectiveness will usually not be key controls.

Key controls often will be detection controls because such controls are inherently redundant with prevention controls. Prevention controls are more desirable from a design and operating viewpoint because generally it is better to do things right the first time than to have to be constantly fixing problems that have been detected. However, the effective operation of detection controls will also indicate whether associated prevention controls are effective. Reliance on detection controls also necessitates some reliance on their associated correction controls. When a control detects a problem, is the response to investigate and initiate corrective actions prompt and effective?

Accordingly, start the identification of key controls by zeroing the implementation of all the prevention controls. This should not be taken to imply that the system would be better or adequate without the prevention controls. If they did not exist, the quantity of problems detected and requiring correction usually would be very large and correction would be very expensive.

Next, zero the implementation for all the detection controls that have moderate to low effectiveness. This generally would be those in the range of 60 percent design effectiveness or less. Also zero all controls that already have low implementation. This typically would be 70 percent implementation or less.

Correction controls require greater care in switching off because the way that they act varies more than with prevention or detection controls. Some correction controls halt the progress of problems but do nothing to remediate the damage that did occur. Other correction controls do little to halt the spread of damage but are essential to remediation. A detailed transaction log would fall into this second category. In any event, carefully zero the implementation of those correction controls that appear to be least essential.

Now look at the model's estimate of total exposure. If it is still less than the amount selected as material, try zeroing additional detection controls one by one until the exposure approaches materiality. The controls with implementation still not set to zero are the initial selection for key controls.

Conversely, if the exposure exceeds materiality, try switching some of the more effective controls back on until the exposure drops back below a material amount. These can include prevention and correction controls as well as detection controls.

Finally, from this selection, consider whether any controls present major cost or effort to test. Keep in mind that the tests can be statistical samples if the population for testing is suitable. If any of the controls would present significant trouble to test, switch their implementation to zero and restore some other controls to their estimated implementation and consider whether they might be more practical to test.

Step 19. Derivations of the Models

The control and risk models that we present here have their complete Excel code open to view and change. When might changes be appropriate?

In the course of our presentations in this book, we have noted a few situations in which the structure and formulae in the illustrative models might be changed. These situations include the following:

- When access controls are so important that the section of prevention controls might be split into one section for access and another section for other prevention controls after access has been attained
- When corrective activities might require one set of controls to halt the "progress" of consequences while another set of controls might reverse and remediate the consequences that happened before damage was halted

We are sure that users will encounter other situations in which the models illustrated in this book are not well suited to the task and other innovative changes would provide more reliable results. Readers should not only feel free to make such changes, they are obligated to do so if their preliminary model does not treat the relevant factions in a suitable manner.

Step 20. Testing Procedures

Compliance with controls often can be determined by statistical attribute samples of transactions. This is a standard audit technique generally known as *compliance testing*, or *tests of transactions*. Sample sizes can often be quite limited and still provide adequately reliable statistical estimates. Compliance rates of more than 95 percent can often be supported by samples of only a couple of dozen randomly selected transactions. If the importance of the control requires much higher compliance rates, the sample size can grow quite large.

Tests can take either of two primary forms. First, the test might examine documentation prepared in its execution or follow-up. This approach is often appropriate to verify controls exercised by people, such as reconciliation.

Alternatively, the test might reperform the function of a control and compare to see whether the results agree. This approach is particularly useful when the operation of a control feature cannot be observed because it is embedded in a computer programmed routine. Test data can be submitted, but care must be exercised to avoid polluting legitimate files. When the test also is accomplished using a computer program, the test is called *parallel simulation*.[1]

Testing techniques can be a much larger discussion. A college course in auditing requires many weeks of study of a thick textbook. The primary point in this discussion of the assessment process is that so-called conversational auditing is not sufficiently reliable for compliance with SOX. Reliable audit tests are required.

Step 21. Reassessment Using Tested Results

This, essentially, is a repeat of Step 12, followed by repeating Steps 13 through 16 as necessary. The conclusion is a report by management to the audit committee.

Once all these procedures are completed, the system and controls should have been fully documented, tested, and assessed. This does not mean that the opinion on the adequacy of internal control is what was desired.

What remains is to improve the system to:

A. Remediate any problems that were found to be significant and not corrected by the internal controls.
B. Redesign any aspects of the system that exceed an acceptable level of risk.
C. Redesign any aspects of the system in which controls are excessive for all objectives.

Some remediation and redesign should be expected following any assessment. No system is ever perfect, and changing conditions will create imperfections even if none existed before.

Step 22. Interpreting Model Results

Proper interpretation of valid model results is a bit more complex than it appears at first glance. The quantitative model produces six primary results:

1. Expected actual incidents of a problem
2. Detected incidents of a problem
3. Expected residual incidents of a problem
4. Control rating
5. Expected consequences
6. Exposure

First, remember that each of these results is a risk probability. Within any particular time span, random fluctuations could cause the actual occurrences to be significantly different from predictions. The more numerous the occurrences, the more likely that they will trend to the mean probability and approximate the model's forecast. Conversely, the fewer the occurrences, the more effect randomness might have during a particular time.

Second, the model predicts based on conditions at a point in time. These conditions can and will change, so the model will become less precise as time progresses. The model should be updated for known changes in conditions every time it is used, which generally will be for each quarterly report.

Third, the interpretation of the dollar effect of incidents really depends as much on which problems occur as on which consequence is affected. Some problems, by their nature, will have only fractional effects on a transaction; other types of problems can affect multiple transactions with each incident.

> For example, an error in a ZIP code input might cause the application of an incorrect sales tax rate, whereas a breach of access security might expose hundreds of thousands of customers to fraudulent transactions on their accounts.

Next, each of the prediction outputs is influenced by several input factors. We rarely are able to obtain precise data on the actual contribution by each individual factor, so we usually only see the result of the combined factor contributions. This can leave open questions. Is a difference between forecast and observed incidents due to random variations, too much optimism with inherent risk factors, too much credit to control environment factors, too much credit to the design of the controls, or what? Although long-term experience with modeling a system might eventually provide clues to these questions, we might never obtain conclusive evidence of which factor contributes exactly now much.

On the other hand, are these uncertainties any worse than the uncertainty left by an intuitive or a formal qualitative approach? The professional standards for CPAs repeatedly note that professional judgment must be applied to these assessments. At times, "professional judgment" seems to be a euphemism for intuition. At worst, the quantitative approach opens up that judgment to view its detailed assumptions and considerations. At best, it allows collaboration by several professional and subject-matter experts to reach clearly reasoned group judgments.

Step 23. Remediation and Improvement

One of the common interpretations of results is that the organization needs to or can do better. If material weaknesses are found, the primary immediate task is to remediate the consequences as well as redesign the controls to attain a satisfactory level of control.

Remediation can be an extremely time- and money-consuming project. Some large companies have spent tens of millions of dollars and years of time to restate prior years' financial statements and to reengineer their systems. In the meantime, they have been hindered from obtaining additional capital and even been delisted from stock exchanges. Of course, investors file civil suits for securities fraud and the like.

System improvements are somewhat more pleasant but also can be quite expensive. Many companies have concluded that their "legacy" computer systems are beyond repair and have taken on sizable replacement projects.

Summary

The purpose of this book is to enable quantification of risk and control assessments, not to provide a cookbook for control of any particular system. Therefore, the problems, risk factors, controls, and consequences used to illustrate quantitative assessment are not presumed to be comprehensive or applicable to any particular instance of an information system. The reader and others involved in such an assessment must identify and consider those problems, risk factors, controls, and consequences specific to the system they are assessing.

Note

1. W. C. Mair, "New Techniques in Computer Program Verification," (Tempo, Touche Ross & Co., 1971); W. C. Mair, "Parallel Simulation: A Technique for Effective Verification of Computer Programs," EDPACS, Automation Training Center, Inc., 1975; W.C. Mair, D.R. Wood, K.W. Davis, *Computer Control & Audit*, (Orlando, FL: The Institute of Internal Auditors, 1976).

CHAPTER 13

Monitoring Internal Controls

S ection 404 of the Sarbanes-Oxley Act (SOX) mandates quarterly management assessments of a company's internal controls over financial reporting. The rules promulgated in July 2003 by the Securities and Exchange Commission (SEC) further endorse portions of the Internal Control Framework published in 1994 by the Committee of Sponsoring Organizations of the Treadway Commission (COSO). One of the essential elements in that framework is the function of monitoring. COSO released *Guidance on Monitoring Internal Control Systems* in January 2009. This chapter supplements that guidance. It considers the implementation of monitoring procedures and ways in which the monitoring function might be assessed based on quantitative modeling.

COSO Monitoring Guidance

COSO's *Guidance on Monitoring Internal Control Systems* (COSO—Monitoring) interprets the original COSO Framework and does not change or add anything to that framework. Its publication was, in part, a response to the many complaints by public companies regarding the cost and resources they were expending to comply with SOX. Another reason is that COSO also perceives monitoring as an important method to enable small companies to apply the COSO Framework at reasonable cost. COSO concluded that these companies' problem was, in part, identification and testing of excessive detailed key controls, the effectiveness of which could be more efficiently verified by leveraging monitoring procedures. Indeed, the role of monitoring is, in the authors' view, the most significant contribution of the COSO Framework.

COSO—Monitoring consists of three volumes that provide:

1. Core concepts
2. Detailed applications of the concepts
3. Case examples of the concepts

Unlike the COSO Framework, the *Monitoring* publication focuses on the financial reporting objective. It does, however, provide some useful examples of monitoring for the other objectives.

COSO—Monitoring addresses what can go wrong with systems of internal control and recommends either ongoing or separate evaluations of controls to promptly identify when control over significant risks is failing at an unacceptable level, when risks have changed and rendered the controls ineffective, or when communication and followup is unsatisfactory. COSO—Monitoring further describes numerous examples of monitoring controls and techniques that reinforce each of the five primary control components. It does not present these examples as preferred or "best practices" but simply as examples illustrating recommendations.

The term *key control* is not found in the original COSO Framework nor in the PCAOB or AICPA pronouncements. COSO now, in its *Monitoring* publication, recognizes the term in recognition of its wide popular use.

COSO is fairly consistent in stating that "controls prevent or detect." We prefer to say that "controls prevent or detect and correct." COSO—Monitoring slips a couple of times and includes the word *correct* as one of the functions of control (Vol. II, para. 60). COSO—Monitoring addresses the "impact of a control's failure." We do not view a control failure as *causing* anything. Only the occurrence of problems causes any harmful impact. If a control is badly designed or not properly implemented, no impact or consequences automatically occur. A harmful impact will only occur if something also happens that it should have controlled.

We strongly recommend that readers of this book also study the complete text of COSO—Monitoring.[1]

In essence, monitoring is a way of saying that management should make sure that what they tell people to do actually is done. In the Army they say, "What gets done is what gets inspected." More specifically, when management tells people to follow certain control procedures when they handle information that is needed to prepare financial statements, they must follow through and make sure that this happens. SOX only addresses financial statements issued to the public, but obviously, the idea has broader merit and objectives.

Because management is required to report their assessment quarterly and a full assessment of all material systems involves a formidable effort, management will prefer to rely on some extension of their monitoring of internal controls to ascertain that their previous assessment of internal controls is or is not still accurate.

The way that management tells people to do things depends on the size and complexity of a company. A company with few employees, all physically working in one location, might be told what to do orally by the boss walking into their offices or cubicles.

Most public companies have outgrown this alternative and tell people what to do by publishing written policies, procedures, guidelines, and instructions and by conducting training. Modern technology might allow distribution of these communications via an internal computer network or the Internet. Rather than publishing materials on paper, they might distribute DVDs, webcasts, or online file servers. The methods can vary according to the availability of the various technologies and their cost.

Even without communication from the top, competent employees often know much of what needs to be done. A competent accountant should not have to be told to reconcile the bank account. A competent systems designer should not have to be told to incorporate edits of data formats into a computer program. A competent controller should not have to be told to read recent accounting pronouncements. Adequate controls can exist even without specific direction from the top.

Recognizing that possibility, we also must recognize that specific management direction should produce a higher assurance that these things really do get done. The accountant might think that someone else is reconciling the bank account; the systems designer might assume that the programmer will include appropriate edits; or the controller might leave new accounting pronouncements to the CPA firm. Management can avoid or resolve these problems by giving direction and monitoring activities.

Monitoring is the control over controls. It sees that appropriate control functions really function and that they remain appropriate to the circumstances. If we can agree that we want or need to have this monitoring, what could go wrong?

Potential Consequences

The focus of SOX is on financial reporting and associated investor protection. The SEC, in its SOX implementation rules, cites the control objectives of the COSO Framework but reduces those objectives to financial reporting, compliance with Sarbanes-Oxley, and safeguarding assets. The COSO objectives of effectiveness and efficiency of a company's operations and a company's compliance with all applicable laws and regulations are otherwise excluded from concern. Although these financial reporting objectives are generally phrased in positive terms, the adverse consequences that correlate to them include:

- Erroneous record keeping
- Unacceptable accounting
- Loss or destruction of assets, especially due to internal fraud
- Sanctions for violations of Sarbanes-Oxley

The viewpoint for these consequences is directly the reporting company but indirectly the effects on investors and corporate executives. A material adjustment decreasing net income by, say, 5 percent, might amount to only $1 million, but it might trigger a decrease in the total market capitalization of a $20 million loss to the shareholders. In addition, if the chief financial officer were accused of securities fraud through deliberate accounting misstatements, that CFO could be charged with violations carrying up to 25 years in prison and so cast doubts in the securities market on all the company's past financial reports.

The Control Environment

The "tone at the top" sets the organization's attitudes toward internal controls as well as everything else. Actions speak far louder than words. Everyone in the organization observes and interprets the boss's facial expressions, casual comments, and body language. Leaders must always be conscious of this fact and be careful to communicate only what they intend.

Much of the perception of tone within an organization is defined by what happens when a policy is violated. If top management knows of the violation and does nothing, the message is that the policy is not important and everyone is free to ignore it. If top management reacts in some extreme manner, especially if it is perceived as excessive or disproportionate punishment, the tone might be set that discourages innovation or risk taking. If punishment is directed at the messenger rather than the true source of the problem, top management should not expect to receive candid information in the future.

> For example, a CEO was known internally as "the flamethrower." He was totally unreceptive to any news that anything was not happening the way he wanted it. He would react with verbal abuse and demote managers for any failure. Of course, everyone quickly learned to leave the bad news to someone else, and the company was close to bankruptcy when the board finally replaced him.

Time and Resource Constraints

Every situation can only fit within the constraints of time and resources. Although the quality of financial reporting is seriously important to investors, not every company will be able to do a perfect job all the time. One of the inherent limitations of "reasonable assurance" is that perfection is impossible and not all risks can be eliminated. What is "reasonable" in one company might be beyond the resources of another. In addition, though a company might design its systems to be highly reliable, installing those designs takes time.

Reliability and Competence of Personnel

Good people can make almost any system work adequately, and poor ones can make a mess out of the best-designed system. A new computer system might help people do their jobs more easily and reduce costs, but computers never really solve problems.

Personnel Turnover

A corollary to having good people is keeping them. High turnover or the loss of an essential person can seriously disrupt internal control.

Systems Changes

Although an automated system cannot provide reliable internal control by itself, one can generate enough of a mess to overwhelm the people trying to make it work. The period immediately following significant systems changes is especially dangerous. Tests during systems development can rarely anticipate the entire breadth of challenges presented to the system in operation. Everyone should expect that some things will be found that do not operate the way they should in a new system—including some of the controls.

Segregation of Duties

Segregation or separation of duties is traditionally regarded as an internal control. We prefer to view it as an element of the control environment because it really cannot be tested or relied on to function reliably. Segregation of duties might exist only on an organization chart, whereas the real people share tasks or leave their work open to anyone with access. They also might conspire or agree to tacit or overt violations of policies or procedures. Segregation of duties, including independence of controls from the subject of control, can be proven a weakness if it does not exist, but it is very difficult to prove that it does exist.

Management should establish or continue their policies of segregating and separating duties. The policies have value. However, one should not automatically assume that this or any control policy is consistently followed or is fully effective.

Potential Monitoring Problems

Problems in this context are anything that could cause one of the consequences described previously. They especially include anything that could cause a previous control assessment to change for the worse.

Out-of-System Transactions

Some accounting transactions and events occur outside any of the established recording systems. This includes acquisitions of other businesses, distribution agreements, special sales or purchase agreements, and many other contracts. These events bypass the usual systems because of especially large size, changes from normal terms, and high-level policy changes. They carry a high risk of inappropriate accounting because the accountants might not be informed of the event or of all its significant details. The accountants need to be informed of all details to determine which are significant to the proper accounting treatment. Other people should not filter this information first.

> For example, a new lease contract was negotiated, but at the last minute it was changed to a longer period than in the original draft. The accountants were given a copy of the initial terms but not of the late change. The change made the difference between treating the lease as an operating lease or recognizing it as a capital lease.

The transactions most vulnerable to being overlooked by accountants usually involve no immediate exchange of cash. Transactions involving cash are much harder for accountants to miss, because they normally keep a close watch on bank activity. Awareness of the cash portions of the transaction, however, still risks inappropriate accounting if the accountants are not also aware of all the other details.

Sarbanes-Oxley specifically recognizes the potential risks of this problem. It requires assessment of the internal controls over transactions that do not fit within the established information systems.

Deterioration in Control Compliance

The simplest failure to control a problem is the failure of someone to perform a control activity. They might not realize they are supposed to perform some action, think someone else is doing it, or just not find the time to do it.

If they did it before, why would they stop doing it? The reason might relate to personal distractions, health, anger, or any of the things to which humans are prone.

> For example, a bank reconciliation might not be completed because the bank statement is being sent by the bank to a person who is on sick leave.

A more complex issue exists when the control activity is to be done by a computer system. Computers usually are quite reliable, but the computer might report no exception if no one set up a new bank account on the system. Changes to the program code during some maintenance could also disrupt a control function that had been operating properly.

Detection without Correction

Detection controls might be operating properly, but the related corrective activities are not.

> For example, the responsible accountant might complete all bank reconciliations and identify bank transactions not on the books but fail to follow through and actually record those unrecorded transactions in the general ledger system.

Implementation Only When Inspection Is Anticipated

In another form of noncompliance, the responsible staff might be negligent in their duties but make special effort to fulfill those duties when a visit from the internal auditors is announced. If the auditors' tests are too predictable, they might test proper functioning of the control, which is then suspended immediately after their departure.

> For example, delinquent bank reconciliations might be completed immediately prior to arrival of the auditors, complete with recording of bank transactions out of their proper accounting period.

Forged or False Documentation of Implementation

An employee could report implementation of controls but lie or falsify his report. This might be deliberate or due to a misunderstanding of what is involved in the proper completion of the control procedure. Routine audit procedures are not completely reliable in detecting false documentation and might have rendered a better assessment than justified.

> For example, an accounting clerk might sign off that he completed all bank reconciliations but honestly not realize that completion means he must also deliver adjusting entries to the general ledger accountant.

Change in the Nature of Consequences

Even when prescribed controls are scrupulously performed, they can become inadequate or ineffective because of changes in the potential consequences of problems. Very commonly, this happens because of some change in outside requirements or regulations.

> For example, documentation of the monitoring of controls might have been sufficient for internal purposes but is no longer sufficient to comply with the requirements of Sarbanes-Oxley.

Change in the Nature of Potential Problems

Changes in potential risks commonly occur because of changes in the technology or methods used in a process. Security over access becomes a larger issue when technology gives outside parties direct access to company records.

> For example, a sales system is changed from having internal sales personnel provide address changes to allowing customers to update their own address information over the Internet. Whole new problems of privacy and bogus transactions arise.

Changes in Inherent Risks

Inherent risks also are changed by changes in the technology applied or the methods used. A new computer system will present new problems when it stores new information never acquired before or it gives access to a new group of users.

> For example, a system used for recording sales taken over an 800 number by trained and experienced clerks will encounter new problems when the company allows sales orders to be entered directly by customers over the World Wide Web.

Changes in Volume or Value of the Opportunities for Problems

Small systems that handle immaterial levels of transactions or assets might tolerate mediocre controls because the benefits of improvements do not justify their costs. When the traffic through a system grows, however, this balance will change and problems that were minor in size could become major.

For example, a Y2K problem in a computer system rendered a company temporarily unable to deliver one of its products. The product was minor to the business at the time, and manual processing was able to serve in replacement until the cause was located and the system was corrected. The next year, the sales of the product increased by tenfold, and the manual "workaround" would not have been sufficient.

Disregard of Problems by Supervisors

Actions speak louder than words. Everyone knows this and acts accordingly. If supervisors or managers communicate by either words or actions that they really do not care whether certain controls are applied, many employees will respond to meet their expectations. Supervisors and managers must understand and be convinced that important controls really are important and that part of their job is to see that those controls are carried out.

Fraud

Much of SOX is intended to prevent or deter the kinds of fraud allegedly perpetrated in several major business failures. Criminal fraud requires trust, intent, deceit, and financial harm. Unfortunately, intent can appear from unintentional acts, and press coverage can lead to financial harm without real removal of funds. As with independence, management must look at their actions and words from a detached viewpoint.

Unfortunately, real fraud can happen at any level. Controls must be robust enough to prevent or detect the kinds of problems that might be intentional. SOX requires that potential whistleblowers be given the opportunity to make confidential reports and criminalizes any actions to retaliate against an employee who bypasses internal reporting protocols.

Other Problems

These problems each cause a potential consequence regarding the primary control objective of financial reporting to the public investors. Of course, other problems might occur that lead to other consequences.

Although these potential problems are typical to many organizations, each organization will have some unique characteristics that either exclude some typical problems or add some atypical ones. The assessment of internal control must, therefore, inquire about the potential for these and other problems and assess the inherent risk of each based on the inherent factors as well as the control environment.

Controls Over Controls to Assure Effective Monitoring

Many of the activities discussed here will help prevent or detect and correct the problems just discussed. Although this is the primary objective, note also that compliance with SOX necessitates documentation of the operation of these controls to enable audit testing.

Financial Involvement in Business Activities

The CFO must be actively involved in all business activities to recognize those with new or different accounting implications. This involvement should include a specific concern for addressing situations that do not fit within the routine information systems. In practice, this might be accomplished by membership on an executive committee that meets regularly and frequently and that openly discusses all pending deals, contracts, transactions, and so on.

> For example, a CEO made a deal to sell a small Spanish subsidiary for its local accounting net worth, which he believed was approximately $25 million. He overlooked the fact that the direct parent of the subsidiary was actually incorporated in Switzerland, which arguably invented conservative accounting. Under Swiss accounting, profits of a subsidiary were ignored on the parent's books, whereas losses were recognized. On the Swiss books, the Spanish subsidiary had a net worth of less than $2 thousand.

If the CFO is primarily expert in financial specialties other than accounting and controls, the chief accounting officer, chief internal auditor, chief legal officer, or other experts might need to be included in this inner circle.

Separate Control Group

Controls are more reliable if the people applying them are independent of the people performing the tasks being controlled. Specialists are unconcerned with taking blame for causing the problems and can be trained to focus on the control tasks.

> For example, in banks, a separate credit department often monitors the credit worthiness of customers granted credit by the commercial lending department. The lending officers are motivated to make loans, whereas the credit analysts provide checks and balances.

Independent Ratings

An outside party can be engaged to provide an independent assessment of risky situations. Not only does the independence lend credibility, it also can usually obtain a broader economic perspective.

> For example, in addition to the internal credit department, a bank might subscribe to the credit ratings of a recognized credit agency.

Audit Committee

"Nose in, hands off" is the colorful way that the National Association of Corporate Directors describes the function of a board of directors. The same applies to the audit committee of the board, except that the audit committee is supposed to possess superior knowledge and expertise on the subject of financial reporting and internal control.

Sarbanes-Oxley grants significant new powers to the audit committee. They must have the independent authority to fire and hire external auditors, subject to proxy vote, and demand budget allocations for auditing that they deem adequate. Some companies also are reorganizing their internal audit departments to report directly to audit committees.

Although the independent audit committee is not traditionally viewed as an internal control because it does not report to company management, it still should be considered in assessing internal control of the enterprise. A good audit committee will ask the right questions and help recognize changes in the business environment that have control implications.

Supervisory Review

The first line of control is direct observation of the activities by supervisory personnel. Supervisors must read the reports prepared for them and talk to the people who work for them. When doing so, they must inquire about problems being encountered and abnormal situations. They must ascertain that their employees have the time and resources required to perform their duties with high quality where it counts.

System Internal Monitors

Most information systems include features that provide monitoring functions. These include a variety of management reports, cumulative and comparative statistics, and programmed alerts. Such ongoing features generally are timelier than periodic activities and more likely to detect problems before they become material.

For example, many inventory management systems include programmed features to initiate cycle counts and comparisons of recorded versus actual quantities on hand. Cycle counts can be an
important monitor of primary controls over recording inventory
transactions and more timely than comprehensive physical counts.

Track and Compare Detected Problems

Trends and comparisons of problems detected within systems can provide
a valuable perspective on the overall system. Trends that show increasing
problems or anomalies must be investigated to identify the causes, including
whether preventive controls have lost their effectiveness.

Detection Controls

Detection controls are a common and plentiful type of control over most
functions and problems, but they also can indicate the degree to which
prevention controls are effective. Detection controls will only detect problems that have evaded prevention efforts. Large rates of detection imply that
prevention controls might be improved.

Redundant or Compensating Controls

Controls that become ineffective might be compensated for by other controls over the same system. Although redundancy increases operating costs,
some extra cost might be justified by the protection remaining when primary
controls are not effective enough, deteriorate, or fail.

For example, although the company relied on cycle counts to monitor
and maintain the accuracy of its inventory throughout the year, it
also conducted complete physical inventory counts of each ware-
house once a year.

Periodic Monitoring Activities

As previously noted, most information systems include some monitoring
functions. Some of these are continuous; others occur periodically. The
duration of the period between occurrences is important. Periodic controls
should be exercised more frequently than would be necessary to detect
material discrepancies. An objective is to avoid material accounting adjustments. The organization should not wait to do something until it expects a
material adjustment.

For example, a company customarily waited until late in its fourth quarter to review the collectability of accounts receivable. This could result in a large adjustment that included amounts that it should have recognized in earlier quarters.

Financial Analysis

The analysis of financial reports should start immediately as the numbers become available. Outsiders will demand explanations of the financial reports as soon as they are released, and internal analysts must be prepared to explain every deviation from trends, prior periods, and public expectations. This could happen even before the formal publishing of the management discussion and analysis.

One possible explanation that internal analysts must always consider is that the change in a trend or other anomaly is due to an error in financial reporting. This is particularly true if the financial reports seem obviously contrary to events. Better to correct the statements before release and avoid an incredible explanation.

Counterparty Feedback

Counterparties to transactions are customers, vendors, brokers, and others who do business with the company. They will complain when invoices, payments, or the like deviate from agreements or are not timely. Such complaints should be included in the company's monitoring and considered as potential indicators of internal control breakdowns.

For example, deductions and adjustments claimed by customers against their invoices could indicate control weaknesses in the billing or delivery systems.

Internal Audit

Most internal audit departments perform periodic audits of implementation with prescribed control procedures. They usually are the only people other than top management who have the authority to follow potential problems that cross over portions of the organization's structure.

Internal audits can be quite intense and exhaustive. The anticipation that work will be inspected can also motivate employees to perform all their duties conscientiously and retain documentation and other evidence that they complied.

The primary weakness of auditing is that by its nature, it is usually periodic. Employees might relax and become negligent after they pass an audit and anticipate that months or years might pass before another.

Some organizations have experimented with "continuous auditing" in response to this issue. Continuous intense inspection is essentially some form of close supervision. Auditors should not be used in lieu of supervisors or their unique value will not be realized. Neither should auditors be used in lieu of staffing with sufficient control personnel. Auditors should inspect and report to senior management. Hardly any company has such a large internal audit staff that it can still cover the entire organization without reassigning audit staff when an examination is complete. Continuous monitoring is good, but it is not the job of the auditors.

Internal auditors might also serve to assist in the periodic assessments of internal controls and to advise on alternate solutions to eliminating weaknesses. This raises some questions of internal audit independence, but the independence issue is more decided by to whom they report.

External Auditors

External auditors cannot be considered internal controls, at least not without compromising their independence. This can still present a dilemma when the CPA firm is essential in the proper financial reporting in some highly specialized area of financial reporting, such as income taxes. Many small public companies cannot obtain or afford a qualified tax expert on their staff. Some companies hire another CPA firm to provide advice and services that would conflict with the CPA firm engaged to audit.

Regulatory Examinations

Regulators are another, albeit unpopular, source of monitoring. Regulated industries are accustomed to periodic examinations, which resemble audits. The primary difference usually relates to the differences between GAAP and regulatory financial reports and their power to impose sanctions if they find problems with reporting or compliance.

Whistleblowers

Children grow up understanding that someone who runs to the teacher and tells on other children is a tattletale and unpopular. Employees who bypass their supervisors to report suspicious or improper situations are also subject to the stigma of spies, informants, or malcontents. Most employees recognize this and are reluctant to push their doubts or disapproval to higher levels.

Sarbanes-Oxley includes a provision that requires companies to set up a confidential informant system and then protect whistleblowers from retaliation. Although the actual use of this mechanism is not a control that management is able to rely on, it should be considered as one more safeguard over internal abuses and failure to respond to reports of problems.

Upstream Reporting of Problems

Employee reports of problems within or caused by company systems should go beyond merely making corrections. Good systems of internal control emphasize avoidance and prevention of problems because detection and correction are much more expensive and prone to additional errors. Problems and corrections should be reported not only to the person directly responsible for making the correction but also at least one level higher. If the problem involves other departments or other business units, the reports should at least reach the lowest level of common supervision.

> For example, reports regarding inventory corrections to shipments between internal plants or warehouses should include informing the manager over all the involved units.

Management Followup of Problems and Weak Control Assessments

Management sometimes is tempted to presume that a hearty exhortation to "do better" will fix a problem. In fact, when problems overcome the controls, the responsible staff often was *unable* to deal with them effectively, not that they did not try. This then implies that management must redesign the controls, allocate more resources, or take some other action beyond telling people to do better.

Without such management action, the problems usually recur. Repeated problems and recurring admonitions in internal audit reports present a serious warning that management is not taking effective action.

> For example, a repeat finding of a problem or control weakness in an internal audit report should be highlighted and affect the report's conclusions.

Periodic Management Review of Problems and All Control Assessments

This final monitoring control is specifically required under Section 404 of the Sarbanes-Oxley Act. Of course, top management and lower levels of management are free to increase their monitoring beyond the statutory minimums.

Decisive Discipline When Justified

Discipline has become a politically incorrect word in today's permissive society. Certainly, the dark stories of taskmasters using physical brutality over a subjugated mass of workers are *not* what we mean. Discipline can be as moderate as an oral "suggestion" that something is better done differently. The employee might have a better method or idea, and possibly the control or other activity should not be required as prescribed. If a control activity really is important and an employee is uncooperative, direction that is more emphatic might be appropriate. Threats generally are a bad idea until the supervisor really sees no alternative.

Although respect and consideration must accompany discipline, a trivial "slap on the wrist" also can communicate the wrong policy to employees. Controls that are important to the avoidance of serious problems must be required even if enforcement is distasteful. The other employees are watching to see what happens in response to a serious violation of policy.

Assessing the Monitoring Function Under COSO

Monitoring can also serve in lieu of some detailed testing of key controls. If a monitoring function can be tested and shows that the key control was functioning consistently and effectively, the monitoring control becomes the key control. This can be an important solution to the expense of testing numerous controls as well as leverage in assessing controls within small companies.

The COSO Framework specifies monitoring as one of the essential components of effective internal control. Section 404 of SOX requires that management's assessment of the effectiveness of internal controls over financial reporting be documented. A control model of the monitoring function can satisfy this documentation requirement (see Exhibit 13.1).

Within this example, we have illustrated:

1. Sample monitoring problems across the top row of the model
2. Potential inherent and control environment factors
3. Potential controls associated with prevention, detection, and correction of monitoring issues.

For further information on this model and the formulas used in its preparation, please review Chapter 8, Quantitative Control Concepts.

Summary

The control component of *monitoring* is, arguably, one of the most significant points of the COSO Framework. Monitoring of detection controls provide the means to monitor prevention controls, and monitoring also

Quantitative Monitoring Assurance Model																			Control
Monitoring	Documentation Reference		Noncompliance	Software Disabled	Inspection Only	False Documentation	Change in Problems	Change in Consequences	Change in Inherent Risks	Change Opportunities	Management Disregard	Fail Corrections	Management Overide	Fraud	Certification Omissions	Tampering with Records	Obstruction	Retaliation Against Whistleblowers	Cost
Opportunities>			4	4	4	4	4	4	4	4	4	4	4	4	4	4	4	4	
Units of measures>			Quarter	Quarter	Quarter	Quarter	Quarter	Quarter	Quarter	Quarter	Quarter	Quarter	Quarter	Quarter	Quarter	Quarter	Quarter	Quarter	
Inherent Risk Factors																			
Nature of monitoring			0.2	0.3	0.2	0.05	0.2	0.1	0.1	0.1	0.2	0.2	0.05	0.02	0.05	0.02	0.02	0.02	
Unrealistic expectations													0.1						
Financial distress						0.05	0.1						0.1						
Personnel turnover			0.1								0.2	0.2	0.1	0.1	0.2	0.1	0.1	0.1	
Systems changes				0.2			0.3		0.3			0.1							
Inherent Risk =			**30.0%**	**50.0%**	**20.0%**	**10.0%**	**60.0%**	**10.0%**	**40.0%**	**10.0%**	**40.0%**	**50.0%**	**35.0%**	**12.0%**	**25.0%**	**12.0%**	**12.0%**	**12.0%**	
Control Environment																			
Tone at the top			0.3		0.2	0.6					0.6		0.7	0.2	0.9	0.4	0.6	0.8	
Reliability of personnel			0.3	0.1	0.3	0.3				0.2		0.2		0.2		0.2		0.2	
Competence of personnel			0.1	0.3			0.3	0.3	0.1	0.1		0.2							
Segregation of duties			0.5		0.5							0.5		0.6					
Audit committee							0.1	0.3	0.2		0.4		0.3		0.8				
Environment Risk =			**22.1%**	**63.0%**	**28.0%**	**28.0%**	**56.7%**	**34.3%**	**57.6%**	**72.0%**	**14.4%**	**32.0%**	**14.7%**	**25.6%**	**0.4%**	**48.0%**	**40.0%**	**16.0%**	
Preliminary Risk =			**6.62%**	**31.50%**	**5.60%**	**2.80%**	**34.02%**	**3.43%**	**23.04%**	**7.20%**	**5.76%**	**16.00%**	**5.15%**	**3.07%**	**0.10%**	**5.76%**	**4.80%**	**1.92%**	
Potential Incidents			**0.26**	**1.26**	**0.22**	**0.11**	**1.36**	**0.14**	**0.92**	**0.29**	**0.23**	**0.64**	**0.21**	**0.12**	**0.00**	**0.23**	**0.19**	**0.08**	
Prevention Controls		**Implementation**																	
Separate control group		0.9	0.9	0.2	0.98	0.6					0.4					0.8			
External control agent		0.7	0.8	0.3	0.98	0.4	0.2									0.9			
Legal counsel		0.9												0.5	0.9	0.5	0.5	0.8	
CAO on executive committee		0.9					0.7	0.5	0.4	0.5	0.7	0.5	0.6		0.8		0.8	0.8	
Prevention Risk =			**8.36%**	**64.78%**	**3.71%**	**33.12%**	**31.82%**	**55.00%**	**64.00%**	**55.00%**	**23.68%**	**55.00%**	**46.00%**	**55.00%**	**5.32%**	**5.70%**	**15.40%**	**7.84%**	
Actual Incidents			**0.02**	**0.82**	**0.01**	**0.04**	**0.43**	**0.08**	**0.59**	**0.16**	**0.05**	**0.35**	**0.09**	**0.07**	**0.00**	**0.01**	**0.03**	**0.01**	
Detection Controls																			
Supervisory review		0.6	0.7	0.3	0.8	0.4	0.7	0.2	0.2	0.4		0.2		0.6	0.8				
Redundant controls		0.99	0.4	0.4	0.6	0.8	0.1					0.6							
Detection control		0.99	0.6	0.6	0.5	0.7	0.1	0.1	0.2	0.2				0.6					
Detected problem trends		0.7	0.6	0.9	0.6	0.1	0.2	0.1	0.7	0.7		0.4		0.6					
Internal audit		0.2	0.95	0.8	0.3	0.8	0.6	0.5	0.8	0.7	0.5	0.7	0.4	0.4					
Periodic reassessment		0.7	0.1	0.2	0.1	0.1	0.7	0.8	0.7	0.8	0.4	0.6	0.4						
External audit		0.25	0.9	0.8	0.4	0.6	0.6	0.7	0.6	0.7	0.8	0.7	0.7	0.6					
Whistleblower call line		0.1	0.1		0.2	0.2	0.1				0.4		0.4	0.2		0.2	0.3		
Financial analysis		0.9	0.1	0.2	0.1	0.05	0.3	0.4	0.3	0.4	0.1	0.2	0.1	0.1	0.9	0.1	0.1	0.4	
Regulatory exams		0.3	0.2	0.1	0.1	0.2	0.2	0.3	0.1	0.1	0.6	0.6	0.3	0.2		0.2			
Detection Risk =			**4.08%**	**3.42%**	**4.21%**	**2.64%**	**10.49%**	**14.03%**	**9.28%**	**6.02%**	**37.14%**	**7.12%**	**43.44%**	**9.88%**	**9.88%**	**83.83%**	**88.27%**	**64.00%**	
Detected Incidents	**Monitor**		**0.01**	**0.04**	**0.01%**	**0.00**	**0.14**	**0.02**	**0.09**	**0.02**	**0.09**	**0.05**	**0.09**	**0.01**	**0.00**	**0.19**	**0.17**	**0.05**	
Correction Controls																			
Discipline		0.8	0.8	0.1	0.8	0.95					0.7	0.4	0.8						
Follow-up assessments		0	0.6	0.4	0.7	0.4	0.9	0.9	0.9	0.9	0.1	0.2	0.5						
Redesign control		0.9	0.2	0.95	0.3	0.2	0.9	0.9	0.9	0.9	0.5	0.5	0.1	0.4		0.4			
Upstream reporting		0.7	0.6	0.6			0.6		0.6	0.6		0.6	0.4						
Correction Risk =			**17.12%**	**7.74%**	**26.28%**	**19.68%**	**11.02%**	**19.00%**	**11.02%**	**11.02%**	**24.20%**	**21.69%**	**23.59%**	**64.00%**	**100.00%**	**64.00%**	**100.00%**	**100.00%**	
Residual Risk =			**1.714%**	**7.056%**	**1.089%**	**7.219%**	**6.478%**	**16.700%**	**12.338%**	**9.009%**	**12.396%**	**14.996%**	**26.121%**	**37.156%**	**5.320%**	**5.366%**	**15.400%**	**7.840%**	
Residual Problems =			**0.00**	**0.09**	**0.00**	**0.01**	**0.09**	**0.02**	**0.11**	**0.03**	**0.03**	**0.10**	**0.05**	**0.05**	**0.00**	**0.01**	**0.03**	**0.01**	Loss
Control Rating			**0.98**	**0.93**	**0.99**	**0.93**	**0.94**	**0.83**	**0.88**	**0.91**	**0.88**	**0.85**	**0.74**	**0.63**	**0.95**	**0.95**	**0.85**	**0.92**	Value
Consequences:																			Per Occur
Erroneous records			0.99	0.99	0.99	0.99	0.99				0.7	0.9	0.9	0.9		0.9	0.7		
			0.00449	*0.08802*	*0.002414*	*0.008005*	*0.087267*	*0*	*0*	*0*	*0.019993*	*0.086378*	*0.048381*	*0.041092*	*0*	*0.011128*	*0.020698*	*0*	1,000,000
Unacceptable accounting			0.05	0.05	0.05	0.05	0.05				0.8	0.8	0.9	0.5		0.5			
			0.000227	*0.004445*	*0.000122*	*0.000404*	*0.004407*	*0*	*0*	*0*	*0.022849*	*0.076781*	*0.048381*	*0.022829*		*0.006182*	*0*	*0*	5,000,000
Loss/Destruction of assets			0.01 *4.54E-05*	0.01 *0.000889*	0.01 *2.44E-05*	0.01 *0.000809*	0.01 *0.000881*	0.1 *0.002291*	*0*	*0*	*0*	*0*	*0*	0.9 *0.041092*	*0*	0.4 *0.004946*	*0*	*0*	500,000
Sarbanes-Oxley sanction														1.0	1.0	1.0	1.0	1.0	250,000
			0	*0*	*0*	*0*	*0*	*0*	*0*	*0*	*0*	*0*	*0*	*0.045657*	*0.000213*	*0.012364*	*0.029568*	*0.006021*	
																		Exposure	**1,376,485**

EXHIBIT 13.1 Example of Monitoring Model

can provide leverage to minimize the number of key controls that require testing. Our quantitative model provides a unique framework for assessing the monitoring of controls.

Note

1. The Committee of Sponsoring Organizations of the Treadway Commission (COSO), *Guidance on Monitoring Internal Control Systems*, ISBN 0-87051-795-3, 2009.

CHAPTER 14

Accounting Policies and Procedures

The Accounting Environment

Reliable public financial reporting is the enabler of our capitalist society. Whether equity, debt, or some hybrid or derivative in between, the basic decisions to invest capital in an enterprise are dependent on financial reporting.

The key to fair and complete financial reporting is to tell the investing public those things about the enterprise that *should* influence their decisions. These things are considered *material*. Of course, each investor makes decisions on his own, without informing those pundits who each day explain that the market moved up or down because of some typhoon in the Pacific or some anticipated government policy shift. Consequently, materiality is in the eye of the beholder. Sometimes a difference of 1 ¢ in earnings per share from published predictions can appear to cause a large change in a stock price. At other times, even an announcement that earnings will be restated by an unknown large amount sometime when a company figures it out does not seem to cause any movement in that company's stock price. No rule measures what really is material to investors, but internal and external accountants are supposed to apply general guidelines and their own judgment to decide whether something is material.

In this environment, enterprise management must publish financial reports that are accurate within the boundaries of materiality. Their activities need to be organized into a system that extracts everything that is needed and assembles it in the format prescribed by generally accepted accounting principles (GAAP).

The Sarbanes-Oxley Act of 2002 (SOX) sets requirements dealing with internal controls over corporate public financial reports on roughly 14,000 publicly reporting companies in the United States. One of the concerns specified in the SEC Rules regarding SOX is the "...controls related to the selection and application of appropriate accounting policies."[1]

In this context, accounting policies include both the presentation of classifications and amounts on the primary financial statements as well as the numerous supplementary schedules and disclosures in the notes and elsewhere. They include the methods of implementation as well as the observance of the FASB or other authoritative pronouncements.

The accounting policy selection process is highly dependent on knowledge of business events and current interpretation of GAAP. A reasonable person from outside the accounting profession might assume that GAAP is a stable and uniform set of standards. However, many forces in the larger environment initiate or force changes in GAAP. One of the most common examples is the ingenious creation of new types of financial instruments.

Even without outside influences, GAAP allows certain discretionary alternatives, such as valuing inventory on the basis of "first-in, first-out" (FIFO) or "last-in, first-out" (LIFO). A more controversial alternative used to allow employee awards of stock options to be either classified as an expense or merely disclosed in notes to the financial statements.

Although the CFO and the CEO must personally sign the company's certificates of compliance with SOX, the CFO might *not* be the primary person deciding on appropriate accounting. The title of that person might be chief accounting officer (CAO), controller, or some similar designation.

In addition to the literal policy, many accounting disclosures involve estimates. The investing public often appears to ignore the existence of uncertainty in these estimates, as evidenced by reactions when earnings announcements miss market expectations by even a cent. Accountants and auditors know very well that estimates of future events will always bring adjustments to actual figures as time passes. The accuracy of the estimates will depend on the nature of the customers (consumer or commercial), the economic climate, the stability of experience as a predictor, the methods used to develop the estimates, and the inherent potential for surprises.

Accounting estimates can be as simple (but not as easy) as estimating the amount of accounts receivable that will never be collected due to borrowers' refusal or inability to pay. The resultant amount for "allowance for doubtful accounts" normally is disclosed, but the accuracy of past estimates is not.

Other estimates can involve forecasting obligations for disbursements or irregular cash flows from investments. Some of these are used in further calculations of discounted present values, so estimates of the distant future have less effect than imminent events.

> For example, the 2004 scandals regarding Fannie Mae's financial reporting arose partly from its failure to adjust mortgage prepayment estimates when interest rates dropped in 1998 and refinancing boomed. Because expense amortization continued to be based on obsolete cash-flow assumptions, Fannie Mae wrongfully postponed recognition of $400 million in additional amortization expenses.[2]

GAAP requires disclosure of the estimates that play a material role in financial statements, and some discussion of the inherent uncertainties, but very little professional literature provides advice on prudent or customary procedures to minimize the uncertainty of estimates.

The authoritative literature of GAAP encompasses a huge quantity of writings by the following:

- Securities and Exchange Commission (SEC)
- Financial Accounting Standards Board (FASB)
- Accounting Standards Executive Committee (AcSEC) of the American Institute of Certified Public Accountants (AICPA)
- Emerging Issues Task Force (EITF) of the AICPA
- Industry Guides (AICPA)
- Academic textbooks

Although not relevant to SOX, many other sets of accounting standards besides GAAP are used in the United States. These include:

- Internal Revenue Code
- Government Accounting Standards
- Statutory accounting standards for specific regulated industries (i.e., insurance, a.k.a. SAP)
- International Financial Reporting Standards (IFRS)
- Accounting standards of nations other than the United States
- Management accounting practices (e.g., the standard cost method for valuation of inventories)

Most companies must issue at least two types of financial reports applying different accounting principles. These usually are GAAP and tax, but for some international companies they might be all of the previously listed methods.

A bachelor's degree in accounting is usually sufficient to be a corporate accountant, but it's not enough to become a CPA. The master's in science in accounting for a CPA normally requires about five years of college to complete. Even then, a degree will probably not cover, or even acknowledge, all the alternative accounting standards and codes listed here. No wonder a poor accountant can get confused about what to do.

Conversion from GAAP to IFRS

The SEC has announced its plan to convert all accounting by U.S. public companies from rules-based U.S. GAAP to principles-based International Financial Reporting Standards (IFRS) in phases extending to 2016. The first step in this conversion is to negotiate a common set of principles that bring U.S. and international principles into convergence. Accordingly, no one yet knows exactly what accounting principles will be in force when adoption becomes effective in the United States. Presumably the final IFRS will consist mostly of the present set, with some changes to be determined when all the authorities agree that some U.S. principles should amend the existing set.

This conversion will force reeducation of substantially every accountant in the United States. Furthermore, the content, terminology, and format of financial statements will be changed, so all *users* of financial statements prepared under IFRS will also have to be reeducated to learn to read them with proper understanding. College curricula must be converted, but the accounting faculty has to learn the new system first. The Uniform CPA Examination will also have to switch from GAAP to IFRS at an appropriate time. A great deal of planning is required if the proposed timetable is to be met. All these changes will present an abundance of added opportunities for problems with the selection and implementation of accounting policies and procedures.

One of the primary themes of preference for IFRS is that it is much more concise than current GAAP literature and places more responsibility on corporate management to select and apply appropriate policies and procedures. To predict some of the implications of this change, we might look back to the days in the United States before the Accounting Principles Board (1959 to 1973) or the Financial Accounting Standards Board (1973 to present) existed.

Even into the 1960s, financial statements and disclosures were much more abbreviated than today. Financial statements were limited to a balance sheet and statement of income. Notes fit at the foot of the page and covered little more than whether inventory was calculated on the LIFO or FIFO basis. No one presented a funds statement or changes in equity. Until 1972, issuers of financial statements assumed that users already knew GAAP well enough to understand the statements, so accounting policies were not explained. A popular objective was to keep things simple enough to be understood by the "widows and orphans," whether that was ever true or not. IFRS will not turn things back this far.

However, IFRS could allow more divergence in accounting interpretations by companies viewing similar situations. Without detailed rules covering the multitude of possible situations, reasonable people will very likely apply different analogies or different degrees of emphasis to their situations and thereby report different results for very similar circumstances. This issue was one of the primary reasons that U.S. GAAP evolved into the rules-based system we have today. At the same time, the detailed rules have been criticized for leaving loopholes, for not adequately covering all situations, and for rigidly forcing unreasonable results under some circumstances.

Conversion to IFRS is not likely to produce widespread changes in existing accounting policies other than those mandated in the new principles. Any change in accounting will still require a justification of the reasons and effects as well as concurrence from the external auditors. IFRS is fairly similar to U.S. GAAP. It is not going to abandon double-entry bookkeeping. It still addresses assets, liabilities, revenues, and expenses. Still, a recent AICPA presentation listed more than five dozen significant areas in which GAAP and IFRS differ. Another publication by Deloitte Touche Tohmatsu[3] lists 214 differences that will be "common."

Whenever the adoption of IFRS occurs for a particular company in the United States and whatever the principles it pronounces, all companies must prepare their information systems to accommodate IFRS. This differs from accommodating changes that already occur in GAAP only in degree.

In a parallel project but with different IT systems implications, the SEC has also announced new conversion plans to XBRL. These initials stand for *extensible business reporting language,* which is intended to enable easier line-item comparison between financial statements and development of databases for comparative financial analysis. It essentially requires that all public reporting companies adopt a universal taxonomy for their general ledgers and encode their financial reports submitted to the SEC according to the system. This doesn't quite mandate universal standardized general ledger accounts, but it does standardize the description of most accounts across most industries.

The XBRL system will obligate corporate accountants and IT support to recode documents filed with the SEC with coding that is similar looking to the HTML used in Web pages. Just the way many software packages provide HTML encoding without having to learn HTML, software is available to help with XBRL encoding. Some general ledgers will have to be redesigned to conform to the XBRL definitions, and some general ledger software will have to be replaced or updated. Companies will still have to use XBRL after conversion to IFRS, but with codes that conform to the IFRS account definitions. Depending on the specific extent of the changes in a particular company and the support from the software vendor, XBRL has a high potential to be a very major conversion.

The purpose of this book is to enable quantification of risk and control assessments, not to provide a cookbook for control of any particular system. Therefore, the problems, risk factors, controls, and consequences used to illustrate quantitative assessment are not presumed to be comprehensive or applicable to any particular instance of a system to select and apply accounting policies and procedures. The reader and others involved in such an assessment must identify and consider those problems, risk factors, controls, and consequences specific to the system they are assessing.

What Can Go Wrong with Accounting Policies and Procedures?

Accounting is a difficult subject. A great number of things can and do go wrong in its proper implementations. These potential problems include:

- Uninformed chief accounting officers
- Incompetent accounting staff
- Incomplete facts
- Undisclosed side agreements
- Misinterpretation of accounting principles
- Overlooked essential attributes
- Form over substance
- Recent changes in accounting principles
- Misclassified transactions
- Computational errors in applications
- Fallacious underlying assumptions
- Unreasonable underlying estimates

Uninformed Chief Accounting Officers

The CAO must be intimately aware of all significant activities, transactions, events, agreements, and plans of the enterprise. Only then will the CAO be able to ensure that all matters that should be accounted for or disclosed are properly included in the financial statements. Omissions are the easiest type of error.

To be informed, the CAO must at least sit at the table when business transactions are being discussed by the top executives. Only by firsthand knowledge can the CAO determine which considerations have accounting implications and which do not. The CAO should not rely on some other executive to filter the considerations and decide what the CAO should know.

Incompetent Accounting Staff

By *incompetence*, we do not intend to insult anyone's mental capabilities or education. Competence simply means that an individual possesses the specific knowledge, skills, and proficiency to do a specific job well. The practice of accounting requires extensive familiarity with a body of knowledge encompassing not only the accounting principles that are current but also economics, business law, taxation, and industry practices and regulations. A college degree and professional certification provide evidence of expert knowledge but not necessarily the level sufficient for the job of CAO. Additional evidence of competence includes previous work experience, continuing professional education, and specific experience with public company reporting. Updated education in IFRS will be especially important when the United States converts from GAAP.

Even all these attributes cannot guarantee competence in all aspects of the job. No one person is able to memorize everything necessary to know about accounting standards or personally do every task involved in preparing financial statements. The CAO must also employ competent assistants and advisors.

SOX emphasizes that the independence of external accountants prohibits them from auditing anything that they, in effect, did themselves for the company. Although they can advise regarding accounting policies, they are prohibited from prescribing what accounting policy is appropriate.

Competence is an issue not only of quality but also of quantity. Many companies that disclosed material weaknesses in their SOX reports indicated that they lacked *sufficient* competent staff. The number of people available was not adequate to reliably address all the tasks requiring competence in the various skills. The obvious solution is to go out and hire the needed personnel. However, if these people must be expert in some scarce skill—for example, accounting for derivative financial instruments—attempts to hire will find that people competent in this particular skill are not readily available.

Incomplete Facts

The selection of appropriate accounting methods often requires consideration of subtle facts and details. Reliance on a "terms sheet" or other summary description of a contract might omit some detail that the person preparing the summarization did not realize is relevant. The chief accountant must also be competent in understanding business contracts.

Undisclosed Side Agreements

One special case of incomplete facts occurs when side agreements are not included in the provided documentation. The very existence of side agreements is usually unnecessary and implies some intent to conceal information.

Misinterpretation of Accounting Principles

GAAP encompasses a large collection compiled by the FASB in a Codification available on the Internet. Consideration of relevant sections with the facts of a particular question require a high level of expertise. Even then, experts might not agree that one interpretation is more appropriate than another. Some accounting decisions are made based simply on the preference of the decision maker.

For example, the selection of an accounting policy for inventory valuation permits either LIFO or FIFO. No authoritative GAAP pronouncement favors one over the other.

As IFRS is applied to accounting in the United States, misinterpretation of GAAP will be replaced by misinterpretation of IFRS. At least it will resolve the previous question regarding LIFO inventories; LIFO will not be accepted.

Misinterpretation will also take a different form. Under GAAP, rules for application are quite detailed and specific. IFRS reverses the approach back to the days in the United States before FASB or the APB. Accountants will be expected and allowed to focus on the underlying economic issues. This will inevitably result in differing conclusions among informed and well-intentioned accountants.

Overlooked Essential Attributes

Even when all the relevant facts are presented or available, an expert accountant might still overlook something important. This is especially high risk when the organization has many separate accounting centers in diverse lines of business and locations.

Form Over Substance

The evolution of accounting pronouncements in the United States over the past several decades has produced voluminous prescriptions for accounting treatments under very specific facts. A skillful person can sometimes manipulate the terms of a transaction to fit the prescribed conditions, even when the economic substance is contrary. Critics are calling for "principles-based" accounting while characterizing current accounting as "rules-based." One of the underlying principles should be substance over form. This means that the accounting treatment should assign priority to the economic substance of the transactions and disregard the legal form if it contradicts.

Recent Changes in Accounting Principles

Because the basic structure of modern accounting has existed since the fourteenth century, one might expect that it would be stable by now. Everyone in the practice of accounting knows that this is not true and that accounting standards, interpretations, guidance, and explanations flow in a torrent, particularly during the later months of each calendar year. Some of the new pronouncements respond to new business practices; others reverse previous pronouncements without anything having changed in the real world. Existing accounting policies must be reconsidered whenever a new FASB pronouncement is exposed or issued. The conversion to IFRS will require a comprehensive reconsideration of all accounting practices.

Misclassified Transactions

Once the responsible company officers decide on the appropriate accounting policy in the circumstances, the information systems must be made to recognize, classify, and summarize the affected transactions according to the policy. This might require redesign of information systems, changes in programming logic, and training of personnel. High risk exists that the proper accounting might not occur until all these essential tasks can be completed. Both IFRS and XBRL will very likely require modifications to both general ledger and application software for the business cycles.

Computational Errors in Applications

Some accounting policies require complex calculations of present values, option pricing, mortality, morbidity, failure probability, or other mathematical values. Errors in such calculations could be easy to commit but difficult to recognize on review. Detailed recalculation tests might be necessary.

Fallacious Underlying Assumptions

The appropriate implementation of many accounting policies requires assumptions about future conditions.

> For example, future yield from investment instruments is often an assumption needed to determine current rates of income recognition.

> Assumptions are often the weak link in a financial projection.

Unreasonable Underlying Estimates

Some accounting policies require estimates of future cash flows, claims rates, statistical correlations between financial instruments, and other predictions. Although no knowledgeable accountants presume perfection in such estimates, they allow opportunities for deliberate manipulation as well as honest errors.

Reliance on Application Systems

In addition to the potential problems we've described, residual problems from application systems that feed into financial reporting can cause erroneous financial reports. This risk is one of the primary concerns in assessing the control over every information system that contributes to financial objectives.

Even after application systems are well controlled, serious financial errors can emerge during the steps to transfer and adapt the application results. Application constraints and the evolution of accounting procedures often cause a need for an interim process following the extraction of results from the application. This interim process is usually implemented using Excel, or some comparable software.

The final preparation of financial reports is the last opportunity to detect errors that evaded earlier controls. Accordingly, we must consider the control activities in the preparation process that can serve to detect such problems.

An attentive analysis of preliminary financial results can often recognize an accounting treatment that is out of sync with the other results. Whether due to an error or an unusual but legitimate occurrence, investigation and explanation are necessary before the statements are released.

Controls Over Accounting Policy Selection and Application

Some of the possible controls that can counteract these potential problems include these:

- Reference literature
- Personnel selection
- Code of ethics
- Outside consultation
- Written communications
- Training and education
- Quantitative estimation methods
- Supervision and review
- Analytic review
- Audit
- Regulatory examination or investigation
- Whistleblowers
- Counterparty treatment
- Adjusting entries
- Audit committee
- Restatement

Reference Literature

An accounting department needs a library of current accounting literature relevant to the company's industry. Access to electronic libraries can save money and provide better assurance of current updates. The AICPA provides subscriptions to its online library of professional literature. Some accounting reference works are accompanied by a CD-ROM for faster research. FASB provide the authoritative *Accounting Standards Codification* in an online, searchable structure. Some issues are so volatile that dedicated web sites monitor developments (e.g., http://fasb.org/derivatives/issuindex.shtml). Other issues might only be addressed in some obscure speech by an SEC commissioner.

Personnel Selection

The selections for employment of the CAO and senior staff are very important hiring decisions. The human resources department should verify applicants' education, certifications, and previous experience.

Code of Ethics

SOX requires that responsible senior executives annually sign a code of ethics that promises full, fair, and honest disclosures. Such sign-offs often also query concerning conflicts of interest and other conduct issues. Signers should be warned that improper responses might be deemed to be fraud.

Outside Consultation

The primary party for outside consultation on accounting issues is the company's independent accounting firm. All the major accounting firms employ special experts in professional standards that are available to the accountants assigned to each client. SEC rules require disclosures that effectively discourage a public company from engaging a rival to its accounting firm for advice regarding appropriate accounting policies. The SEC refers to this practice as *opinion shopping*. Furthermore, AU Section 625, "Reports on the Application of Accounting Principles," contains standards for accountants who are asked to provide an opinion on an accounting matter to another auditor's client. If company management cannot agree with its regular accounting firm, the issue must be taken to the audit committee.

Written Communications

Once an accounting policy decision is made, it must be clearly communicated to everyone involved in its application. For nonrecurring situations, this communication might occur via memoranda or email. For recurring situations, most companies maintain a controller's manual containing a complete, current set of all accounting procedures. Notes to the financial statements must also disclose policies, although usually in less detail.

Training and Education

Professional accountants are required to obtain continuing professional education as a condition for renewal of their CPA license and AICPA membership. Typically this amounts to 40 hours of coursework per year, but the appropriate level can vary according to the individual's professional classification or the nature of current issues. Certainly the conversion to IFRS will require at least 40 hours of education by itself. Even if the accounting department personnel do not carry active licenses, they still need continuing professional education to remain competent and effective.

Quantitative Estimation Methods

Reliable estimates are better produced by quantitative methods than by personal intuition. Even when intuition deserves a high level of trust, it could provide an *appearance* of influence by some company agenda. Mathematical regression analysis and other operations research techniques can deliver more objectivity and measure uncertainty.

Even formal mathematics can produce unreasonable results, and some important factors of causation cannot readily be fit into mathematical models. In practice, many enterprises apply quantitative methods together with intuitive judgment.

Supervision and Review

Supervision of activities and review of work products are the most basic types of control over all accounting activities. All reviews should be evidenced by the date and a name or initials for control documentation purposes.

Analytic Review

Before any financial reports are released to management or the public, a skilled accountant should closely review the various results being reported. This means viewing the draft report as though she is a user in senior management or an outside analyst. It usually involves comparing the current period draft with the most recent previous period and with the comparable period in prior years. It also involves calculation of common ratios and metrics such as earnings before interest, taxes, depreciation, and amortization (EBITDA); days of receivables; inventory turnover; and other non-GAAP metrics. Such analysis will usually reveal some set of disclosures that should be expected to draw questions. The answers might reveal a situation in which the accounting policy or its application is inappropriate or questionable. If the accounting is correct, it has revealed some business issue that might be important to management's discussion and analysis.

Audit

Investors view the external auditors as the final control over a company's accounting policies. The audit committee of the board of directors will customarily meet in private with the partner in charge of the external audit team and inquire regarding scope, independence, improprieties, and suitability of accounting. SOX specifies that they are to be informed of all material adjustments to the financial reports initiated by the external auditors. Of course, management will prefer to resolve any issues with the external auditors before this point.

Regulatory Examination or Investigation

The SEC retains authority over the accounting policies of public companies, even after the external auditors have expressed their opinions. Various other regulatory authorities also have authority over statutory reports, which can differ from GAAP reporting. The Enforcement Division of the SEC can initiate an investigation of any financial reports that arouse its concern. This is really the final control protecting investors, but a public company definitely wants to avoid this step.

Whistleblowers

SOX requires that each audit committee establish procedures to receive direct, confidential, and anonymous concerns about financial reporting. This facility might reveal a serious problem, but it cannot be relied on. Significant courage is required to make open accusations. Right or wrong, whistleblowing can kill a career. Anonymous accusations often lack sufficient detail to pinpoint the real problem, and since they're anonymous, investigators have no one to ask for more details.

Whistleblowers have been responsible for revealing serious misstatements, but they also have been the source of incorrect, unsubstantiated, and irrelevant accusations. Certainly they are not an internal control on which any assessment can rely.

Counterparty Treatment

Generally, investors expect mirror treatment of the same transaction by both sides of the parties involved. If one company treats a transaction as a lease, the other would be expected to treat it as a lease and not as a sale. Although mirror treatment is not an accounting standard, inconsistent treatment can certainly raise questions. Consistent treatment is sometimes a subject covered in a contract or other formal agreement, and the parties are free to exchange views of their planned interpretations, even without contractual agreement.

Adjusting Entries

The significance of accounting adjusting entries depends on who initiates them. Adjusting entries initiated by some internal level of accounting personnel could represent a designed correction control and be evidence that the detection and correction controls are working as planned. At worst, the adjustment might indicate a weakness in preventive internal controls. Even if an entry is part of a planned response, any adjusted material should be reported to senior management. Adjusting entries initiated by external auditors carry greater significance because they imply some inadequacy in the company's internal accounting application. Audit adjustments are presumed material and must be reported to the audit committee.

Audit Committee

The audit committee of the board of directors is charged by SOX with resolving any disagreements between the external auditors and company management. These disagreements include any remaining debates over appropriate accounting policies and practices. SOX also enables the audit committee to require company funding for legal counsel and other advisors they might require to accomplish these duties.

Restatement

The ultimate correction to problems in accounting policy selection and application is restatement of public financial reports. Restatement after such reports are released to the public carries potentially serious consequences, but failure to do so might be viewed as fraud.

Restatements have become common in recent years. At one extreme, they might cause the company's stock price to move a few percentage points; at the other extreme, they might lead to delisting of the stock from a public stock exchange.

Although such restatements are always embarrassing to management, the investment markets' reaction to an announcement of a restatement is hard to predict. The reaction depends on the company's explanation of the accounting issues and estimated size. A restatement of depreciation will probably draw a much different reaction than a restatement of sales.

Accounting Policy Control Model	Documentation Reference	Problems — Uninformed CAO	Incompetent Staff	Incomplete Facts	Undisclosed Side Agreement	Misinterpret GAAP	Overlook Attribute	Form Over Substance	Overlook Change in GAAP	Misclassify Transactions	Computational Error	Inappropriate Assumption	Inappropriate Estimated	
Opportunities>		4	4	4	4	4	4	4	4	4	4	4	4	
Units of Measure>		Quarter	Quarter	Quarter	Quarter	Quarter	Quarter	Quarter	Quarter	Quarter	Quarter	Quarter	Quarter	
Inherent Risk Factors														
GAAP volatility		0.05	0.05	0.05		0.1	0.2	0.05	0.3	0.05	0.02	0.05	0.05	
Material nonrecurring trans		0.1	0.1	0.1	0.05	0.1	0.1	0.2	0.05	0.05	0.1	0.1	0.1	
Nonsystem transactions		0.05	0.05	0.05	0.02	0.05	0.05	0.05	0.05	0.1	0.1	0.05	0.1	
Inherent Risk=		20.0%	20.0%	20.0%	7.0%	25.0%	35.0%	30.0%	40.0%	20.0%	22.0%	20.0%	25.0%	
Control Environment														
Tone at the top		0.3		0.2	0.6	0.2	0.1	0.6	0.1	0.1	0.1	0.5	0.5	
Reliability of personnel		0.2	0.1	0.4	0.2	0.2		0.3	0.4	0.5	0.6	0.2	0.3	
Competence of personnel		0.1	0.5	0.4	0.2	0.7	0.6	0.3	0.5	0.6	0.5	0.2	0.3	
Segregation of duties														
Other elements														
Environment Risk=		50.4%	45.0%	28.8%	25.6%	19.2%	36.0%	19.6%	27.0%	18.0%	18.0%	32.0%	24.5%	
Assessed Risk		10.08%	9.00%	5.76%	1.79%	4.80%	12.60%	5.88%	10.80%	3.60%	3.96%	6.40%	6.13%	
Application Consequences				yes						yes	yes			
Potential Incidents		0.40	0.36	0.23	0.07	0.19	0.50	0.24	0.43	0.14	0.16	0.26	0.25	
Prevention Controls *(Implementation)*														
Reference literature	152 0.9		0.4	0.2		0.7	0.5	0.6	0.8	0.2	0.3	0.1	0.2	
Personnel selection	153 0.8		0.7											
Code of ethics	153 0.99			0.3	04			0.4				0.1	0.1	
Consultation	153 0.7		0.8	0.1		0.8	0.7	0.7	0.8			0.2	0.3	
Written communication	153 0.9	0.5	0.7	0.4	0.4	0.4	0.4	0.2	0.3	0.7	0.5	0.1	0.2	
Training and education	153 0.9		0.8	0.2		0.6	0.3	0.4	0.8	0.7	0.4	0.1	0.2	
Quantitative est method	154													
Audit committee	155 0.99		0.4	0.1		0.2	0.1	0.4	0.5			0.2	0.2	
Other prevention control														
Prevention Risk=		55.00%	0.78%	25.35%	38.66%	3.84%	11.81%	4.49%	1.27%	11.23%	25.70%	46.83%	31.48%	
Actual Incidents		0.22	0.00	0.06	0.03	0.01	0.06	0.01	0.01	0.02	0.04	0.12	0.08	
Detection Controls														
Supervision and review	154 0.95	0.5	0.7	0.3		0.3	0.6	0.5	0.7	0.7	0.8	0.5	0.5	
Analytic review	0.7					0.3		0.3	0.4	0.4	0.3	0.2	0.2	
Audit	154 0.99	0.5	0.4	0.5	0.3	0.8	0.7	0.7	9.9	0.7	0.7	0.5	0.6	
Counterparty treatment	155 0.4		0.3	0.6	0.7	0.6	0.5	0.5	0.7				0.2	
Whistleblower	155 0.02	0.05	0.1	0.2	0.9	0.7	0.1	0.1	0.1	0.1	0.1	0.1	0.1	
Regulatory exam	154 0.3	0.1	0.1	0.1		0.1	0.1			0.2	0.2	0.1	0.1	
Other detection control														
Detection Risk=		25.69%	17.24%	26.14%	49.91%	8.64%	10.22%	10.17%	1.89%	6.95%	5.46%	22.07%	16.33%	
Detected Incidents		0.10	0.06	0.06	0.04	0.02	0.05	0.02	0.01	0.01	0.01	0.06	0.04	
Correction Controls														
Adjusting entry	155 0.98	0.9	0.7			0.9	0.9	0.9	0.98	0.9	0.98	0.9	0.9	
Restatement	156 0.6	0.6	0.8		0.6	0.6	0.6	0.6	0.8	0.2	0.7	0.5	0.2	
Audit committee	155	0.8	0.8	0.5	0.3	0.8	0.2		0.1			0.3		
Other correction control														
Correction Risk=		7.55%	16.33%	100.00%	64.00%	7.55%	7.55%	7.55%	2.06%	10.38%	2.30%	8.26%	10.38%	
Residual Risk=		0.0%	12.3%	20.0%	0.0%	10.9%	8.5%	10.2%	3.1%	3.3%	2.3%	2.9%	5.0%	
Residual Problem=		0.07	0.00	0.06	0.02	0.01	0.01	0.00	0.00	0.00	0.00	0.03	0.02	
Control Rating		0.83	1.00	0.75	0.68	0.99	0.98	0.99	1.00	0.98	0.98	0.87	0.92	Value per occurrence
Consequences:														
Erroneous records		0.99	0.6	0.05	0.025	0.05			0.05	0.9	0.9	0.9	0.9	$ 50,000
Unacceptable accounting		0.05	0.2	0.05	0.5	0.99	0.7	0.9	0.9					$ 500,000
Loss/Destruction of assets		0.01	0.2	0.05		0.1								$ 50,000
													Exposure	20,472.64

EXHIBIT 14.1 An Accounting Policy Control Model

These controls, and others, can reduce the likelihood and impact of problems with accounting policies and procedures. They can be assessed using a model as illustrated next.

An Accounting Control Model

The model in Exhibit 14.1 is a hypothetical example of the issues and controls to be expected. When IFRS goes into effect, the inherent risk estimate in the first row for "GAAP volatility" should be changed to "IFRS changes" and probably increase by a large degree.

Notice that within this model, we have included a row for "Application Consequences" in the vein of our interdependent systems chapter. This illustrative model clearly reveals that accounting policies and procedures are a complex situation to control effectively. Perhaps this helps to explain why so many reputable companies have admitted to accounting problems and restated their financial reports.

The "... controls related to the selection and application of appropriate accounting policies ..." receive well-deserved special mention in the SEC Rules regarding Sarbanes-Oxley. The art of accounting only grows more complex with new forms of structuring enterprises, new investment instruments, new ways of transacting business, and more reliance on systemic controls by government. Many of the financial disasters that triggered the legislation of SOX were primarily deceptive accounting methods—whether deliberate or negligent—not any breakdown of bookkeeping at the transaction or system level. Enterprise controls of the accounting process are the means to the end of fair presentation.

Notes

1. SEC Final Rule 33-8238, management's "Report on Internal Control Over Financial Reporting and Certification of Disclosure in Exchange and Periodic Reports," p11. August 14, 2003.
2. *Wall Street Journal*, December 16, 2004.
3. Deloitte Touche Tohmatsu, "IFRSs and U.S. GAAP: A Pocket Comparison," 2008.

CHAPTER 15

Business Process Applications

The bulk of financial control assessments address the various transaction processes and applications within an organization. These commonly include the major accounting cycles and processes such as:

- Invoicing, receivables, and collections
- Purchasing, payables, and payments
- Payroll, benefits, and taxes
- Inventory
- Investments and their valuation
- Bank accounts
- Income taxes
- General ledger, closing entries, and accruals

Of course, many others could exist, depending on the business model and industry. This chapter presents a generic example of the approach to assessing these major processes.

Our objective in this book is *not* to repeat the definitions and descriptions of various controls that are readily available elsewhere in the risk/control or auditing literature. Rather, our objective is to summarize the way we classify and include common application controls in our quantitative model. In a few cases where we differ from the common treatment of a particular control, we go into some depth to explain our difference.

Application Components, Structure, and Architecture

Most modern application systems are built on some database architecture, but many legacy systems still exist that apply batch processing to flat master files. The specific architecture will affect some of the inherent risks and the location of some of the controls.

The basic components of an application system that processes transactions are the inputs, processes, and outputs. By contrast, examples of business computer applications that do *not* process transactions include:

- Word processing
- Presentations and graphics
- Design and engineering (for example, CAD/CAM)
- Plans and projections

Transactions fall into two major categories: inputs from external sources and internal processing.

The first major category is input transactions that are submitted from some external source and are put into the application system by one of the following methods:

- The source records data on a paper document, which is transcribed to a computer medium
- An operator records data from a source, in person or remotely
- The source directly enters the data via a workstation with controlled access
- The source directly enters that data via a personal computer connected to an open network (the Internet)

The mechanism for data entry can include:

- Pen or pencil
- Keyboard
- Menu and mouse
- Barcode scanner
- Optical character recognition (OCR)
- Audio recognition

Note that an application system does not begin or end with the computer components. Input transactions usually are initiated by some human engaging in some business activity, and many computer applications require human interaction for information, consideration, evaluation, or action. These human inputs to automated applications must be included as components of any application system in a quantitative risk analysis.

For example, the transaction flow of a payroll application starts with employees working on the job and ends with them filing W-2 forms with their income tax returns.

Aside from input transactions, the other major category is internal transactions that are initiated by processing under some programmed conditions, most commonly a date or the passage of time.

The term *transaction* has different meanings for accountants than for information technology personnel. Transactions in a computer system include many more types of data and functions than accounting transactions. Some of these other transactions are focused on operations objectives; a few are purely for compliance. Still others are administrative to the operation of the application.

Processing of accounting transactions is essentially rather simple. In essence, it is the summation of monetary amounts by general ledger account classifications within accounting periods. The essential data elements are:

- Accounting category or general ledger account ID
- Date the event occurred (not the date processed)
- The monetary amount, which sometimes must be calculated

Other important accounting characteristics usually can be inferred from the essential elements. Positive amounts can be assumed to be debits or credits, according to the nature of the application and general ledger account.

Of course, real system processing usually is more complicated than this.

For example, the monetary amount of a single payroll transaction could require the input of hours worked each day and the identity of the worker. The computer then looks up the employee's hourly rate, benefits, withholding rates, and department. It must compute base pay, shift premium, overtime, gross pay, various deductions, various tax withholding amounts, and net pay. Each category of expense and liability must be accumulated according to its appropriate general ledger account.

Outputs from an application can include these:

- Documents
- Reports
- Transactions for downstream applications

For example, a payroll application might generate either a paycheck or a bank deposit advice. Periodically, it must generate tax documents, benefit payments, and management reports. Summarized accounting data will be produced either in the form of a report or by a direct interface to the general ledger application. Output transaction data will be passed as inputs to pension and retirement benefit application systems.

Processing takes place between the initiation of input or internal transactions and the outputs. As illustrated earlier, processing often is required to convert raw data into the classifications, dates, and amounts used in accounting transaction entries. Other functions of processing can relate to operating functions (for example, shipping an order), administration (hiring an employee), internal control (identifying delinquent receivables), compliance (calculating tax-basis depreciation), or support (summarizing telephone usage).

Multiple Instances

In organizations with multiple locations, many locations often have duplicate installations of the same application software, and the same model can be used for all, with adjustments only for differences in activity and implementation.

> For example, branches of a bank will each have copies of the software needed to perform the operations and accounting suitable to a branch.

Ideally, each of the multiple installations of the same application will be identical in every way. Realistically, this is sometimes not feasible, so a different configuration will demand a slightly different assessment model.

The scope of testing is another complication presented by multiple instances of an application system. Most external auditors will be satisfied by testing a representative sample of the locations, plus any locations that are individually material. Effective monitoring can also provide assurance that all locations are implementing the same controls.

The purpose of this book is to enable quantification of risk and control assessments, not to provide a cookbook for control of any particular system. Therefore, the problems, risk factors, controls, and consequences used to illustrate quantitative assessment are not presumed to be comprehensive or applicable to any particular instance of any application system. The reader and others involved in such an assessment must identify and consider those problems, risk factors, controls, and consequences specific to the system they are assessing.

What Can Go Wrong with Applications?

Typically, application problems are classified by input, process, and output. However, some problems might not fit into these categories due to the different methods permitted by technology.

Input problems

- Event or transaction not recorded
- Event or transaction recorded more than once

- Input data inaccurate
- Input data incomplete
- Input recorded but lost

Process problems

- Process against wrong file or database
- Process against wrong record or segment
- Processing incomplete
- Processing incorrect
- Processing untimely
- Processing inappropriate
- File or database lost
- Program lost
- People lost

Output problems

- Output improperly distributed
- Privacy violated
- Output late
- Output lost
- Excessive error correction
- Unsupported output

Other problems

- Unlimited access
- Management override

Typical Application Controls

We find that organizing controls by their function allows the best assessment of their effectiveness against each type of problem. The following is an example of the classifications of some common application controls:

Prevention Controls

- Application training
- Documentation
- Help screens
- Authorization
- Access identification
- Access authentication
- Rotation of duties

- Default option
- Secure custody
- Encryption
- Passwords

Authorization is cited in COSO as an important control objective. In reality, authorization is a prevention control that might or might not be important in a particular context. Economic exchanges and events must be recorded, whether or not they are authorized. Sales normally need not be authorized if they are for cash, with no credit being granted.

> For example, no one authorizes a customer to put a can of beans into his shopping cart, except by opening the doors to the grocery store. The store might monitor its customers and object if someone tries to leave with the beans without paying, but that is a different type of control. Inventory pilferage must be recorded because it happens, in spite of it being decidedly unauthorized.

Authorization is a control only to the extent that it regulates the source of input data to the information system. The primary intent is to prevent untrained personnel from introducing errors or corrupting files. An important secondary purpose is to prevent incompatible activities that might enable fraud.

Detection Controls

- Visual verification
- Overflow edit
- Format edit
- Completeness edit
- Check digit
- Limit or range edit
- Validity edit
- Relationship edit
- Approval
- Balancing
- Reconciliation
- Proof
- Suspense file
- Aging
- Matching
- Redundant process
- Summary process

The various edits are applied mostly to data elements within transactions. Accordingly, an assessment might sometimes break down its analysis to the data element level. However, if the mission is to provide an assessment for SOX compliance, the data elements that are given priority are the date (format and range edit), the account categories (validity edit), and the amount (range edit). The other edits apply more to data used for operating objectives (such as a check digit on a part number).

Balancing, reconciliation, and proof are related but progressively stronger controls to detect problems with the integrity of record keeping. Balancing simply matches the total value of one file or list with another. Reconciliation is applied when the totals do not match to identify those items that make up the difference. A proof not only reconciles the totals, it also reconciles the debit and credit activity and will reveal offsetting differences within the details.

Correction Controls

- Reverse and reenter
- Lockout access
- Discrepancy message
- Discrepancy log
- Discrepancy report
- Transaction trail
- Backup
- Recovery
- Automated error correction
- Upstream resubmission
- Remediation project

Correction controls are underrated by the COSO Framework. The implication is that once an error is detected, one merely reverses it and reenters the transaction correctly. Oh, if only it were so simple.

Speed is very important in error correction. Consequences can multiply as time passes, and correction is much easier if the responsible people are making the correction immediately, while the cause is still clear and obvious.

When errors arrive across the Internet, prompt action might be the only salvation, because the task could be virtually impossible once the source disconnects or logs off.

If immediate correction is not possible due to delays in detection or because time has brought secondary consequences, correction can get extremely expensive. Companies that report material weaknesses can spend millions and millions of dollars hiring consultants and project contractors to unravel and repair financial misstatements, sometimes going back years.

Application		INPUT (Problems)				PROCESS						
Generic Application		Not recorded	Recorded more than once	Inaccurate	Incomplete	Recorded, but lost	Wrong file or DB	Wrong record or segment	Incomplete	Incorrect	Untimely	Inappropriate
Rate by liklihood/probability												
Opportunities>		10000	10000	10000	10000	10000	10000	10000	10000	10000	10000	10000
Units of measure>	per year	Trans	Trans	Trans	Trans	Trans	Trans	Trans	Trans	Trans	Trans	Trans
Average Value		200	200	200	12	200	200	200	200	200	5	200
Std Deviation		50	50	50	3	50	50	50	50	50	1	50
Inherent risk factors												
Nature of problem		0.02	0.02	0.05	0.05	0.02	0.01	0.01	0.02	0.05	0.05	0.03
Fraud appeal		0.01	0.01				0.01	0.01				0.02
Factor #3												
Factor #4												
Factor #5												
Inherent risk=		2.0%	3.0%	6.0%	5.0%	2.0%	2.0%	2.0%	2.0%	5.0%	5.0%	5.0%
Control Enviorment												
Tone at the Top		0.3	0.3	0.2	0.2	0.1	0.1	0.1	0.1	0.2	0.3	0.2
Reliability of persn		0.3	0.3	0.5		0.2	0.2					
Competence of persn		0.1	0.1	0.6	0.1	0.1	0.1	0.1	0.1	0.1	0.2	0.2
Element #4												
Element #5												
Segregation of duties			0.2									
Element #7												
Enviornment risk=		44.1%	35.3%	16.0%	72.0%	64.8%	64.8%	81.0%	81.0%	72.0%	56.0%	64.0%
Preliminary Risk=		0.88%	1.06%	0.96%	3.60%	1.30%	1.30%	1.62%	1.62%	3.60%	2.80%	3.20%
Potential Incidents=		88.2	105.8	96.0	360.0	129.6	129.6	162.0	162.0	360.0	280.0	320.0
Prevention controls	Implementation											
User training	0.9	0.2	0.2	0.6	0.7	0.2	0.2	0.2	0.6	0.6	0.3	0.6
Documentation	0.7	0.4	0.8									0.7
Help screens	0.95				0.7					0.7		0.8
Authorization	0.95											0.8
Access ID & authentication	0.95						0.8	0.8				0.8
0	0											
Rotation of duties	0.8											0.7
Default option	0.7				0.7							
Secure custody	0.8					0.8	0.6	0.6				
Encryption	0.5											
0												
0												
Prevention risk=		59.04%	36.08%	46.00%	6.32%	29.52%	10.23%	10.23%	46.00%	15.41%	73.00%	0.14%
Upstream Problems=								12.0	17.8	32.3		
Actual Incidents=		52.1	38.2	44.2	22.8	38.3	25.2	34.4	106.9	55.5	204.4	0.5
Expected value		$10,415	$7,637	$8,832	$273	$7,652	$5,049	$6,877	$21,373	$11,095	$1,022	$91
Detection controls												
Visual verification	0.99	0.7	0.3	0.7	0.3		0.4	0.4		0.6		0.7
Edits: Overflow	0.99		0.2							0.3		
Format	0.95			0.7	0.8					0.7		0.7
Completeness	0.99				0.9				0.9		0.7	0.6
Limit/range	0.99			0.6			0.8					
Relationship	0.99			0.6						0.6		0.5
#REF!												
Check digit	0.95			0.7	0.7		0.5	0.6	0.6	0.7		0.6
Approval	0.95		0.7	0.8	0.7		0.6	0.7	0.7	0.8		0.8
Balancing	0.95	0.8	0.9	0.9	0.8	0.9	0.8	0.7	0.8	0.7	0.7	0.7
Reconciliation	0.8	0.95	0.95	0.95	0.95	0.8	0.9	0.9	0.9	0.7	0.8	0.7
Suspense file	0.8	0.9	0.9		0.7	0.8		0.8			0.7	0.6
Aging	0.99		0.8	0.6	0.6	0.8	0.7	0.8	0.9	0.7	0.9	0.7
Matching	0.9	0.9	0.95	0.9	0.8	0.8	0.6	0.8	0.6	0.6	0.6	0.7
Redundant process	0.99			0.9	0.9	0.9	0.9	0.7	0.7	0.9	0.8	0.8
Summary process	0.98			0.8	0.8	0.8	0.8	0.6	0.6	0.8	0.7	0.5
0												
0												
Detection Risk=		0.09%	0.01%	0.00%	0.00%	0.01%	0.04%	0.00%	0.00%	0.00%	0.03%	0.00%
Detected Incidents=		52.0	38.2	44.2	22.8	38.3	25.2	34.4	106.9	55.5	204.3	0.5
Expected value		$10,405	$7,637	$8,832	$273	$7,651	$5,047	$6,876	$21,373	$11,095	$1,022	$91
Correction controls												
Lockout access	0.98		0.8									0.8
Discrepancy message	0.6	0.7	0.8	0.9	0.9	0.6	0.9	0.9	0.8	0.7	0.7	0.7
Discrepancy log	0.99		0.8	0.5	0.5	0.5	0.5	0.8	0.7	0.8		0.8
Discrepancy report	0.9		0.8	0.5	0.5	0.5	0.5	0.95	0.8	0.9	0.6	0.8
Transaction trail	0.3		0.9	0.5	0.5	0.9	0.95	0.95	0.95	0.95	0.7	0.9
Backup w/recovery plan	0.9					0.95						
Supervisory action	0.7			0.3			0.3					0.5
Automated error correction	0.9			0.7	0.6							0.5
Upstream resubmission	0.95	0.9		0.8	0.8		0.8	0.9	0.9	0.8		0.8
Correction risk=		8.41%	0.48%	0.76%	1.20%	1.88%	1.73%	0.14%	0.46%	0.39%	21.08%	0.05%
Residual risk=		5.016%	0.175%	0.350%	0.076%	0.559%	0.181%	0.015%	0.213%	0.061%	15.405%	0.000%
Residual Incidents=		4.4	0.2	0.3	0.3	0.7	0.4	0.0	0.5	0.2	43.1	0.0
Expected value		885	37	67	3	145	89	10	99	44	216	0
Control rating		0.950	0.998	0.996	0.999	0.994	0.997	0.9997	0.997	0.999	0.846	0.999999
Consequences:												
Erroneous records		0.99	0.99	0.99	0.99	0.9	0.9	0.3	0.95	0.95	0.95	0.8
		4.379988	0.183135	0.333084	0.270133	0.651902	0.134138	0.047338	0.490881	0.208005	25.88118	0.000168
Unacceptable accounting		0.05	0.08	0.3	0.2	0.2	0.3	0.2	0.4	0.3	0.3	0.3
		0.221212	0.181286	0.100934	0.054572	0.217301	0.089426	0.019932	0.148752	0.153267	12.94059	6.31E-05
Loss/Destruction of assets		0.01	0.1	0.01	0.1	0.1	0.3	0.05	0.01	0.1	0.01	0.1
		0.044242	0.018499	0.003364	0.027286	0.072434	0.134138	0.002491	0.004958	0.021895	0.431353	2.1E-05
Exposure												

EXHIBIT 15.1 An Application Assessment Model

			OUTPUT				OTHER				Control
File or DB lost	Program lost	People lost	Improper distribution	Privacy violation	Output late	Output lost	Excess error correction	Unsupported output	Unlimited access	Management override	Cost
10000	260	260	10000	10000	260	260	10000	10000	10000	10000	
Trans	Days	Days	Trans	Trans	Days	Days	Trans	Trans	Trans	Trans	
200	7700	7700	200	200	250	7700	200	200	200	200	
50	800	800	50	50	10	800	50	50	50	50	
0.01	0.01	0.01	0.02	0.02	0.02	0.01	0.03	0.02	0.05	0.01	
			0.01	0.02		0.02		0.01	0.02	0.01	
1.0%	1.0%	1.0%	3.0%	4.0%	2.0%	3.0%	3.0%	3.0%	7.0%	2.0%	
0.1	0.1	0.2	0.1	0.1	0.2	0.1	0.3	0.1	0.2	0.3	
0.1	0.1		0.1	0.2	0.1	0.1	0.2	0.1	0.1		
										0.2	
81.0%	81.0%	80.0%	81.0%	72.0%	72.0%	81.0%	56.0%	81.0%	72.0%	56.0%	
0.81%	0.81%	0.80%	2.43%	2.88%	1.44%	2.43%	1.68%	2.43%	5.04%	1.12%	
81.0	2.1	2.1	243.0	288.0	3.7	6.3	168.0	243.0	504.0	112.0	
0.1	0.1		0.6	0.6	0.2	0.2	0.6	0.4	0.4	0.3	
							0.6	0.9			
			0.9							0.6	
		0.7							0.9	0.8	
0.8	0.8		0.6	0.7		0.8			0.9		
			0.9	0.9					0.9	0.7	
32.76%	32.76%	44.00%	13.16%	1.61%	82.00%	29.52%	19.78%	23.68%	1.43%	4.90%	
26.5	0.7	0.9	32.0	4.6	3.1	1.9	33.2	57.5	7.2	5.5	
$5,307	$5,312	$7,047	$6,394	$930	$768	$14,361	$6,646	$11,508	$1,441	$1,097	
							0.7				
			0.7	0.7			0.8				
0.6						0.8					
0.8						0.7		0.8			
				0.7	0.7	0.7				0.5	
				0.6	0.6	0.6				0.5	
15.48%	100.00%	100.00%	33.50%	33.50%	30.70%	3.24%	30.70%	11.05%	100.00%	50.50%	
22.4	0.0	0.0	21.3	3.1	2.1	1.8	23.0	51.2	0.0	2.7	
$4,486	$0	$0	$4,252	$618	$532	$13,895	$4,606	$10,237	$0	$543	MONITOR
				0.9						0.95	
				0.8							
0.7			0.7				0.8	0.8			
0.7											
0.7								0.9			
0.95	0.95					0.95					
		0.7	0.7	0.7	0.7	0.7	0.8	0.7	0.8	0.6	
1.30%	14.50%	51.00%	51.00%	0.96%	51.00%	7.40%	9.15%	7.74%	3.04%	58.00%	
5.432%	32.760%	44.000%	8.869%	0.551%	54.155%	3.069%	7.327%	4.248%	1.429%	3.879%	
4.4	0.7	0.9	21.6	1.6	2.0	0.2	12.3	10.3	7.2	4.3	Loss
880	5,312	7,047	4,310	317	507	1,493	2,462	2,065	1,441	869	
0.95	0.67	0.56	0.91	0.99	0.46	0.97	0.93	0.96	0.99	0.96	Value per Occur
										Sum	$250
0.9	0.7	0.3	0.3		0.3	0.4	0.6	0.4	0.3	0.9	
3.959583	0.48294792	0.27456	6.465587	0	0.608272	0.077566	7.38559	4.129241	2.1608294	3.905817	62.034
0.1	0.1	0.7	0.1		0.2	0.5	0.5	0.7	0.2	0.9	400
0.439954	0.06899256	0.64064	2.155196	0	0.405515	0.096958	3.692795	7.226171	1.440553	3.905817	34.204
0.3	0.05	0.05	0.01		0.05	0.05	0.1	0.05	0.2	0.5	2,000
1.319861	0.03449628	0.04576	0.21552	0	0.101379	0.009696	1.230932	0.516155	1.440553	2.172121	7.847
										Exposure=	$44,884

EXHIBIT 15.1 *(Continued)*

An Application Assessment Model

The illustrative model displayed in Exhibit 15.1 is a generic application that serves as an example only. It shows how all the modeling elements fit together in typical relationships.

As described in Chapter 8, Quantitative Control Relationships, we model the inherent risk of a problem (input not recorded) by estimating the probabilities of occurrence due to various risk factors and adding the various risk factors (not to exceed 1.00). In Exhibit 15.1 this is just one factor amounting to 2 percent.

Then we list and estimate the inherent risk reduction from the environmental factors, and calculate the joint probability that all will fail. In the exhibit this calculation is $(1 - 0.3) \times (1 - 0.3) \times (1 - 0.1) = 0.7 \times 0.7 \times 0.9 = 0.441$.

The inherent risk times the environment risk is $0.2 \times 0.441 = 0.88$. When the number of opportunities (10,000) is considered, the model calculates that approximately 88.2 incidents will possibly occur in one year.

Assessing control requires not only an estimate of each control's effectiveness over each problem, but also the reliability that the control will actually be applied to every incident. In the exhibit this calculation for the first potential problem calculates $[1 - (0.2 \times 0.9)] \times [1 - (0.4 \times 0.7)] = 0.82 \times 0.72 = 59.04\%$ as the prevention risk. When the probable number of actual incidents that will occur is considered, the model calculates that $(88.2 \times 0.5904) =$ approximately 52.1 will evade prevention. An application model that is dependent on a supporting system and its controls must be designed to incorporate incidents of problems that are put upon it by the upstream system. We explore a method for modeling this in the next chapter.

Detection and correction failure risk is calculated in the same manner as prevention, and yields risks of 0.09 percent and 8.41 percent, respectively.

The detection risk is fairly low, and we calculate that $[52.1 \times (1 - 0.0009)] = 52.0$ out of the 52.1 actual incidents will be detected.

Although detection is strong in this instance, not so for correction. The model calculates that $(52.1 \times \{.0009 + [(1 - .0009) \times .0841]\}) =$ approximately 4.4 incidents will remain as uncorrected residual problems.

Applications are also subject to incidents of problems caused in a support system, such as the network, server, or database. Such incidents have already occurred and cannot be subject to application prevention controls. The application must detect such problems and can attempt to correct them, but correction might also be dependent on corrections to the system that was the source of the problems.

Not recording input will almost always (99 percent) have consequences, producing erroneous records 4.38 of the times. This allows for instances when the omissions offset or somehow are not relevant. However, unacceptable accounting will probably result from only 5 percent of the incidents, producing this consequence only once every four or five years (22 percent of the years). Finally, the inputs not recorded will probably cause loss or destruction of assets in only about 1 percent of the incidents. This is $4.4 \times .01 = 0.044$, or roughly every 23 years.

When the estimated instances are accumulated for each type of consequence, and each is given an estimated typical value, the product of these sums equals $29,567 total exposure. Whether this is material depends on the overall totals of the affected accounts.

Summary

Applications normally provide the bulk of the systems needing risk and control assessments. Only those applications that are determined to affect the assessment objectives need be fully assessed, of course. An application can serve both financial reporting objectives and internal operating objectives. As a result, some seemingly important controls might not be key to financial reporting. Careful analysis of this can reveal that fewer controls are really key to the objective than one would intuitively expect.

A quantitative model of application risks, controls, and consequences is usually structured around the potential problems with input, processing, and output functions, plus a few other potential problems that don't fit into any category. Application systems can occur in multiple copies and be subject to residual incidents of problems that occur in supporting systems.

CHAPTER 16

General and Infrastructure Systems

The Environment

General systems encompass a variety of functions that service and support application systems. This chapter presents a generic example of the approach to assessing these important support systems. These systems include:

- Internal development of new application systems
- Purchase and installation of commercially developed application systems
- Operating system software
- Database management system software
- Network hardware and software
- Communications hardware and software
- Server hardware and disk arrays
- Maintenance and changes to all of these systems

Some general systems can be viewed as another type of transaction processing; others exist mostly as a constant condition of activity.

For example, development of new application systems or projects to maintain or change application systems, essentially process transactions in the form of projects. Network operations, on the other hand, focus on continuous availability, speed, and performance.

CobiT for Control of IT

Control Objectives for Information and Related Technology (CobiT) is the product of the IT Governance Institute, an educational foundation associated with the Information Systems Audit and Control Association (ISACA). In their approach, applications and facilities are classified as separate systems, with facilities being one of the general infrastructure systems, together with technology. Data is a component of application systems. People fulfill a huge variety of roles, but in the context of resources they serve as part of systems and controls.

Like COSO, CobiT has much broader goals than simply financial reporting. It is directed toward IT governance, control, and assurance. This covers everything that IT provides to a business.

CobiT is structured around four *domains*, or phases of the systems development process. These domains are:

1. Planning and organization
2. Acquisition and implementation
3. Delivery and support
4. Monitoring

Within these domains, CobiT lists 34 high-level *control objectives*, also referred to as *naturally grouped processes*. These objectives contain a mixture of what we would mostly characterize as meta-controls and control environment factors. An example is "Manage data." This sounds laudable, but what does it mean?

Next, CobiT lists 7 information criteria and 5 IT resources to which some or all of the 34 control objectives/processes could apply. The information criteria are positive statements that are the reverse of many adverse consequences. They are:

1. Effectiveness
2. Efficiency
3. Confidentiality
4. Integrity
5. Availability
6. Compliance
7. Reliability

The IT resources are:

1. People
2. Applications
3. Technology (operating systems, DBMSs, networks)
4. Facilities
5. Data

The CobiT Framework contains 318 detailed control objectives, some of which are simply direct statements that a particular control is necessary. The authors have a fundamental disagreement that control should be an objective in and of itself, but these 318 criteria also presume many generalities that simply might not apply. If some do not apply, could there be some that are omitted because they apply only in rare instances or because the environment has changed since CobiT updated its list?

CobiT appears to presume that systems are designed with clear and stable objectives, expertise, and awareness. In reality, systems were developed before anyone currently in the IT department can remember, and they do not meet the current business objectives. Moreover, many businesses today use off-the-shelf IT solutions software rather than developing it in-house.

In April 2004, the IT Governance Institute, publishers of CobiT, also published a mapping of CobiT to Sarbanes-Oxley.

At some businesses, an IT staff could be shorthanded and green, with nobody knowing what is going on with the business except what they find on the SEC's EDGAR site or from a Bloomberg terminal. Too cynical a picture? Not at all! CobiT tells us a lot about how to do it right, but it does not give much guidance to assess the consequences when it was not done right.

What Can Go Wrong with General Systems?

The following are examples of a few of the major types of general and infrastructure systems and some of the most common things that can go wrong with them.

Internal Development of New Application Systems

The design and programming of an application system is a complex and risky project. Many development projects exceed their authorized budgets and some never complete an acceptable system. Internally developed systems might also contain more errors than purchased programs; however, they may be necessary when highly customized solutions are required.

Purchase and Installation of a Commercially Developed Application System

The main alternative to internal systems development is purchase from a software vendor. The proliferation of computer technology has created such large markets for many applications that few applications are so unique that no commercial version is available. Commercial software is usually cheaper than internal development and usually lowers risk of failing to deliver acceptable operation.

This does not mean that the commercial software alternative is cheap or foolproof. The basic licensing fees can be significant, and the system might require expensive hardware, staff support, and vendor maintenance. Many commercial systems are, in substance, specialized programming suites that must be adapted and configured to a specific company and use. Conversion might also require collection and conversion of data. The time and cost of adaptation and conversion can eclipse the cost of the basic software.

Maintenance and Changes to Application Systems

Once installed and running, all applications will encounter some requirements for maintenance or changes. Internally developed systems will require an internal programming staff to develop the modifications; commercial software vendors will usually make periodic upgrades or patches available.

Either way, maintenance changes will be necessary to fix bugs, adapt to changing operating systems and database management systems, and offer functional improvements. Unfortunately, the changes can also introduce new bugs or render linked systems incompatible.

Operating System Software

Each computer uses an operating system (OS) for basic user operations and controls. Microsoft, with Windows, holds a near monopoly on operating systems for personal computers; Apple has its proprietary OS, and several operating systems (UNIX, Linux, Windows, etc.) share the market for network servers.

Operating systems are highly complex pieces of software. In spite of its monopoly market position, Microsoft Windows has been notorious for crashing during routine use. As operating and security vulnerabilities are identified and corrected by the manufacturer, users must watch for releases of the corrections (patches) and install them.

Database Software

Database software manages the transfer and storage of data in many applications. Most modern systems link related segments using internal pointers, which sometimes can become corrupted during normal operation or unscheduled interruptions. Most database systems include a corrective control to reindex the database when directed by the user or an IT technician.

Database management software is also the usual location for edits and reasonableness tests of data elements submitted as inputs or generated by application software. This provides uniformity, consistency, and reliability to the editing controls.

Network Hardware and Software

Most businesses interconnect their many computers via a wired or wireless network. Several generic architectures exist, each implemented by further alternative hardware and software components. In some instances, an alternative exists between a component being provided by hardware or software.

Networks can experience failures or slow performance. Networks also present major access and other security concerns. The public Internet network has become a playground for malicious worms, viruses, spam, fraud, and information theft.

Communications Hardware and Software

Once a network connection is established, various hardware and software components provide the services that use the network. These include email agents, Web browsers, host/server configurations, and others. Many of these services should be considered general systems that support access to business applications.

Because most of these systems are sold widely, their foibles are watched for a slipup that can be exploited by malware or other problems. As soon as a vulnerability is discovered in a popular product, the word spreads quickly among the hacker community. Exploits of the vulnerability often occur within hours. A race ensues, with the vendor trying to develop and distribute a remedial patch before exploits penetrate many systems. Users must be notified and ready to install the patch as soon as it is available so as to protect their software and data.

Email

Email has become the method for much of the formal and informal communications within many companies. It is widely relied on to communicate many business matters and policy announcements and to transfer work products in the form of spreadsheets, reports, and images as attachments to email messages. It is also used to communicate rumors, jokes, personal conversations, social announcements, and other nonbusiness matters.

Email systems distribute and store everything they receive. This two-edged sword assists retrieval of useful documents together with "smoking guns." The first thing civil or criminal investigators seize is all the email files they can reach with their subpoenas or warrants. Failure to promptly deliver complete records can be punished by devastating penalties and judicial rulings. Delivery of incriminating communications can give the opposition devastating evidence, even when it was unofficial and unintentional.

For example, a major investment banking firm was fined and found guilty by summary judgment after it repeatedly claimed that all subpoenaed email materials had been delivered—and then repeatedly found more.

Another investment company delivered emails that showed that internal experts had major doubts about the quality of certain investment products it was offering to the public, while management told buyers that they were safe.

Controls over General Systems

Like the problems, available and appropriate controls depend on the nature of the system. We will not attempt to provide a comprehensive list of alternative controls; we simply describe a few examples of the most common or important ones. CobiT provides an excellent source for a more comprehensive listing of recommended controls in each of the several IT domains.

Acceptance Testing

Every change to any software component must be tested to assure its proper installation and functioning in the specific environment, before it is relied on to maintain business systems.

Supervision

Expertise in *how* to do something will usually assure steady employment, but expertise in *why* it is done will promote the expert to management. Good, effective supervision involves frequent observation, review, and comprehension of what is important and why. IT supervision of general systems must include understanding not only the technical nuances but also the potential consequences to applications and the total enterprise.

Physical Security

Access and protection of the physical IT assets are fundamental necessities. A multitude of hazards exist that can be reduced by limiting access and by providing physical protection.

Electronic Security

Security over computer operations and networks is a major challenge in the current environment. The Internet can be connected to every type of computer system, even when it is not authorized. When systems are connected to the Internet, some security problems have proven very difficult to control, and the environment changes rapidly to present new and altered threats. Intranets and other network systems also present access issues.

Some of the common electronic security controls include:

- Firewalls
- Spam filters
- Traffic monitoring
- Encryption
- Passwords

Computer and network security is so complex and volatile that most organizations with any significant vulnerability employ security specialists or consultants.

Backup and Recovery

This corrective control will be needed by every computer user; the only uncertainty is when. Backup copies of computer software and files can be generated continuously or periodically, depending on the hardware configuration and importance of the files. Recovery procedures should be carefully planned and occasionally tested because backups can be destroyed by inept recovery.

Contingency Planning

Most modern enterprises are deeply dependent on their IT systems. Hazards that disrupt or deprive the enterprise of system resources can quickly bring the business to a complete halt. Every organization must plan for how it will continue operation in the face of a disruptive event.

Redundancy

Many strategies to survive disasters and disruptions rely on redundant resources: database arrays, network circuits, processing facilities, and so on. Clever allocation of tasks and resources can avoid redundant costs.

Infrastructure Model

We have chosen to use the example of a network system to illustrate the modeling of an infrastructure system (see Exhibit 16.1). Networks have

Quantitave Assurance Model Template		Documentation Reference	Problems						Control		
Infrastructure or Supporting Network			Wrong Server	Open Access	Service Disrupted	Service Slow	Malware Download	User Spoof	Cost		
Rate by likelihood/probability											
Opportunities >			1000	1000	220	220	1000	365			
Units of Measure>		per year	Site access	Site access	Days	Days	Site access	Days			
Inherent Risk Factors											
Nature of problem			0.5	0.5	0.2	0.1	0.1	0.1			
Internal abuse			0.1	0.2	0.1		0.1	0.1			
External abuse					0.1	0.1	0.1	0.1			
Inherent Risk=			60.0%	70.0%	40.0%	20.0%	30.0%	30.0%			
Control Environment											
Tone at the top			0.3	0.2	0.1						
Reliability of Personnel			0.3	0.3	0.3						
Competence of Personnel			0.3	0.4	0.3						
Segregation of duties											
Environment Risk=			34.3%	33.6%	44.1%	100.0%	100.0%	100.0%			
Preliminary Risk=			20.58%	23.52%	17.64%	20.00%	30.00%	30.00%			
Potential Incidents=			205.8	235.2	38.808	44	300	109.5			
Prevention Controls		Implementation									
Fire wall	N-1	0.9	0.99	0.9			0.9				
User ID and Password	N-2	0.99		0.95				0.8			
Password rotation	N-3	0.8						0.8			
Prevention Risk=			10.90%	1.13%	100.00%	100.00%	19.00%	7.49%			
Actual Incidents=			22.4	2.7	38.8	44.0	57.0	8.2			
Detection Controls											
Access log	N-9	0.99	0.7		0.5		0.5				
Malware detection software	N-10	0.99	0.9			0.9					
Wrong password counter	N-11	0.99	-0.5			0.9					
User notify	M-1	0.7			0.99	0.75	0.2				
Network monitor software	N-12	0.99			0.99	0.9		0.6			
Detection Risk=			3.35%	149.50%	0.61%	2.61%	9.37%	2.23%			
Detected Incidents=			21.7	-1.3	38.6	42.8	51.7	8.0	Monitor		
Correction Controls											
Malware removal software	N-22	0.97					0.8				
Wrong password 3X shutout	N-23	0.99						0.7			
Network Administrator action	M-2	0.9	0.95	0.9	0.9	0.8	0.6	0.9			
User action	M-3										
Correction Risk=			14.50%	19.00%	19.00%	28.00%	10.30%	5.83%			
Residual Risk=			1.892%	1.584%	19.495%	29.883%	3.555%	0.594%			
Residual Problems=			3.9	3.7	7.6	13.1	10.7	0.7			
Control Rating			0.98	0.98	0.81	0.70	0.96	0.99	Number of Incidents	Value per occurrence	
Consequences:											
Process against wrong file or database			0.05	0.99			0.3	0.99	7.7		Appl problem
			0.1947237	3.687786	0	0	3.1997696	0.644313			
Process against wrong record or segment			0.4				0.3	0.1	4.8		Appl Problem
			1.5577895	0	0	0	3.1997696	0.065082			
Processing incomplete			0.8				0.3	0.1	6.4		Appl problem
			3.1155789	0	0	0	3.1997696	0.065082			
Wasted labor			0.8		0.9	0.7			19.1	$160	$3,061
			3.1155789	0	6.809006	9.203822	0	0			
Loss/Destruction of assets			0.01	0.3	0.2	0.1	0.8	0.8	13.0	$2,000	$26,076
			0.0389447	1.1175109	1.513113	1.314832	8.532719	0.520657			
Insert if more									**Exposure=**		$29,136

EXHIBIT 16.1 Model of Network Infrastructure

become pervasive in the past 20 years, with both internal and Internet connections to substantially every workstation and server.

The potential problems and controls in this example are, like a network itself, immersed in technological jargon. Nevertheless, such technical issues can bring devastating consequences and must be rigorously assessed.

The purpose of this book is to enable quantification of risk and control assessments, not to provide a cookbook for control of any particular system.

Therefore, the problems, risk factors, controls, and consequences used to illustrate quantitative assessment are not presumed to be comprehensive or applicable to any particular instance of any general or infrastructure system. Readers and others involved in such an assessment must identify and consider those problems, risk factors, controls, and consequences specific to the system they are assessing.

Summary

Chapter 10 discussed the core concepts of interdependent systems. IT systems provide abundant examples of the dependency of computer application systems on the IT infrastructure. The risk and control implications of these interdependencies can be difficult to grasp for people who are not familiar with technical functions. Other times, the interdependencies can be so familiar that they are overlooked.

The significance of system dependencies depends on what is dependent. Senior IT and operations managers should be able to contribute essential information on what allows other things to work.

CHAPTER 17

Trusted System Providers

The Environment

A consistent and important trend in the evolution of information technology has been the migration of functions and controls. If we look back to the earliest computers in the 1950s, each machine was self-contained, and the program software had to include instructions for the most mundane operating tasks. These were the days before compilers, operating systems, database management systems, and networks. The only trusted providers were the manufacturers of the hardware and the electric power utility company. Contrast this with our current dependence on:

- Computer manufacturers
- Peripheral manufacturers
- The electric power utility
- Network component manufacturers
- Network line providers
- Network software providers
- Email agent software
- Internet service providers
- Operating system providers
- Database software providers
- Communications software providers
- Application software providers
- Programming language providers
- Application service providers (ASPs)

Each of these linked components must function properly for the entire system to function. A breakdown, malfunction, or "crash" can stop everything. In a modern business, if the network is down, you might as well send the employees home. They might be able to do little or nothing.

How Much to Trust Trusted Systems?

In general, service providers are the buy solution to a make-or-buy decision. The primary reasons for outsourcing include:

- Use of a provider might avoid requirements for scarce capital.
- Service is beyond the resources of the user.
- Providers can deliver at lower cost than the user can provide internally. This might reflect economies of scale or efficiencies of specialization.
- Providers can deliver better quality than an internal source. This might involve reliability or speed.

Often the decision is so obvious that no formal make-or-buy analysis is attempted. Hardly anyone is going to attempt to develop his own computer operating system. The time, cost, and effort for a user to build her own replacement for Microsoft's Windows, for example, would be absurd. Neither is anyone likely to build his own telephone network or buy his own electric power plant.

Many other instances involve more consideration. Should a company develop its own inventory management system or purchase one from a software vendor? Should it design a payroll system, purchase it, or contract with a payroll service? A company might even consider its own assembly of personal computers directly from purchased components if they cost less than buying standard models from recognized manufacturers.

A company could keep many of these functions in-house, or it could outsource its noncore functions. Although the economics might differ, many of the potential problems do not.

Users must still be concerned with manufacturing and design defects in their business systems, no matter who put them there or who operates them. One might assume that a software vendor would have greater resources to thoroughly test newly developed or updated software than would an in-house development staff, but this does not provide absolute assurance that purchased software is free of bugs. Users of trusted providers must still test, control, and monitor the products and services they purchase.

The purpose of this book is to enable quantification of risk and control assessments, not to provide a cookbook for control of any particular system. Therefore, the problems, risk factors, controls, and consequences used to illustrate quantitative assessment are not assumed to be comprehensive or applicable to any particular instance of a system outsourced to or acquired from an independent provider. Readers and others involved in such an assessment must identify and consider those problems, risk factors, controls, and consequences specific to the system they are assessing.

Provider Problems

Providers are vulnerable to many of the same types of problems as the user would be if the user kept the service in-house. Failures in trusted systems fall into three major categories: design, manufacture, or service.

Design Defects

A designer of a system to be used by multiple customers must anticipate a variety of environments and needs. This is much more challenging than designing a good system for a single user. A flexible design will permit extensive options and preferences for every primary function. The system must operate under a variety of operating systems and networks. Complete compatibility can be very elusive.

Design defects, particularly in software, are often difficult to detect, although they are present as soon as the device or program is installed. The Y2K problem was caused by early constraints in legacy systems and poor design in recent ones.

One special type of design defect might not be considered an actual defect at all. The computer code that goes into a software product could be acquired from a variety of sources. Very often, the lower cost of skilled programmers in developing nations causes the primary designer to subcontract portions of the development to such resources.

> For example, in China, local subcontractors have been known to install "back door" access to the software they design. This can be motivated by industrial espionage or as a device to evade controls applied by the Chinese government to monitor use of the Internet by dissidents.

Certainly industrial espionage is a serious problem that should be classified with computer abuse and fraud. The creation of back doors to evade foreign political controls is seen by some as an acceptable accompaniment to the software. An informed decision of this type belongs to the board of directors or the audit committee.

Manufacturing Defects

Manufacturing errors in software usually mean that the CD-ROM or other media containing the programs cannot be loaded and installed. This type of defect is usually obvious rather quickly. Manufacturing defects in hardware could be subtler. The device might work properly for a time but then fail. Anything with mechanical moving parts will eventually wear out, and the accumulated effects of heat can cause integrated circuits to fail.

Service Defects

Service failures from trusted providers also could be obvious. When the power goes out or the telephones have no dial tone, everyone notices. The same could be true for an Internet service provider or remote application provider. Power surges or brownouts can also harm delicate electrical circuits.

Other service defects might more subtle. Does the payroll servicer adequately protect the privacy of employees? Does the software vendor promptly provide users with patches to correct design vulnerabilities that are discovered?

CONTINUITY OF SERVICE   Service providers can go out of business, leaving customers without support or the resources necessary to support themselves. They also can be overwhelmed by customer demands and decide that your company has a lower priority than another. Denial-of-service attacks over the Internet can also obstruct customer service.

CUSTOMER DISSATISFACTION   Service providers are in business to earn their own profits. If they are to cost less than the customer would pay "making" the product internally, they must be sufficiently more efficient that they can earn their profit and still price their product below a user's costs. This efficiency often comes by limiting the customer's options and choices to the vendor's standards. These limits sometimes force the user to conform their operations to fit the provider rather than operate in the manner they previously preferred.

USER OPERATING ERRORS   An external provider presents another requirement for communication of necessary procedures and practices. Some providers have difficulty communicating in the language of the users, whether English in general or the user's industry jargon. Some fail to communicate at all. A user is likely to make errors or omissions in operating any type of system—a likelihood that grows substantially if the user is uninformed.

Internal Controls Over Trusted Systems

Trust, but verify! Although a user might have assurance that the provider's controls are reasonably effective, compensating controls will give additional assurance and monitor the provider's controls.

Generic Controls

The following controls are commonly available to manage problems with service providers. Many must be applied or agreed upon before the contract with the servicer is signed. Retrofitting some of these controls might be resisted by the provider.

A service provider may occasionally resist revealing the requested risk and control information with the explanation that it is proprietary or confidential. This is especially common with source code to software. If the user organization accedes to this refusal, the user must plan to implement compensating controls.

STRONG CONTRACTS AND SERVICE-LEVEL AGREEMENTS (SLAs)   An SLA spells out in detail what the provider will do during the term of its service and what falls under the responsibility of the user. A well-defined SLA is essential to maintaining amicable relations between provider and users.

EVALUATE PROVIDER STABILITY   When a user adopts a system from a provider, it becomes dependent to some degree on the future availability of that provider for a warranty of the system, maintenance, and continuing services. A disruption of the provider is just as serious as a disruption of an internal provider, but the user does not have the access, resources, and flexibility he or she would have dealing with an internal interruption. To avoid this situation, a user can investigate the strength of the financial, personnel, and other resources of the provider he or she plans to trust. Source code can be held in an escrow by a trust company. The provider's continuity plan can be reviewed by an independent expert. Existing customers can be contacted for detailed references. These efforts and others can lend some assurance that the provider can be trusted before an agreement is completed.

OPERATIONS DOCUMENTATION   Many software providers attach some indexed text file to a help command on their menus. They might also provide a link through the Internet to more extensive instructions on their web sites. A few still print and distribute paper manuals with their product installation discs. The electronic aids are preferred by both users and providers because they can be readily updated for changes in new versions and are cheaper to distribute.

THIRD-PARTY CONTROL ATTESTATION REPORTS   Generally accepted auditing standards (GAAS) permit reliance on assurances prepared in accordance with an SAS No. 70 type II report, as described in Auditing Standards AU Section 324. In essence, the independent auditor of the service provider (the service auditor) acts as an agent or proxy for the independent auditor of the company receiving the service (the user auditor). Of course, this is necessary only if the user auditor determines that key controls reside within the systems at the service provider.

For this to work, the service auditor must be aware of which servicer controls the user relies upon, and the servicer must agree to allow and support the work necessary for the service auditor to attest to them.

In practice, a service provider usually provides the same or very similar services to several users. Accordingly, key controls of each and every user must be covered by the service auditor's report.

TYPICAL OPERATING CONTROLS A trusted system needs to include all the normal prevention, detection, and correction controls that the user would develop if the system were provided from internal resources. One of the reasons to outsource a system might be that it is better controlled and tested by experience than the user could do internally at a reasonable cost.

These controls include both programmed controls in the software provided as well as detection control reports that the user must investigate and correct.

A user organization is just as responsible for the information produced by a trusted system as it is for one developed internally. If it is relevant and important to the quality of the information, the trusted system will be subject to the assessments and tests required under SOX. Accordingly, the provider should include detailed control documentation for the assessment process by the user.

PASSWORD ROTATION Over time, passwords can be inadvertently disclosed or observed. To reestablish the confidentiality of a password, many organizations mandate a periodic change of each password. The period might be a year or a day, but commonly it is 30 or 90 days.

Changing passwords is a bother to users, and many will procrastinate if possible. Many computer networks include software that times the changes of passwords, gives a warning that a change will be needed within X days, and nags for the change.

FIREWALLS All modern computers are equipped with ports that accept input signals from outside the machine, across some network. A firewall closes off ports that are not assigned a current use and monitors the signals arriving through the open ports according to criteria for legitimacy. A trusted system that provides inputs across a network should be assigned a unique port.

A firewall can be set up with hardware or software. The hardware type is more robust against penetration; the software type is more flexible and easier to monitor. Penetration attacks via the Internet are so pervasive that a firewall is mandatory for any computer that can be connected to the Internet.

ACCEPTANCE TESTS   Just as any competent IT department tests the software that it develops, so must be the software that is leased or purchased. Trusting a provider does not mean that provider is perfect. An outside provider might not anticipate some peculiar characteristic of your hardware and software configuration. A system that has been installed with no problems dozens of times elsewhere can still fail when it encounters some new configuration.

POST-IMPLEMENTATION REVIEWS   Shortly after a system is installed or major changes are made to it, the user should conduct an in-depth review to determine that the system and its users are coordinated and functioning as intended. This differs from acceptance testing in that it takes place some-what later and focuses on achieving intended objectives rather than simple functionality.

SCHEDULED AND UNSCHEDULED MAINTENANCE   Most software providers pro-vide scheduled updates of their systems that can add valuable features and correct minor defects that have been discovered. If the defect is serious enough, the provider should notify all its users and deliver a patch to fix it as soon as possible. One of the major problems with this practice is users who do not install the patch or upgrade promptly and leave the system vulnerable to everyone else who has learned about the defect.

A Trusted Provider Assessment Model

This section presents a sample trusted provider assessment model, shown in Exhibit 17.1. At the top of the model, we have estimated the number of opportunities at 8500, an approximate number of working days in a typ-ical fiscal year. We have also elaborated risks for six potential problems: design defects, manufacturing defects, service defects, continuity of service, customer dissatisfaction, and embedded malware.

The consequences of these provider problems will mostly be passed downstream to dependent application systems in the form of application problems that are not contained by application prevention controls. A few of the consequences are retained in the direct environment, such as wasted labor and loss of assets (money or operating assets).

Quantitative Assurance Model Template											
Application											
Trusted Payroll Provider				**Problems**						Control	
Rate by liklihood/ probability	Documentation reference		Design defect	Manufacturing defect	Service defect	Interruption of service	Dissatisfaction with service	Embedded malware		Cost	
Opportunities> **Units of measure>**		per year	220 days	220 days	220 days	220 days	220 days	220 days			
Inherent risk factors											
Nature of problem			0.05	0.01	0.1	0.05	0.1	0.01			
Fraud appeal			0.05			0.01	0.1				
Inherent risk=			10.0%	1.0%	10.0%	6.0%	10.0%	11.0%			
Control Environment											
Tone at the Top			0.3	0.3			0.1	0.2			
Reliability of persn			0.3	0.3	0.5	0.2	0.1	0.2			
Competence of persn			0.3	0.5	0.6		0.1	0.1			
Segregation of duties								0.2			
Environment risk=			34.3%	24.5%	20.0%	80.0%	72.9%	46.1%			
Preliminary Risk=			3.43%	0.25%	2.00%	4.80%	7.29%	5.07%			
Potential Incidents=			7.5	0.5	4.4	10.6	16.0	11.2			
Prevention controls (Implementation)											
Service-level agreement	SLA	0.9	0.2		0.5	0.2	0.6	0.2			
Provider stability evaluation	0	0.98			0.1	0.3	0.1				
Operating documentation	0	0.9	0.2		0.3	0.1	0.4				
Firewall	0	0.99			0.7		0.5				
Operating controls	0	0.9	0.6	0.3		0.3		0.3			
Prevention risk=			30.93%	73.00%	36.22%	11.81%	26.55%	30.23%			
Upstream Problems=											
Actual Incidents=			2.3	0.4	1.6	1.2	4.3	3.4			
Detection controls											
3rd-party attestation	SAS 70	0.99	0.7	0.3	0.5	0.7	0.5	0.7			
Operating controls	0	0.9	0.1	0.3	0.7	0.7	0.5	0.6			
Acceptance test	0	0.95	0.7	0.9	0.6	0.3	0.1	0.7			
Post-implementation review	0	0.7	0.9	0.9	0.9	0.3	0.7	0.4			
Detection Risk=			3.46%	2.75%	2.97%	6.42%	12.82%	3.41%			
Detected Incidents=			2.3	0.4	1.5	1.2	3.7	3.3		MONITOR	
Correction controls											
Unscheduled maintenance	0	0.8	0.95	0.95	0.9	0.9	0.7	0.97			
Password rotation	0	0.97			0.3		0.8				
Scheduled maintenance	0	0.95	0.95	0.95	0.9		0.7	0.98			
Source code escrow	0	0.9			0.9						
Operating controls	0	0.9	0.7	0.5	0.3	0.3	0.3	0.3			
Correction risk=			0.87%	1.29%	2.96%	2.75%	10.76%	0.25%			
Residual risk=			1.330%	2.924%	2.118%	1.062%	5.895%	1.103%			
Residual Incidents=			0.1	0.0	0.1	0.1	0.9	0.1			
Control rating			0.99	0.97	0.98	0.99	0.94	0.99		Value	
Application Problems:									Sum	per Occur	
Erroneous paycheck			0.99	0.99	0.8	0.99	0.9	0.8		$500	$625
			0.09932661	0.01560023	0.07455512	0.11099971	0.85093566	0.0984421	1.249859		
Privacy violation			0.05	0.1	0.1	0.2	0.1	0.1		1,000	145
			0.0050165	0.00157578	0.00931939	0.02242418	0.09454841	0.0123053	0.14519		
Excessive costs			0.01	0.02	0.01	0.1	0.01	0.5		2,500	211
			0.0010033	0.00031516	0.00093194	0.01121209	0.00945484	0.0615263	0.084444		
								Exposure=			$981

EXHIBIT 17.1 Example Trusted Provider Model

Summary

Service providers can be vital and integral to all kinds of functions and processes. Their service might range from being a simple supplier to providing complete management of a major business function. When their service constitutes a component of a system that is subject to a risk and control assessment, both their controls and user controls must be formally included and documented in the assessment, and then tested to the extent that the servicer is providing key controls.

CHAPTER 18

Reporting on Internal Control

The Environment

The ultimate audience to a report on internal control over financial reporting is the investing public. Although this includes the proverbial "widows and orphans," the most influential audience is the handful of securities analysts who follow the company. These people judge the reliability of the company's financial reports, independently predict its earnings, and recommend whether investors should buy, hold, or sell their stock in the company.

Analysts would prefer to receive something more than a boilerplate report that signals a rating by counting the number of paragraphs. On the other hand, space will limit the explanations of the considerations involved in an assessment. Sarbanes-Oxley only requires public disclosure of material weaknesses, if any, that exist at the ending date of the reporting period. The SEC also requires that additional information provided to securities analysts and investors be simultaneously or promptly provided to the public (Regulation FD—Fair Disclosure[1]). Section 302 of Sarbanes-Oxley prescribes public quarterly reports disclosing significant changes in internal controls during the preceding quarter. The form and content of public reports on internal control assessments are prescribed by PCAOB AS-5, paragraphs 85 through 98.

The audit committee should require considerably more detail. Although they also must receive an overall assessment, they should be given brief descriptions of every system included or excluded from the assessments. This will allow them to appraise the scope of the evaluation. They also must be given expanded descriptions of any material weaknesses as well as any significant discrepancies or any instances of fraud of any magnitude in any function. Communications by the CPAs with the audit committee and board of directors are prescribed by SAS Nos. 115 and 117.

Condensed results from control assessment models can fulfill many of the needs of the audit committee.

The quantitative control assessment models we have presented express risk as probabilities with values between zero and one. This is in accordance with the conventional mathematics of probability. Unfortunately, this convention is not particularly readable or readily convertible into normal human comprehension. It puts all the digits behind a decimal point, and small probabilities are preceded by countless zeros. This simply does not communicate risks well to board members or executives.

A slightly better format for presentation to these individuals is percentages. Spreadsheet software can easily be set to format numbers as percentages. However, small probabilities still end up with decimals and leading zeros.

For presentation purposes, verbal expressions often communicate better. A 1 percent risk can be stated as 1 in 100. Psychologists tell us that people react more to such statements because they focus on the numerator as being a real incident. The "one" will happen; the only questions are how often and when.[2] Comparison with a familiar, but rare, hazard, such as being struck by lightning (400,000 to 1, according to the National Weather Service), might help provide a frame of reference.

Results of Modeling

The control models described in the preceding chapters contain an abundance of detail regarding the relationships of individual control features to specific problems and systems. They go far beyond the level of information needed by the CEO, CFO, and audit committee to comply with SOX.

On the other hand, they do *not* directly answer the essential question: Does the company have reasonable assurance that it has effective internal control over the contents and presentation of the public financial statements? This final answer can only be decided by company management and the board of directors after they digest the results of the models of the design and tests of internal controls.

SOX and the rules promulgated by the SEC in its implementation discuss but never directly quantify what is meant by *reasonable* assurance or *effective* control. Management must decide what is reasonable in the circumstances and what is sufficiently effective. This decision is part of the control environment. The models produce both qualitative and quantitative measures that can assist in these decisions. Then the external auditors must agree.

Start with presuming that all the individual controls and levels of compliance really operate in the manner contained in the models. The most important information is:

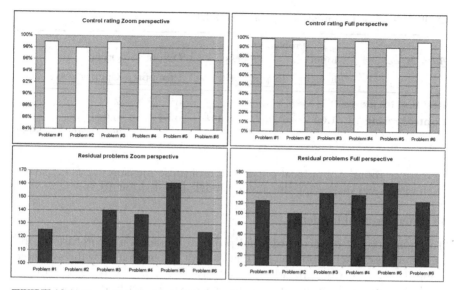

EXHIBIT 18.1 Chart Perspectives Influence Perception

- The nature of the problems considered
- The quantities of expected residual incidents
- The control ratings
- The total exposure

By hiding the other cells, the view of each model can be reduced to these essential results (see Exhibit 18.1).

The Nature of the Problems

The lists of considered problems should include everything that could go wrong with the financial reports and cause a material misstatement. The completeness of these issues is so important that it should have been agreed on at the top level before any models were completed. The nature of the problem is a qualitative consideration. The potential problems must include the concerns of all parties to the assessment.

Control Ratings

The quantitative control ratings should describe how good the controls are over each significant potential problem (see Exhibit 18.2). Management must decide whether 90 percent is reasonable or whether the problem deserves 99

EXHIBIT 18.2 The Quantitative Assessment Model

Basic Model	Problems				
	Input	Process		Output	Other
	Inaccur	Inapprt	File lost	Unsupprt	Open access
Residual Incidents	0.03	3	4	85	2
Control rating	**1.00**	**0.90**	**0.35**	**0.64**	**0.94**
					Exposure $959

percent or more. A graphical presentation of these measurements is usually preferable over displaying the actual models (see Exhibit 18.3).

Expected Residual Incidents

The quantities of expected residual problem incidents are forecasts of the occurrences of each problem type that will not be eliminated by the available controls. They do not include the severity of the problem, except that it might be significant in the aggregate or we would not bother assessing it. Again, management must decide whether the forecasts indicate tolerable levels according to the qualitative nature of the problems.

Again, a summary graphical presentation is usually preferred over the detailed quantitative model (see Exhibit 18.4).

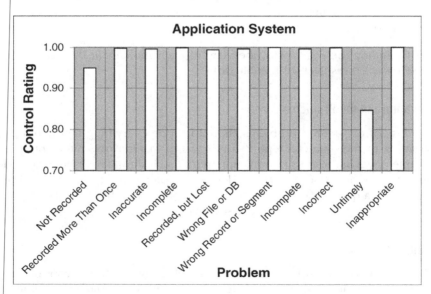

EXHIBIT 18.3 Graphical Presentation of Control Ratings

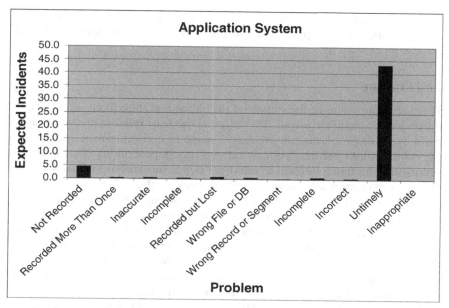

EXHIBIT 18.4 Expected Incidents

The estimates of residual incidents are not the final word on this subject. What remains are the unknown unknowns. These are the things that are totally off the radar. They are whatever can happen that no one has even thought of. A popular book refers to these things as *black swans*, in recollection of the discovery of such birds in Australia in the nineteenth century. This is where probability and mathematics stop but management continues. Although we can quantify the monetary exposure from expected incidents, as discussed below, we cannot associate any values to the unknowns. Instead, management needs to anticipate and provide for surprises. While the arrival of a black swan does not follow any schedule, its consequences can be categorized by the damage it can cause.

> For example: A serious business interruption might be caused by a great variety of problems. These include fire, tornado, hurricane, terrorist attack, demonstration against a neighboring business, or so many other, unexpected things that any list will still omit something. The risk of any one of these extraordinary incidents is extremely small, but the risk of some one of them is not trivial, and must be considered.

All-risk insurance is one prudent risk management strategy, but money might not be able to restore operations. Accordingly, insurance should be accompanied by a contingency plan that provides for restoring the essential operating functions. No one can predict a black swan, but prudent risk management can anticipate their existence and provide an appropriate risk management strategy.

Total Exposure

The aggregate value of the expected problems and their likely severity culminates in the total exposure. This value is the least reliable metric because many types of problems can produce a range of consequences, and no single value for loss per incident can express this. A probability distribution or statistical confidence interval would be a better measurement, but the state of the art of control assessment cannot yet deliver this value with reliability. The SEC rules suggest that future disclosures of qualitative and quantitative measures could provide comparative assessments of different companies.

Until a sufficient body of knowledge can be obtained, the value of the loss used for the occurrence of each uncorrected problem going into the total exposure should be a pessimistic appraisal rather than a simple transaction average. Neither should it be an absolutely worst case. The worst case for many problems leading to misstated financial reports is bankruptcy and prison sentences. A total exposure that is an amount material to the financial statements probably indicates a material weakness.

Perception of Risk

Another effective presentation method is visual, in graphs or charts. The perspective of a graph is important to the perception of risk. All graphs should hold zero as the base minimum value for the y-axis, thus showing the entire image. A graph that zooms in so that the minimum value is the lowest actual value displayed will exaggerate the appearance of the relative risks. If the values are all very close and thereby difficult to differentiate, especially if they are very high so that they all appear to be nearly 100 percent, a graph that zooms in might be acceptable only if the full perspective is also shown in another chart (See Exhibit 18.1).

Summary

Only management can decide what is reasonable and effective enough. Of course, they then will be second-guessed by the audit committee, the full board of directors, the independent external auditors, outside securities analysts, and the SEC, just to name a few. Naturally, management will want advice before committing themselves.

Management's report on their internal controls over financial reporting is at a point in time: fiscal year-end. Unacceptable levels of control during periods prior to year-end need not affect their year-end report, but significant changes in the system of internal control from prior reports must be disclosed. Neither can management take advance credit for planned improvements. Any changes necessary to avoid or eliminate material weaknesses must be in place and available for testing before year-end.

Disclosure of significant changes in internal control should be fairly common and routine. Such changes include significant improvements as well as deterioration. Of course, we would not expect deterioration except in infrequent situations such as the integration of a major acquisition. Improvements, however, should follow any report of a material weakness or installation of a major new IT accounting system.

Notes

1. Securities and Exchange Commission, 17 CFR 243.100–243.103.
2. D. Wessel, "Vioxx, Tsunami Present the Puzzle of Risk," *Wall Street Journal*, January 6, 2005.

CHAPTER 19

Review and Acceptance of Assessments

The ultimate responsibility for risk management and control assessment is placed on the CEO and the CFO. The Sarbanes-Oxley Act requires quarterly filings by these executives, stating the effects of any changes in internal controls plus annual statement of their opinions regarding internal control of financial reporting. Their assessments must be endorsed with an opinion from the company's independent accountants. The audit committee of the board of directors is charged with oversight of these assessments and opinion statements. Recognizing that these individuals rarely have the time to personally conduct the detail work to make the required assessments, this chapter describes how they can fulfill their responsibilities while delegating the detail work to middle management and staff of the company.

Summary Description of the Assessment Model

The quantitative assessment model described in this book is an extension of the concepts presented in the COSO Framework of 1994. The COSO control framework is endorsed in the SEC rules guiding compliance with Section 404 of SOX. The COSO Framework discusses a "risk-based" approach to risk management and control assessment but does not describe how this might be quantified. This modeling structure is intended to rectify that omission.

The ultimate risks that are our concerns are called *consequences.* In the aggregate, they can be measured in dollars and called the *exposure.* Consequences are the reverse of *objectives* because objectives are the destination, whereas consequences are the risks of not getting there. Along the road are various hazards, which we call *problems,* that might disrupt or divert our path. *Controls* are designed to prevent or detect and correct potential problems before they produce serious consequences. Controls must be designed to be effective against all significant problems and must be implemented in a way that ensures their appropriate use. Because no system is perfectly controlled, those problems that occur and are not corrected in a timely manner in spite of all efforts are known as the *residual incidents*, and their likelihood is their *residual risk*. For further information regarding the definition of these terms, see chapter 8 on our quantitative modeling methodology.

The assessment approach currently (2009) in general use relies on professional judgment to assess the significance of risks. The controls that are deemed to be the minimum essential to reduce the exposure below the level of materiality are called the *key controls*. For management or outside auditors to render their control assessment opinions, they must verify the effectiveness and implementation of the key controls by testing them.

The authors respect the professional judgment of business executives and independent accountants, but we doubt whether any human can mentally grasp the complete web of relationships in any sizable public company without the assistance of quantitative risk models. This web includes several accounting cycles, encompassing multiple application systems, all supported by a complex infrastructure of information technology systems and human decisions. Some of these application and IT systems could be repeated in hundreds of instances across the organization. Comprehension of the problems and risks across even a medium-sized organization can be extremely challenging, and a large organization can take years to comprehend.

Even if all this information could be analyzed, distilled, and condensed in the minds of the CEO and CFO, how can they explain it sufficiently to satisfy the outside auditors and audit committee? They must deliver their condensate in some form of lucid documentation. We believe that the results from quantitative models best provide this documentation.

Basic Modeling Concept

Our control model is structured in a matrix format, as shown in Exhibit 19.1. The columns depict potential problems, the first few rows address inherent risks and the control environment, while the next several rows depict the various control functions: prevention or detection and correction. The final rows depict the adverse consequences, which can be focused or broad. Improper financial reporting is one focused consequence, whereas a decrease in the stock price would be a broader consequence.

Each cell in the control rows of the model is quantified as the likelihood that the particular control will be effective against the particular problem. A joint probability formula calculates the net probability that all the controls in each function might fail. If the controls work, the problem is averted. If

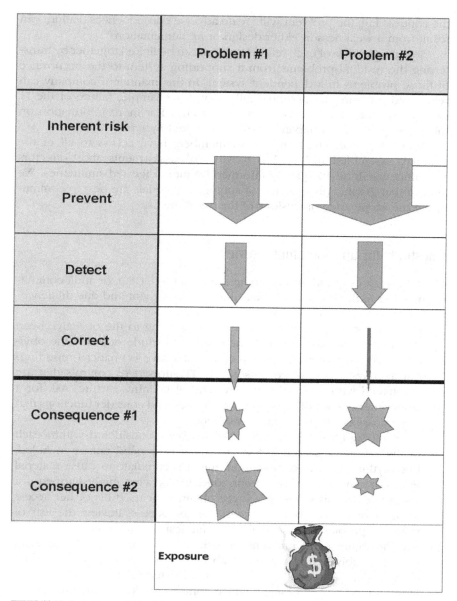

EXHIBIT 19.1 A Control Model

the controls fail, the problem will create adverse consequences. Failure can result from a weakness in either design or implementation.

Separate models of each relevant system can be linked together by transferring the residual problems from a supporting system to the occurrence of those problems in a dependent system. In this manner, a company can relate and measure the potential fallout of, for example, failure of the IT network on the billing and collections systems. For more information on this topic, please see Chapter 10, Interdependent Systems.

While top executives and board members have access to all of the materials assembled and used to provide risk assessments, most directors and officers will be adequately informed by more digested summaries. We believe that graphic presentation of summary materials are best to communicate the scope and conclusions of the assessments.

Questions for an Assessment Review

The following 12 questions are suggested for a CEO, CFO, or audit committee member in the conduct of their ultimate assessment and due diligence:

1. Has every relevant function and system leading to the objective been included in the assessments? These should include not only the obvious internal accounting systems (if the objective is financial reporting) but also systems that are outsourced, IT support of controls that are automated within the systems, and critical IT infrastructure. Ask for a comprehensive list of the systems addressed and consider functions that were possibly omitted from assessment.
2. Have all significant potential problems been considered within each of the systems assessed in Step 1? Trivial risks need not be included, but anything that, in combination, might accumulate to cause material errors or omissions must be considered. Ask what might happen if a disgruntled or dishonest employee obtained or used his or her access to do harm. What about outsiders gaining access? Review the lists of potential problems for several of the highest-risk systems.
3. Are the estimates of inherent risks plausible? These should represent what probably would happen if absolutely no controls were present. Review some estimates for the systems selected in Step 2.
4. How did the assessors select which controls are key to limiting consequences? If the key controls exist in multiple instances of the process or system (i.e., in multiple subsidiaries, plants, branches, stores, or locations), what proportion of those units were tested? What were the results of their tests? Did the test results cause the rejection of any controls from being relied on? Also ask what would happen if a manager attempted to override key controls.

5. Inquire how the assessors validated their models. Quantitative modeling has been enabled by the availability of commercial computer software. Some of the skills and expertise once required of the person developing the model have been replaced by features within the software to the extent that someone might create a model that is not valid for the circumstances. All models must be validated before they are relied on.

6. The most efficient method for managing control is to monitor, continuously or periodically, their effectiveness and implementation. Ask which key controls are monitored continuously and how frequently the ones that are monitored periodically receive coverage. Inquire about which additional controls are also monitored but are not included as key. Ask which monitoring activities were tested.

7. Study the estimates of residual risks. These are the problems that the models indicate will still occur in spite of all the controls in place. Consider whether any of these residual risks could cause such severe harm that better control is necessary. If the exposure from them would cause a material misstatement of the financial reports, a material weakness exists. Also, do any of the residual risks indicate a likelihood of fraud?

8. The control assessment models described in this book can be used to calculate a numeric rating or grade for the overall efficacy of control over the various potential problems in each system studied. Ask to see the grades for each major system and a few of the lesser systems.

9. An internal audit function can be a very important monitor of internal controls and of continuous monitoring activities. Review the summary of findings by the internal auditors.

10. Ask to see the aggregation of exposures. The summation of exposures from individual system models may exceed a material level without representing a material exposure if the likelihood of a "perfect storm" is remote.

11. How is the documentation of systems and controls being stored and maintained? Reports must be issued quarterly, addressing changes in controls. Does the company use an integrated database to inventory and maintain its risk and control documentation?

12. The final consideration for acceptance is to compare the findings of the assessments with your personal knowledge of the organization. Does everything appear consistent with your perceptions? Are the conclusions not only supported but also reasonable?

Summary

Within this chapter, we have provided guidance for audit committees regarding the review and acceptance of quantitative risk estimates. Directors and top executives have too many responsibilities to personally prepare and test everything required by risk and control assessments; instead, staff or consultants perform the detail work. However, SOX is quite explicit that the CEO and CFO are still personally responsible for the conclusions of assessments.

Sound risk assessment and management require a blend of detailed analysis and reasoned judgment. The quantitative modeling must not be a crutch but rather a tool to understand when the details are important. Ultimately the CEO, CFO, audit committee, and independent accountants must reach consensus using their consolidated analysis, tests, and wisdom.

Glossary

Consequences The impacts, results, or effects of an incident or event. There may be a range of possible impacts associated with an event. The impact of an event can be positive or negative relative to the entity's related objectives.

Control An activity or procedure that acts to mitigate potential problems.

Control environment Same as in COSO-ERM.

Correction control An activity or procedure that acts to correct incidents of a problem that have been detected. Correction may extinguish the damages, remediate them, or both.

Correction risk The probability that all applicable correction controls will fail to correct a problem.

Detected incidents Incidents of problems that are detected by controls. This is an important metric to monitor.

Detection control An activity or procedure that acts to detect problem incidents.

Detection risk The probability that all applicable detection controls will fail to detect a problem.

Environment risk The probability that the control environment will fail to reduce the incidence of a problem.

Event An incident or occurrence that could have an effect on the achievement of objectives. The impact of an event can be positive or negative relative to the entity's related objectives. See also *incident*.

Exposure Probable losses from future events to which the entity is susceptible. This differs slightly from COSO-ERM.

Incident Synonymous with *event* in COSO-ERM, but only of a nature that causes negative effects.

Inherent risk The probability that a problem might occur in the absence of any control activities to mitigate the problem. Fundamentally the same as in COSO-ERM.

Likelihood Generally the maximum probability in a probability distribution.

Opportunity The number of instances where problems might occur during a year or other span of time. This differs from COSO-ERM.

Potential incident An incident that would probably occur based only on inherent risk, as if no environmental factors or controls act to mitigate.

Potential problem A problem that could arise in a specific system or control subject.

Preliminary risk The probability that a particular problem would occur in spite of the control environment constraints on inherent risk. Calculated as: Inherent risk × Environment risk.

Prevention control An activity or procedure that acts to prevent problems.

Prevention risk The probability that all applicable prevention controls will fail to prevent a problem.

Probability The amount of uncertainty stated as a value between zero and one. Sometimes stated as a percentage or ratio.

Problem An underlying internal or external factor that causes or results in an adverse event or incident. COSO-ERM refers to this as a *cause*.

Residual problems The problems that will probably not be prevented or detected and corrected, and thereby cause consequences.

Residual risk The probability that all applicable controls will fail to mitigate a problem. Fundamentally the same as in COSO-ERM.

Reward A positive event, or the alternative benefit to accepting a risk and it not occurring.

Risk A widely misused word that this book uses only to refer to the *probability* that a problem or consequence will occur. It should not be used to refer to the nature of the problem or the consequence, so it therefore does not describe such adverse incidents or events.

Internal Control Sections of the Sarbanes-Oxley Act

The following text is the complete sections of the Sarbanes-Oxley Act that relate to internal control over financial reporting.

Sec. 301. Public Company Audit Committees

Section 10A of the Securities Exchange Act of 1934 (15 U.S.C. 78f) is amended by adding at the end the following:

"(m) STANDARDS RELATING TO AUDIT COMMITTEES.—
"(1) COMMISSION RULES.— —32

"(A) IN GENERAL.— Effective not later than 270 days after the date of enactment of this subsection, the Commission shall, by rule, direct the national securities exchanges and national securities associations to prohibit the listing of any security of an issuer that is not in compliance with the requirements of any portion of paragraphs (2) through (6).
"(2) RESPONSIBILITIES RELATING TO REGISTERED PUBLIC ACCOUNTING FIRMS.—The audit committee of each issuer, in its capacity as a committee of the board of directors, shall be directly responsible for the appointment, compensation, and oversight of the work of any registered public accounting firm employed by that issuer (including resolution of disagreements between management and the auditor regarding financial reporting) for the purpose of preparing or issuing an audit report or related work, and each such registered public accounting firm shall report directly to the audit committee.
"(3) INDEPENDENCE.—

"(A) IN GENERAL.—Each member of the audit committee of the issuer shall be a member of the board of directors of the issuer, and shall otherwise be independent.

"(B) CRITERIA.—In order to be considered to be independent for purposes of this paragraph, a member of an audit committee of an issuer may not, other than in his or her capacity as a member of the audit committee, the board of directors, or any other board committee—

"(i) accept any consulting, advisory, or other compensatory fee from the issuer; or

"(ii) be an affiliated person of the issuer or any subsidiary thereof.

"(C) EXEMPTION AUTHORITY.—The Commission may exempt from the requirements of subparagraph (B) a particular relationship with respect to audit committee members, as the Commission determines appropriate in light of the circumstances.

"(4) COMPLAINTS.—Each audit committee shall establish procedures for—

"(A) the receipt, retention, and treatment of complaints received by the issuer regarding accounting, internal accounting controls, or auditing matters; and

"(B) the confidential, anonymous submission by employees of the issuer of concerns regarding questionable accounting or auditing matters.

"(5) AUTHORITY TO ENGAGE ADVISERS.—Each audit committee shall have the authority to engage independent counsel and other advisers, as it determines necessary to carry out its duties.

"(6) FUNDING.—Each issuer shall provide for appropriate funding, as determined by the audit committee, in its capacity as a committee of the board of directors, for payment of compensation—

"(A) to the registered public accounting firm employed by the issuer for the purpose of rendering or issuing an audit report; and

"(B) to any advisers employed by the audit committee under paragraph (5)."

Section 302 Corporate Responsibility for Financial Reports

(5) the signing officers have disclosed to the issuer's auditors and the audit committee of the board of directors (or persons fulfilling the equivalent function)—

(A) all significant deficiencies in the design or operation of internal controls which could adversely affect the issuer's ability to record, process, summarize, and report financial data and have identified for the issuer's auditors any material weaknesses in internal controls; and

(B) any fraud, whether or not material, that involves management or other employees who have a significant role in the issuer's internal controls; and

(6) the signing officers have indicated in the report whether or not there were significant changes in internal controls or in other factors that could significantly affect internal controls subsequent to the date of their evaluation, including any corrective actions with regard to significant deficiencies and material weaknesses.

Sec 404. Management Assessment of Internal Controls

(a) RULES REQUIRED.—The Commission shall prescribe rules requiring each annual report required by section 13(a) or 15(d) of the Securities Exchange Act of 1934 (15 U.S.C. 78m or 78o(d)) to contain an internal control report, which shall—

1. state the responsibility of management for establishing and maintaining an adequate internal control structure and procedures for financial reporting; and
2. contain an assessment, as of the end of the most recent fiscal year of the issuer, of the effectiveness of the internal control structure and procedures of the issuer for financial reporting.

(b) INTERNAL CONTROL EVALUATION AND REPORTING.—With respect to the internal control assessment required by subsection (a), each registered public accounting firm that prepares or issues the audit report for the issuer shall attest to, and report on, the assessment made by the management of the issuer. An attestation made under this subsection shall be made in accordance with standards for attestation engagements issued or adopted by the Board. Any such attestation shall not be the subject of a separate engagement.

Sec. 407. Disclosure of Audit Committee Financial Expert

(a) RULES DEFINING "FINANCIAL EXPERT."—The Commission shall issue rules, as necessary or appropriate in the public interest and consistent with the protection of investors, to require each issuer, together with periodic reports required pursuant to sections 13(a) and 15(d) of the Securities Exchange Act of 1934, to disclose whether or not, and if not, the reasons therefore, the audit committee of that issuer is comprised of at least 1 member who is a financial expert, as such term is defined by the Commission.

(b) CONSIDERATIONS.—In defining the term "financial expert" for purposes of subsection (a), the Commission shall consider whether a person has, through education and experience as a public accountant or auditor or a principal financial officer, comptroller, or principal accounting officer of an issuer, or from a position involving the performance of similar functions—

1. an understanding of generally accepted accounting principles and financial statements;
2. experience in—
    (A) the preparation or auditing of financial statements of generally comparable issuers; and
    (B) the application of such principles in connection with the accounting for estimates, accruals, and reserves;
3. experience with internal accounting controls; and
4. an understanding of audit committee functions.

Index

Printed in the United States
By Bookmasters